Lecture Notes in Computer Science 4323

Commenced Publication in 1973
Founding and Former Series Editors:
Gerhard Goos, Juris Hartmanis, and Jan van Leeuwen

T0223276

Gavin Doherty   Ann Blandford (Eds.)

Interactive Systems

Design, Specification, and Verification

13th International Workshop, DSVIS 2006
Dublin, Ireland, July 26-28, 2006
Revised Papers

 Springer

Volume Editors

Gavin Doherty
Department of Computer Science
Trinity College Dublin
Dublin 2, Ireland
E-mail: Gavin.Doherty@cs.tcd.ie

Ann Blandford
UCL Interaction Centre
University College London
London, WC1E 7DP, U.K.
E-mail: a.blandford@ucl.ac.uk

Library of Congress Control Number: 2006939792

CR Subject Classification (1998): H.5.2, H.5, I.3, D.2, F.3

LNCS Sublibrary: SL 2 – Programming and Software Engineering

ISSN   0302-9743
ISBN-10   3-540-69553-2 Springer Berlin Heidelberg New York
ISBN-13   978-3-540-69553-0 Springer Berlin Heidelberg New York

Springer is a part of Springer Science+Business Media

springer.com

© Springer-Verlag Berlin Heidelberg 2007
Printed in Germany

Typesetting: Camera-ready by author, data conversion by Scientific Publishing Services, Chennai, India
Printed on acid-free paper   SPIN: 11971344   06/3142   5 4 3 2 1 0

Preface

We present here the proceedings of the 13th International Workshop on the Design, Specification and Verification of Interactive Systems, held in Trinity College, Dublin. The workshop provides a forum where researchers at the intersection of software engineering and human–computer interaction can present and discuss their ideas. The different perspectives and concerns of these two communities were exemplified by the thought-provoking contributions of the invited speakers Jan Gulliksen, who looked at the nature of contact between developers and end users (keynote paper included in this volume), and Ian Sommerville, who looked at construction by configuration as the de-facto paradigm for many real-world development projects.

All papers were reviewed by at least three reviewers. We present here 19 out of 57 submissions, along with a keynote paper and two working group reports. The healthy number of submissions reflects the continuing interest and commitment of researchers in this area. The accepted papers came from a wide range of locations—Belgium, Canada, France, Ireland, Italy, Norway, Portugal, Spain, Sweden and the UK.

Model-driven development remains a strong theme, with papers by Penichet et al., Van den Bergh et al., and Koninx et al. The sophistication and power of the tools now available compared to those presented at earlier editions of the workshop were clearly evident from these presentations. Other uses of models in development are investigated in the papers by Silva et al., which looked at reverse engineering, Lepreux et al., which looks at the visual design of user interfaces, and Potter and Wright, which looks at visualization resource management. Formal perspectives on cognitive aspects of interaction were explored in papers by Roast and Khazaei and Rukšėnas et al. The design of safety-critical systems was the subject of several papers this year, both in terms of engineering (Barboni et al.), requirements (Santos et al.), and evaluation (Thimbleby). There were also two papers on bringing rigorous approaches to bear on the design and development of haptic and multi-modal interfaces, both in terms of specification (Smith) and analysis (Faconti and Massink).

Prototyping and evaluation are always a concern in the development of interactive systems, and work in this area was presented by Petrie and Schneider on mixed fidelity prototyping, by González et al., who looked at modelling early prototype evaluation, and O'Neill et al. who looked at a VR-based approach to evaluation. On the theme of supporting user interface development, a patterns-based approach to adaptive user interfaces was presented by Nilsson et al. Consideration of computer games by Graham et al. was a new topic for the event, and was the subject of a lively working group discussion. The critique of validity in published HCI research presented by Thimbleby struck a chord with many of the participants, with discussion continuing in a working group. One concrete result of this was a strong impetus on presenters to comment on the availability of their software and repeatability of their results!

The interest in the work presented at this year's workshop was evident from the number of questions for each speaker and the many discussions which took place over the three days. Trinity College provided an attractive setting for the conference, and the friendly atmosphere of the event helped to make it an enjoyable as well as an intellectually rewarding experience.

October 2006   Gavin Doherty and Ann Blandford

Organization

Programme Chairs

Gavin Doherty   Trinity College Dublin, Ireland
Ann Blandford   University College London, UK

Programme Committee

Rémi Bastide	Université Paul Sabatier, Toulouse, France
Ann Blandford	University College London, UK
Jose Campos	University of Minho, Portugal
Anke Dittmar	University of Rostock, Germany
Alan Dix	University of Lancaster, UK
Simon Dobson	UCD Dublin, Ireland
Peter Forbrig	University of Rostock, Germany
Nicholas Graham	Queen's University, Canada
Michael Harrison	University of Newcastle, UK
Chris Johnson	University of Glasgow, UK
Joaquim Jorge	INESC-ID, Lisbon, Portugal
Rick Kazman	SEI, Carnegie Mellon University, USA
Panos Markopoulos	Eindhoven University of Technology, Netherlands
Mieke Massink	ISTI-CNR, Pisa, Italy
Laurence Nigay	Université Joseph Fourier, France
Philippe Palanque	Université Paul Sabatier, Toulouse, France
Fabio Paternò	ISTI-CNR, Pisa, Italy
Chris Roast	Sheffield-Hallam University, UK
Kevin Schneider	University of Saskatchewan, Canada
Alistair Sutcliffe	University of Manchester, UK
Harold Thimbleby	University of Swansea, Wales

Reviewers

Sophie Dupuy-Chessa	CLIPS-IMAG, University of Grenoble 1, France
Eduardo Calvillo Gámez	University College London, UK
Yamine Ait-Ameur	LISI-ENSMA, University of Poitiers, France
Giorgio Faconti	ISTI-CNR, Pisa, Italy
Joelle Coutaz	CLIPS-IMAG, University of Grenoble 1, France

Local Organization

Gavin Doherty	Trinity College Dublin, Ireland
Alena Moison	Trinity College Dublin, Ireland
Kris McGlinn	Trinity College Dublin, Ireland
Simon Dobson	UCD Dublin, Ireland

Supporting Organizations

ACM SIGCHI
The British Computer Society HCI Group
IFIP WG 13.5
The Eurographics Association
Department of Computer Science, Trinity College Dublin

Table of Contents

Keynote

How Do Developers Meet Users? – Attitudes and Processes in Software
Development 1
Jan Gulliksen

HCI Research

Validity and Cross-Validity in HCI Publications..................... 11
Harold Thimbleby

Critical Systems

Model-Based Engineering of Widgets, User Applications and Servers
Compliant with ARINC 661 Specification 25
*Eric Barboni, Stéphane Conversy, David Navarre, and
Philippe Palanque*

Usability Requirements for Improving the Infection Module
of a Hospital Intensive Care Unit Information System 39
*Mónica Sara Santos, João Falcão e Cunha, and
Altamiro da Costa Pereira*

Interaction Walkthrough: Evaluation of Safety Critical Interactive
Systems 52
Harold Thimbleby

Model Based Development

Collaborative Social Structures and Task Modelling Integration 67
*Victor M.R. Penichet, Fabio Paternò, J.A. Gallud, and
Maria D. Lozano*

Towards Model-Driven Development of Staged Participatory
Multimedia Events 81
Jan Van den Bergh, Steven Huypens, and Karin Coninx

Integrating Support for Usability Evaluation into High Level Interaction
Descriptions with NiMMiT 95
*Karin Coninx, Erwin Cuppens, Joan De Boeck, and
Chris Raymaekers*

Cognitive Aspects of Interaction

An Investigation into the Validation of Formalised Cognitive
Dimensions.. 109
  Chris Roast and Babak Khazaei

Formal Modelling of Cognitive Interpretation 123
  *Rimvydas Rukšėnas, Paul Curzon, Jonathan Back, and
  Ann Blandford*

Use of Models

Combining Formal Methods and Functional Strategies Regarding
the Reverse Engineering of Interactive Applications 137
  J.C. Silva, José Creissac Campos, and João Saraiva

An Ontological Approach to Visualization Resource Management 151
  Richard Potter and Helen Wright

Visual Design of User Interfaces by (De)composition.................. 157
  Sophie Lepreux, Jean Vanderdonckt, and Benjamin Michotte

Haptics and Multimodality

Exploring the Specification of Haptic Interaction 171
  Shamus P. Smith

Analysis of Pointing Tasks on a White Board 185
  G. Faconti and Mieke Massink

Prototyping and Evaluation

Mixed-Fidelity Prototyping of User Interfaces........................ 199
  Jennifer N. Petrie and Kevin A. Schneider

A Hybrid Approach for Modelling Early Prototype Evaluation Under
User-Centred Design Through Association Rules 213
  María Paula González, Toni Granollers, and Jesús Lorés

Rapid User-Centred Evaluation for Context-Aware Systems 220
  Eleanor O'Neill, David Lewis, Kris McGlinn, and Simon Dobson

Supporting User Interface Development

Using a Patterns-Based Modelling Language and a Model-Based
Adaptation Architecture to Facilitate Adaptive User Interfaces 234
  *Erik G. Nilsson, Jacqueline Floch, Svein Hallsteinsen, and
  Erlend Stav*

Toward Quality-Driven Development of 3D Computer Games   248
    T.C. Nicholas Graham and Will Roberts

Group Discussions

Processes: Working Group Report   262
    Stéphane Chatty, José Creissac Campos, María Paula González,
    Sophie Lepreux, Erik G. Nilsson, Victor M.R. Penichet,
    Mónica Santos, and Jan Van den Bergh

Usability and Computer Games: Working Group Report   265
    T.C. Nicholas Graham, Paul Curzon, Gavin Doherty,
    Philippe Palanque, Richard Potter, Christopher Roast, and
    Shamus P. Smith

Author Index   269

How Do Developers Meet Users? – Attitudes and Processes in Software Development

Jan Gulliksen

Uppsala university, Department of IT/HCI, PO Box 337, SE-751 05 Uppsala, Sweden
Jan.Gulliksen@hci.uu.se

Abstract. This keynote paper argues for an increased understanding of the various roles involved in the development work to be able to achieve the goal of developing increased usability. Human Computer Interaction (HCI) has for a long time been arguing for the sake of the users, but to be able to deliver methods, tools and processes that better fit the needs of developers we should study and understand development work to a larger extent. This paper discusses what HCI and software engineering contributes to each other's disciplines as well as what research contributes to practice. This also means an increased understanding of what research that counts in the academic context. Finally I argue that research should focus more on real problems of real development work, rather than on research that is easily publishable.

Keywords: Usability, User-centered systems design, process, attitude.

1 Introduction

Why do we do what we do? How come we started doing research? What do we think we contribute and who cares?

A couple of years ago I was an opponent on a PhD defense. I asked the defender: *"What is the real objective behind your research?"* The thesis was put together in a standard way, posing research questions in the beginning, examining the state of the art, setting a methodology for answering the research questions, presenting results and discussing them in relation to previous research. However, there was no discussion on the main objective behind the research. I repeated:

What is the main research objective? To make it easier for you, I will give you three options,

1. *You want to change the world*
2. *You want to contribute new knowledge to the world*
3. *You want to get your PhD*

The defender tried to get out of the situation by proposing a fourth alternative. I said: *"Please do, but if you do that I will show that whatever you propose actually is one of the three options I have proposed"*. So, the defender then claimed that he wanted to change the world, and my immediate response was to ask him to explain why. During his explanation as to why his research would change the world it became obvious for

G. Doherty and A. Blandford (Eds.): DSVIS 2006, LNCS 4323, pp. 1 – 10, 2007.
© Springer-Verlag Berlin Heidelberg 2007

him that *that* was not the main objective of his research. He then said that he wanted to contribute new knowledge to the world, and of course I asked him to motivate his contribution. Unfortunately the work he had done had some methodological flaws meaning that the only conclusions that could be drawn from the work was that if he had conducted the experiments a bit differently one might have been able to draw some conclusions over the results. As a consequence of the discussion he finally said: *"I think I want my PhD"*.

It is important here to clarify that this story does not have the purpose of making fun over someone's work or studies, but rather to have this serve as an illustration of the utmost importance of this discussion. To clarify, I mean that any of the answers are equally good. It is excellent if people do want to change the world – that is where and when we really can make a difference. Also it is very good if people do contribute new knowledge to the world. HCI is a field with quite a few white spots on the map, why new knowledge is essential. Also it is very good if people do want there PhD, because industry has a great need of well educated and experienced HCI researchers (even if they are not fully aware of it yet). The important thing is that by asking yourself what your main research objective is before starting you might be able to focus on the really important questions rather than focusing on what is easy to get valid results out of.

2   What Research Is Promoted?

What research is promoted? Given that the competition at conferences within the field has risen tremendously, and given the relative importance of getting publications from a personal merit value point of view, the research questions that people investigate are often set to fit publications not necessarily meaning that it focuses on what is important for the world. Conferences and journals promote quantitative studies before qualitative, positivist research before hermeneutic studies, experimental research before case studies and action research, and hence the research questions that people select are biased towards what easily can be published. Let me take an example. Defining a new evaluation method is relatively easy to do and to evaluate the validity and reliability of such a method is also relatively straightforward and can be done in an experimental setting. But, do we really need a new evaluation method? If the goal is to increase the overall usability of a product is it really the new method that makes the difference? Most likely not, it is the work and knowledge of the people involved in the design and development of the system that makes the difference, and methods may of course provide the hooks that those professionals can hang their knowledge upon, but it is most likely that the knowledge and experience of the person doing the work that makes the difference. On the other hand to really improve a development process in practice will inevitably pose a much bigger challenge. And it is the practice, the context it is set in that pose the challenges. To my experience in 9 cases out of 10 things will happen in research in practice that aggravates the scientific results, yet there are so much knowledge and experiences to be drawn from such cases, yet they are much more difficult to get published in a scientific manner. My argument here is that we should make more efforts of promoting research that actually contributes to changing (and hopefully improving) the world than what is easily evaluated and justified. Research should also be judged based on its contribution to the development of practice or knowledge that is useful for practice.

One of the reasons why this is problematic is that computer science research to its nature is a positivist type of research and therefore research into computer science seldom reaches the level in which it becomes important to judge qualitative terms. One of the most well known professors at my university responded to my discussions around this problem: *"I do not understand your problem. In my research group we invent a new processor and we can measure that it is 5 % quicker than previous processors. That is what I call research."* Hence the problem of improving the practical utility of the research is also a development of the scientific knowledge and breadth of the knowledge from philosophy of science.

3   How Can Research Contribute to the Development of Practice?

I have for a very long time been cooperating with public authorities to improve their system usability and computer supported work environment. The common denominator of a lot of that work is that it is very difficult to specifically point out what our contribution have been? There is not a particular method, tool or technique that they adopt today that directly comes out of our research cooperation. But, at the same time it is clear that our cooperation has had a tremendous impact on the way that they now perform their development. It is clear that the awareness and knowledge about usability and various approaches has developed significantly, at all levels in the organization. But, none of the developed or proposed methods were actually adopted as they were. Rather the organization needed to fell that they were in control and hence they invented and developed their own approaches for these things. To a large extent the approaches were adapted from the approaches proposed from research, or inspired by research activities, but it was very important that the initiative came from the organization.

One of the important contributions that the research has on practice is to emphasize and develop the conceptual framework. This relates both to HCI-related terminology as well as domain terminology. As we are very well aware of, HCI-related concepts such as prototypes, design, evaluation, etc. has very different connotation to different people within the organization. Research can here play an important role in specifying and elaborating the conceptual framework, but it needs to be based on the practice of the developers. This means that we must understand how various concepts are interpreted by the different professionals using it, rather than how the dictionary defines it. We can also make use of this understanding and base the approaches we suggest on the commonly agreed upon definitions. Let me take a couple of examples:

One important distinction one can make is between a user test and a use test. User testing has been used to a large extent to emphasize the importance of letting users test the products and gather knowledge on how systems can be improved based on this. On the other hand, others feel that by using the concept of user testing, we might risk a false understanding that it is about testing the users. Of course this is not the case, and I doubt that many people misunderstands this. The concept of use test would of course be much better in this sense, but then on the other hand some people might mistake it for testing where you actually do not need to involve users. As an expert you might be able to apply a use test.

Another conceptual difference that is often discussed is the variety of concepts relating to any type of User-centered design (UCD). The ISO 13407 standard calls it Human-centered design, arguing that human is a much broader concept than users. On the contrary I have seen examples of the development of cow milking robots that was developed in a user-centered fashion that definitely did not focus on the humans. Another commonly used term is usability engineering, but to my experience usability engineering is much more focused on improving the usability through evaluation rather than focusing on the design in an iterative fashion. I have in other publications below elaborated on the conceptual framework at length and will not go into further detail here. The point is merely that if we want research to improve practice, we need to focus more on establishing a mutual understanding of the language used in the organization/project rather than on the academic conceptual discussion on the definition of various concepts. What practice needs is a common mutual understanding of the basic constructs among those involved in their development?

In addition to understanding the conceptual framework case studies and action research provides some of the most interesting examples of success and failures that we can learn a lot from. Extracting and generalizing the knowledge from various case studies and reapplying different variants of the approaches in other real life action research projects can move us towards a more successful development approach. However, action research and case studies are not very easy to document and publish and may often be open to critique due to the nature of the research approach. This must not stop us as researchers from using the practice as our field of research and generalize and extrapolate from these cases to a more general theory.

Successful UCD requires an understanding of the nature of the work of the people involved. HCI has for a long time been concerned about the users' situation, which has given us several very important studies and theories on the user's situation. However, in terms of having this knowledge contribute to development in practice we have not succeeded very well. Still with a number of user studies, user testing, etc. developers still continue to develop systems the way they have always done. HCI activities always become an add-on to the well-established processes that developers deploy. Therefore I believe that if we want the research to have any impact we need to focus on the main users of all our research results, namely the developers. We must understand the nature of software development and the basic values and attitudes among the developers and how these may be influenced because of the ways in which we communicate and disseminate our research into practice.

4   Understanding Users

Understanding users, analyzing users, living with users, modeling users have been issues that over the years have received a lot of attention. Literature on users shows very different basic values and perspectives of how people view users and their contribution to the development work. This has lead to a wide variety of different myths about users and their involvement in the process:

- **Users have unrealistic requests; we must manage their expectations.** It is not the question of developing exactly what the users requests. It is more the issue of interpreting the users wishes and in cooperation with them analyze what requirements that actually should be put on the system to meet their needs. And, by involving users on a regular basis you avoid unrealistic expectation and the need for managing expectations.
- **Users are not designers.** On the contrary we have experimented with users as designers of the conceptual design and interaction design of their system, with tremendously good results both in terms of the results that these design workshops gave and the efficiency of the process. But, such sessions do not, and should not, deliver formal specifications of the user interface design. They produce low-fidelity prototypes and scenarios and storyboards that show the work with the systems in a way that is understandable to users and that gives developers knowledge of the work beyond what can be captured in the formal models.
- **Users do not want change.** This is partly true – initially the users do not want change but when you start to work with the users on how they may develop and improve their work situation, most users are prone to change and do want to develop the ways in which they work. And if they don't you have either selected wrong users, or not given them the feeling that they actually have the opportunity to contribute.
- **Users adapt to everything.** True, but this should not be taken as an argument that the user's needs and wishes are of less value. Users can adapt to lousy situations and often do so, but their performance, and sometimes even the security, may be heavily influenced if you don't use the user adaptation as an excuse for producing systems that are easier to develop, rather than systems that are easy to use.
- **Users rarely adapt their systems to their specials needs.** Also true, but mostly because the customization and individualization opportunities of the systems often are added on after the initial design of the system and not seen as an integrated part of the system. Careful considerations are required also in the design of the ways in which users can adapt their systems to their special needs.
- **It is all about education and implementation.** Education and a proper introduction of the system to the work setting is of course very important and needs to be planned and carefully conducted. But be ware that the implementation process might reveal a lot of usability problems that should be dealt with to increase the quality of the product. But far too often this is not possible due to delays earlier on in the process.

These different myths have also been conserved and emphasized in various processes and industrial applications. For example in the development of Objectory (the predecessor to Rational Unified Process – RUP), Ivar Jacobsson changed the concepts from users to actors in the description of the method. Originally he intended the methods to focus on the users and their needs, but when this was changed to actors, it also became the concept for a number of other things, leading to a view on actors where there didn't need to be any users available at all. Consequently one of the biggest problems for heavy RUP users is that they risk loosing the perspective that they are actually developing for users. The process became the goal in itself. Of course, processes are useful and necessary, but right now we need to fight back the user perspective in software engineering processes, as this was lost years ago.

Unfortunately this has lead to a deeply rooted basic value of users and what their role is in development that devalues their knowledge and potential contribution. I often meet with developers that work hard to not have to meet with users and consider it as a very tough task when they have to face the actual users of what they have developed. This has also spread into the research community where several researchers argue against user involvement, because it becomes unpredictable and decreases the orderliness of development work. In a personal communication with Larry Constantine a number of years ago he concluded (sort of in an ironic matter): *"Frankly it's about keeping the users on an arm lengths distance"*

5 Understanding Software Development and Developers

If we want to develop methods, processes, tools and techniques that can help developers in producing usable systems, we must understand software development and understand how software developers work. The HCI community has for a long time been advocating a user-centered approach to the development of applications for end-users, but have failed to adopt a user-centered perspective when it comes to looking at what developers need and can make use of to meet the goal of developing usable systems. I would therefore argue that an immature view on developers is potentially very harmful to the goal and our views and perspectives on developers need a much more serious attention.

Over the years in HCI conferences I have heard stories about "technicians" describing them as asocial individuals that never wash or shave, and that smells. In a review of a journal paper I wrote, one of the reviewers gave the following comment:

"Don't waste time with the geeks, unless you like hanging out with them. You'll never get their money. The proper self-assigned job of the authors ought to be to work out how HCI can make its deserved living from guaranteeing increased operational effectiveness, i.e. Value For Money - something the programmers don't give the project."

I have even heard presentations in an ironic manner referring to software developers as psychopaths, according to the definition of psychopaths as people who lack the ability to put themselves in another person's situation and lacking empathic abilities. What is the effect of such an attitude towards developers? Will we ever reach the goal of increasing the usability of systems, if we approach those who actually are going to construct and build the systems in this way. Of course not, and that is probably why we see the few researchers within HCI that deal with the practical application of HCI in practice focusing, not on issues relating to software development, but rather relating to power relations, such as the work on procurement issues and power relations as a way to clarify who should be in charge.

I therefore strongly believe that we need to better understand the nature of the work of software developers. We need to meet the developers in their actual tasks and provide tools, methods, techniques and processes that contribute to their work. *"It's all in a days work of a software developer."*

6 What Does/Can Software Engineering Contribute?

"... there is a prolonged period of confusion at the start followed by a frantic scramble to finish on time at the end" (McCoy, 2002)

Many software engineers that I have met act as if the world would have been much better without people. The ideal software development tool would be a machine that as input took requirements formulated according to a specific syntax and that delivered a perfectly functioning and usable system as output. Even if the utopia is achievable in the future it does not mean that software development in practice in the future will rely less on the activities of individuals involved in the process.

So, in order to understand what software engineering and software engineers can contribute, we need to study what it actually does contribute today, and what its major problems are. What does software engineering contribute (among other things):

- Requirements gathering
- Development processes
- Tools

What does it lack (among other things):

- Ways of facilitating and promoting user involvement
- Ways of supporting informal activities such as design
- Understandable formats for documenting designs

Software engineering is an excellent discipline in bringing orderliness to a tremendously complex process that lack transparency, since software during development rarely gives the users an image of the system to be. But software engineering also lack the humility of seeing its limitations and seeing the vast amount of HCI knowledge that is available for inclusion, rather arguing that HCI must go 90 % of the way towards the integration into software engineering (personal communication with Bonnie John). I believe that until the research has changed its basic values when it comes to these issues, the practice won't change.

7 What's the Contribution of HCI and What Should It Be?

I attended a keynote address that Bill Buxton gave at the Local SIGCHI in Toronto in 2002. In his talk he listed the major inventions of HCI and concluded that all of them were invented before 1982, when the CHI conference was born and when the field became a field of its own. His ironic conclusion was that the academic field of HCI had not contributed much to the practice of HCI. I might agree, that most of the development within the field has taken place outside of academia. However, I doubt that the development would have happened without the birth and growth of the academic field of HCI.

But, why have we not managed to make a significant contribution to the development of practice? One well-known example in Sweden is the development of systems for managing medical records. Despite studies showing the risks involved in developing medical records without considering the user perspective decades ago, organizations keep repeating the same problems over and over again. How come nobody listens to the warnings from researchers within the HCI field? Why have we not succeeded in getting the authority that is required for others to listen to what we have to say?

I believe that the field of Human Computer Interaction, as well as the practice of usability professionals, has a lot of things to contribute to the development process. For one thing the approaches gathered under the umbrella of User Centered Design (UCD) provides several methods and techniques for the process of developing interactive systems with the focus on usability and on the perspective of the users. However, UCD is not easily achieved, given the problematic contexts in which it needs to take place. Therefore UCD in itself has some specific requirements. For successful UCD we need to:

- Get the right support from management
- Determine the importance of usability in the organization
- Actively involve users in the design process
- Use understandable design representations in the development
- Involve usability designers.

Therefore we need to understand the usability profession as well. After all, these are people we must not only cooperate with, but also support. The usability profession is perhaps the most significant impact the HCI community has had on practice. As every profession they are faced with some problems. Some of the major problems we have encountered with the usability profession are:

- Lacking impact in the development process
- Lack of time, resources, knowledge, interest, etc.
- Unclear responsibilities
- Lack of consistency in naming

These problems are neither new nor unique for a newly established profession. Rather they are problems that probably would be easy to overcome if dealt with in the right way. An initial problem with all new roles and professions is that they need to justify their role to a higher extent than other already existing roles. One way of doing this is to alter the work more towards contributing to the design rather than commenting on and evaluating other people's work. The usability professionals must have *"skin in the game"* (Cooper, 1999). UCD professionals who focus on doing "studies", as opposed to generating designs and products, will always be perceived as peripheral." (Siegel & Dray, 2003). The usability person must participate in all the user-centered activities, to prevent valuable information from being lost in the transitions between the activities, in accordance with the principle of integrated design (Gould et al., 1997).

8 Conclusions

At the end of the road, research in HCI and SE, as well as the work of usability professionals all deal with the problem of developing usable systems. I strongly believe that if we want to have any impact on practice, we need to focus more on how our research is implemented in practice and why it fails, and then make use of that knowledge to define new research questions. Over the years our research has produced new methods, tools, processes and roles – yet these have not changed the world to any larger extent. Very few of the methods that have been developed by researchers have been applied by anybody else than the inventers themselves. What is the reason behind this? How come others do not apply the methods to the extent that they deserve?

I believe that the main reason for this is that the development of such methods mainly are based on the market of science – by developing these methods you will get a neight study that is relatively easy to publish. On the other hand a good action research study or case study may be interpreted as theoryless, unstructured and even "sloppy", and hence the opportunities of getting it published is much less. But the potential utility for practitioners is unquestionable. In other words, if you want to change the world a new process or a new tool will most likely not change the practice of developers. The real improvement or development comes when practitioners change their ways of work and ultimately maybe their view on the work and the context for which they are developing. Users become a necessary source of information, not only on the work of today, but also on the potential of the future, instead of being a source of aggravation and disturbance. Usability doesn't happen by accident, but rather comes as a result of a thoughtful and enlightened design process focusing on usability. And how can we manage such a development process?

We need to work on the attitudes and basic values among everybody involved in IT development and use. We need to determine how important usability is for everybody? Further we need to determine who is responsible for usability and how do people respond to this responsibility? Finally, we need to get an understanding of what type of management support (project and overall management support) usability do have? To our experience every developer should get first hand experience from the users using the system. If practitioners can get immediate and first-hand experience of this perspective, that is when the people start to develop and when people tend to change.

References

Cooper, A., (1999) The Inmates are Running the Asylum, SAMS, Indianapolis.

Gould, J.D. Boies, S.J., Ukelson, J. (1997) How to design usable systems, in: Helander, M. Landauer, T.K., Prabhu, P. (Eds.), Handbook of Human-Computer Interaction, Second revision, Elsevier Science B.V., Amsterdam, pp. 231-254.

Jacobson, I., Booch, G., Rumbaugh, J., (1999) The Unified Software Development Process, Addison Wesley Longman Inc., Reading.

McCoy, T. (2002). Usability: Who Cares? In Usability Gaining a Competitive Edge. IFIP World Computer Congress 2002. Hammond, J., Gross, T., Wesson, J. (Eds), pp 283-294. Kluwer Academic Publishers.

Siegel, D., Dray, S., (2003) Living on the edges: user-centered design and the dynamics of specialization in organizations, Interactions, X.5. pp. 19-27.

Bibliography

Following are some of the research that I have been involved in that may provide additional guidance to the issues that this keynote paper is dealing with. I have tried to order them into categories of fields that may seem relevant to your needs.

User Centred Systems Design
Key Principles for User Centred Systems Design – Jan Gulliksen, Bengt Göransson, Inger Boivie, Stefan Blomkvist, Jenny Persson & Åsa Cajander (2003) Behaviour and Information Technology, Vol. 22, No. 6, pp.397-409

Usability professionals
Usability Professionals – Current Practices and Future Development – Jan Gulliksen, Inger Boivie & Bengt Göransson (2006) Interacting with Computers, Vol. 18, No. 4, pp. 568-600.

The Lonesome Cowboy – A Study of the Usability Designer Role in Systems Development – Inger Boivie, Jan Gulliksen & Bengt Göransson (2006) Interacting with Computers, Vol. 18, No. 4, pp. 601-634.

Making a Difference – A Survey of the Usability Profession in Sweden – Jan Gulliksen, Inger Boivie, Jenny Persson, Anders Hektor & Lena Herulf (2004) In Hyrskykari A. (ed.), Proceedings of the 3rd Nordic Conference on Human Computer Interaction, NordiCHI 2004, Tampere, Finland, ACM Press, pp. 207-215

Basic values
Management Perspectives on Usability in a Public Authority – Åsa Cajander, Inger Boivie & Jan Gulliksen (2006) Proceedings of the 4th Nordic Conference on Human Computer Interaction, NordiCHI 2006, Oslo, Norway, ACM Press

Usability And User's Health Issues In Systems Development - Attitudes And Perspectives – Åsa Cajander, Inger Boivie and Jan Gulliksen (in press) In Effie Law, Ebba Hvannberg, Gilbert Cockton and Jean Vanderdonckt (eds.) Maturing Usability: Quality in Software, Interaction and Value. Springer

SE and HCI
Human Centred Software Engineering: Integrating Usability In The Software Development Lifecycle – Ahmed Seffah & Jan Gulliksen, Michel Desmarias (2005) Kluwer Academic Publishers.

The Usability Design Process – Integrating User-Centered Systems Design In The Software Development Process – Bengt Göransson, Jan Gulliksen & Inger Boivie (2003). In the Special Issue on Bridging the Process and Practice Gaps Between Software Engineering and Human Computer Interaction edited by Rick Kazman and Len Bass. Software Process Improvement and Practice, Vol. 8, No. 2. pp. 111-131 Wiley

Usability Design—Extending Rational Unified Process With A New Discipline –Bengt Göransson, Magnus Lif & Jan Gulliksen. (2003) In LNCS volume 2844 "DSV-IS 2003: Issues in Designing New-generation Interactive Systems Proceedings of the Tenth Workshop on the Design, Specification and Verification of Interactive Systems" DSV-IS 2003.

Validity and Cross-Validity in HCI Publications

Harold Thimbleby

Department of Computer Science, Swansea University, Wales
h.thimbleby@swansea.ac.uk

Abstract. Papers in HCI play different roles, whether to inspire, solve industrial problems or further the science of HCI. There is a potential conflict between the different views, and a danger that different forms of validity are assumed by author and reader — deliberately or accidentally.

This paper reviews some of the issues in this complex area and makes practical recommendations. In particular, the paper introduces the term "cross-validity" to help make explicit the issues, problems and means to tackle them.

1 Background

Errors in published scientific papers play different roles. Resolving an error may advance science, it may uncover fraud, or it may remain undetected and delay progress or it may (being undetected) cause inexplicable and apparently unavoidable problems. At another extreme, an inspiring paper may be no less inspiring despite manifest errors — researchers will be stimulated to sort out the errors and inaccuracies they wish to overcome.

Papers can be sound but incomplete; or, a common problem, the analysis correct, but the data flawed. There seem to be many ways for errors to creep in. Papers can be valid in at least three different senses: they may be objectively valid; they may appear valid; or they may be effective for the community (or some sub-community) of researchers. Philosophers may further argue that objective validity is unattainable in any case — there is no rational truth to be 'valid' about in a paper.

In HCI, we have different sources of confusion or possible confusion over types of validity:

- Many techniques in HCI are developed to be used on prototypes or approximations, particularly techniques intended for application in system evaluation (e.g., cognitive walkthrough). It is then a short step to do scientific research with prototypes and approximations instead of real, robust systems.
- Doing good HCI (or usability) involves a particular process, typically starting with something like task analysis, progressing through prototyping and implementation, then evaluation, then iteration. If any HCI publication must show evidence of this process to be valid, then some sorts of HCI may be being excluded. This is a particular problem with doctoral work in HCI, where examiners may expect a three year or longer research project to exhibit all features of the HCI process.

G. Doherty and A. Blandford (Eds.): DSVIS 2006, LNCS 4323, pp. 11–24, 2007.

- HCI is of course multidisciplinary. At worst, one discipline's validity is another's irrelevance. Computer scientists may do work ignoring psychology, and *vice versa*. Mathematicians may do work that cannot be implemented. And so on. Grudin covers these issues very well [9].
- Almost all work in HCI involves a complex system, one or more humans, a task and an environment. Few of these are ever fully defined in a paper, or understood by an author; in fact, the user and environment rarely *can be* defined, and the interactive system itself is rarely available for inspection. In short, work in HCI is based on approximations — that may compromise validity.
- Since a goal of HCI is usability, then it has been argued publications should be usable. If this is believed, then hard papers (e.g., containing mathematical theory) will be published less.
- Usability is the improvement of specific products, for instance in production, whereas HCI as the field of research, for instance refining the principles of design. However the words are defined, there is a conflict on what valid work is. For example, Wixon [20] claims very strongly that the current HCI literature fails — probably because he applies a usability perspective to papers that might not themselves claim to be usability but HCI. Usability professionals read and referee the HCI literature, and their standards, particularly concerning rigour, the significance of errors and handling errors is pervasive in the field. Whether that matters, and if so, from whose point of view, is a crucial point.
- More generally, HCI is a multidisciplinary subject, with disciplines drawn from a very wide variety of traditions. Notions of validity are especially hard to appreciate across disciplinary boundaries, because they are often implicit in the respective discipline's traditions. For example, a mathematician may not appreciate the difficulty in even identifying research questions in a soft approach; a social scientist may not appreciate the difficulty of programming correctly; and a programmer may not appreciate the nature of rigorous experimental methods with human subjects (let alone the ethical issues). A recent book in activity centred design writes, "Leont'ev (1981) created a formal structure [that is] less a representation of reality than a heuristic aid" [6]. To a mathematician this makes as little sense as modal logic must to an activity theorist; yet both can contribute to HCI, and will contribute more if we can find ways to bridge the disciplines — *whilst* remaining true to the disciplinary notions of validity.

Those are brief presentations of deep issues — that we will not resolve in this short paper! The point is to indicate the nature and depth of the problems. What the tensions represent is that there are many ways for author and reader of papers to have differing approaches to validity. Indeed, in HCI this tension seems inevitable. How can we reduce or resolve the tensions? How can we agree to differ where differing is appropriate? Some even argue (with the backing of usability experiments) that validity itself is not a valid notion in HCI [12].

We often have a naïve view of validity. "The scientific researcher writes objectively and is devoted to the pursuit of truth, regardless of pressures such as career progression, financial inducement, fame, or whatever." If we think or teach this simplistic view, then dealing with the reality of error in research will be even harder. Neither readers nor writers of papers will be prepared to guard against potential problems — because they do not expect them. Indeed, referees will not be prepared either, and poor papers will slip through. In turn, the next generation of students will read the poor papers and think that they set the standard to aspire to; thus the next researchers will likely work to lower standards than the ideals of the previous generation.

Errors may mislead readers of a paper and waste time as researchers attempt to reproduce work that has been inaccurately reported. Perhaps worst is when a community ignores minor errors, and standards drop. Perhaps nobody minds if science progresses faster because putting less effort into polishing papers for publication means they can be published faster, but in the long run lowering standards lowers publishing standards. Again: a vicious cycle ensues: poor publications are taken to define the standards of acceptable research, and worse work is then published to appear to be of that standard. New researchers do not learn or appreciate rigour.

The *appearance* of validity is a problem: researchers may read a paper, work from it, but ultimately be wasting their time — does it appear to be valid because its author thought it was (in which case, researchers are helping correct the misconception); does it appear to be valid but isn't because the author was sloppy (in which case, the author is wasting people's time — or the referees of the paper didn't reject it and should have); or perhaps the paper is in some sense fraudulent, and the author intended it to be published, sloppy or not.

Arguably, confusion between the different sorts of validity with respect to the status of a particular paper is *the* problem, certainly a bigger problem than errors, or even fraud *per se*. Confusion in the mind of a reader is worse than confusion (or ignorance) in the mind of a writer as there are usually many more readers than writers. For example, being knowingly inspired to do better is different (and far more constructive) than being misled. But this relies on correctly recognising the status of the paper. Even a fraudulent paper might inspire people. People *wanted* to research on cold fusion regardless of validity: they suspected the Fleischmann and Pons work [5] was fraudulent or exaggerated, but it gave the area a useful impetus and more funding *regardless*.

The difficulty of reproducing research will discourage researchers from trying to build on the foundations of published research; research methods will be understood less, they will be refined less (as fewer people try to use them), and new research will be isolated — and it will also be harder to assess.

In short, we should try to reduce errors, from whatever causes. However, as our knowledge is incomplete, some errors are inevitable: we should also try to improve the detectability of errors. Of course, our attitudes must be realistic and appropriate to purpose: in some areas, we want to be inspired, for instance by futuristic fiction which explores how things might be other than they are, but in other areas, such as flight deck safety in aircraft, we want to be certain, so far as possible, to avoid errors and to make the detection of non-avoided errors as easy as possible. In science, also, we want to report results so that potential or actual errors in our work are as readily detectable as possible.

Notwithstanding Francis Bacon (truth will sooner come out from error than from confusion) [2] and others, Popper [13] was the first to present a systematic argument on the importance of being refutable — and of being *clearly* refutable by being sufficiently precise that errors could be spotted, rather than missed or dismissed. Gray and Salzman's classic though controversial paper [7,8] was an exposé of a widespread relaxed attitude to statistics and experimental method in human-computer interaction. A review of the *Journal of Machine Learning Research* suggests that about a third of its programs are not reproducible [17]; Mlodinow [10] recounts the Nobel Prize winner Richard Feynman's reaction to fraudulent physics, namely he was more concerned at its wasting the time of honest researchers — see also Feynman's discussion of radical honesty [4], which emphasises the central importance of doing science so that potential errors and assumptions are intentionally made clear rather than, as is common, concealed or ignored. There is a large literature on error in science, with [19] being a good review. In computing, tools are available to improve reproducibility [16], a paper that also includes substantial discussion of reproducibility in different disciplines. (I know of no such tools for HCI specifically.)

2   Handling an Error

David Mackay, Alan Blackwell and their colleagues have reported to me that there is an error in my own paper [15]. This particular error resulted from my sloppy proof reading of the paper, which is embarrassing, but I hope that is mitigated by the fact that the error could be, and indeed was, detected.

The Appendix of the present paper briefly summarises the error, and shows alternative approaches to how it can be corrected. Although the case is concrete and (at least to me) interesting, the details have been moved into a self-contained Appendix. The purpose of the present discussion is to generalise, rather than dwell on the specific issues of a particular paper, though of course that paper illustrates the principles.

In terms of the business of science, reporting and correcting a published error is no more than a footnote to a journal's wider business. On the other hand, the paper in question proposes not just a scientific idea advancing research in the field (e.g., under-pinning [18]), but the theory itself is an approach that can be developed further for practical user interface design. The detection and correction of an error in the paper is not just correcting a piece of science publishing, but can also be seen as a parable of detection and correction of errors in practical user interface design. Just as we do not want to mislead researchers, we do not want designers to use methods that allow them to be misled in real design projects: when researchers are misled, time is wasted; when designers are misled, bad systems will be built and lives will be risked. In other words, what at first sight is a criticism of the paper and its author (there was an error) in fact is an argument providing support for applying the approach (the error *was* detected), certainly in safety related applications.

Detailed discussion of the error in the paper is provided in the Appendix A, and the discussion and lessons are summarised in Appendix B.

3   Different Sorts of Error

Although authors may take steps to disguise an error, or an error may be concealed or ignored by accident, in principle errors can be identified. We may distinguish between internal errors: errors that can be spotted by the internal evidence or arguments of paper; errors that can be spotted only by reference to external information (perhaps locked in lab books, or transient and lost); and errors of reportage, which can only be spotted, if at all, by reproducing experiments and collecting more data.

Quite different sorts of problem arise through vagueness and witholding information. Within these sorts of inadequacy, we can see variations:

- Inadequacy due to brevity. The paper is too short. The simplest solution here is to make good use of the internet or FTP to provide supplemental material.
- Inadequacy due to separation. The work was done too long ago (or the paper is being read by somebody some years after it was written). Details are now no longer available — particularly computer-based material. The solution here is to use media like digital libraries and journal repositories that may be archival, or at least far more likely to be archival than the author's resources permit of local storage.
- Due to sloppiness or disregard to standards, the work is vague.
- Due to exaggeration or 'clarification' the work as reported is in some ways better than was actually obtained.

4   Recommendations

This paper has reviewed the role of error in science publication (and has given a 'worked example' centred on and exploring the consequences of an error in one of the author's own HCI papers). So what?

Lessons can be drawn out of the discussion and example, which lead to recommendations for better practice.

4.1   Star Rating

First, it is important that there is a close match between the author's intentions and the reader's understanding of the status of the paper. As an extreme example: a paper written in jest is humourous if the reader recognises it as funny; and a serious paper would not be successful if the readers thought it a joke, and *vice versa* (notwithstanding [14])! A simple idea, then, is that papers should clearly indicate key features of their claim to validity. For example, a star rating could be used — as follows.

A paper that merely claims to be inspirational might have one star. The paper would be refereed on the basis of how inspiring it was, not how reliable it was. Maybe the ideas discussed do not quite work, but nevertheless they are very interesting. A two star paper claims, further, to have got something to work, but perhaps not everything. All the way to a five star paper that claims not only do the ideas work as described, but all background data and programs are available from a server. The exact definitions of the star ratings would depend on the journal (or conference) and the field. A mathematics paper, generally, makes an implicit claim to be five star in this sense — hence the error in my own paper was an issue, because it betrayed the implicit star rating.

Note that an author can improve the star rating of a paper. They can include more data or program code, or provide URLs for readers (and referees) to access the original information. There are many papers, in journals and conferences, that describe systems — but the systems are not available. One may wonder how the actual system implemented and the published paper conform. If we had a culture of awarding stars to papers, there would be a pressure to make papers and what they are about correspond more closely — and be more open to inspection. Indeed, the more stars, the more easily another researcher can build on or reproduce the original work.

Another way of viewing the star rating is answering the question, "does the system described work?" Almost everything in HCI is about an interactive system and the author's experience with it (or the author's experience of a user's experience with it), so something should have worked! So: zero stars for things that do not work; one star for something that almost worked, or worked well enough for a small experiment; two stars for something that really works — but has only be used for the purposes of the paper; three stars for something that not only worked for the paper, but has been developed to work elsewhere as well; four stars for something that has been rigorously tested elsewhere, on different platforms; and five stars for something that is supported to work well anywhere.

4.2   Triangulation

Secondly, authors (and editors and referees) should encourage triangulation: more than one way of justifying a result. If a paper is the only claim to the result, there is no triangulation. One takes the paper on faith (which may be expoited). Triangulation requires alternative routes to the same result — the simplest is that the paper provides URLs so that any reader of the paper can reconstruct for themselves the same results. The discussion of the matrix error above gave several ways in which the same result can be found.

In short, publishing and doing research in a way that promotes triangulation improves the assurance of the results, as well as giving the reader of the paper more choices in reproducing, understanding, or working from the claims made.

4.3   Data, Formal Argument, Programs, etc, Downloadable

Thirdly, many more formal papers in HCI (and papers aspiring to formality) present fragments of formal text. Often the fragments or the notations they are written in are not fully defined. It is of course very hard to abstract out what needs saying for a paper; a full elaboration may take up excessive space. However, mostly, it is a reasonable expectation that the author has actually done the work that the paper abstracts. If so, the work should be available in full, for instance at a URL.

I know of no journal in HCI that has a working mechanism for reporting corrections to papers, let alone a means for encouraging the detection or correction of errors. (Conferences are inevitably in an even worse position.) Why don't journal web sites have explicit correction threads?[1]

As Altman [1] says, if journals are willing to publish subsidiary material on the web, they should explicitly tell authors. More so, journal articles would be improved if it was made clear to readers whether and to what extent the published paper is backed up by subsidiary material; this is a specific form of star rating.

Who would wish to publish papers that announce near their title banner that there is no supporting subsidiary material, if the paper clearly has the nature that there should have been such material (e.g., the paper discusses results obtained from a program; the program presumably exists and was at least once run)? No doubt authors would aspire to the greater prestige of having the right boxes ticked!

4.4   Further Work

Stylistically it is tempting to mix fact and vision. Often fiction is much clearer than the messy reality. What an author plans to do, planned to do, or would rather have done may make a lot more sense that what actually happened. Indeed it is sometimes recommended to write what you want to happen, so that expressing clear goals will guide experimental work; this obviously leaves open-ended the obligation to fix up the writing when the experimental work fails to deliver the original goals neatly.

In some fields, papers fit into standard patterns (e.g., "introduction; previous work; method; experiment; discussion; conclusion; references"). These standard patterns do not help factor out fact from wishes. Many papers, then, would be improved by having a section clearly labelled Further Work, or equivalent, so that the author can explain the simple vision without risk of misleading the reader.

4.5   Clarification and Communal Practice

Finally, we need to sort out these (or better) ideas, because many authors — and doctoral students — are working hard to advance our field, but they may fail in one of two ways:

- They may fail to publish because their notions of validity are not the disciplinary notions of their referees' or examiners'. We will call this the *cross-validity problem*.

---

[1] It was the lack of a working facility in the *ACM Transactions on Computer-Human Interaction* that stimulated the writing of this paper.

– In order to avoid the cross-validity problem (consciously or accidentally) authors may succeed in publishing invalid work that is hard to tell is invalid in any discipline.

4.6   Learning from Other Fields

HCI is not unique in its problems of validity; compared to medical fields, the debate surrounding Gray & Salzman [7] is tame! For example, von Elm and Egger lament the 'scandal' of epidemiological research [3]. Since problems in medical fields have had a longer history than in HCI, various standards have been developed such as the Consolidated Standards for Reporting Trials (CONSORT) and the Standards for the Reporting of Observational Studies (STROBE), etc. I believe it would be an advance if HCI developed or adopted such standards, so that they can be used where applicable — and so that authors can aspire to higher, and explicit, standards in the validity of their work.

Another suggestion from the medical field is post publication peer review [1]. Some HCI journals (such as *Interacting with Computers*), have had reviews, but these have not been sustained.

4.7   An Incomplete List ...

This list of recommendations is incomplete. It raises issues, and suggests solutions. There are many other issues, and other solutions. I hope the list stimulates the HCI community to address the problem of validity, whether incrementally or radically, whether starting from this list or by introducing new ideas. The benefits of improved validity are substantial, and the field clearly has the scope to improve.

5   Conclusions

Theories should be clear and robust enough that errors in their exposition (as in this case) or in their foundations can be reliably and robustly detected. The error reported and corrected in this present paper was essentially a typographical error rather than a conceptual error that needed correction for 'science to progress.' Instead, it can be used to make another point, about the practical application of theory. Had the error or a similar error been made in the design context, it could have been detected and rectified before a faulty product was put into production.

HCI is a very difficult and broad discipline. The difficulties we have in doing good work and reporting it accurately may lead to compromising validity — and to errors. By discussing errors and their role in publication, this paper also suggested some criteria for improving the detectability of errors, and improving the author: reader match of expectations of validity: requiring triangulation, and using a 'star rating' system. As well as a list of recommendations, which are of course of varying value in different subfields of HCI, we introduced the term *cross-validity problem* to enable the community to talk about the central issue explicitly.

To make any recommendations (such as the list above in this paper) work, ways must be found to make the recommendations *sustainable*. Currently, many economic and political factors conspire against improving validity. In the UK, the Research Assessment Exercise attaches no importance to reviewing work for maintaining or improving quality. Instead, it strongly emphasises the value of publishing, and therefore it must tend to increase the volume of publication, and, other things being equal, reduce the standards of validity in publication.

If we do not address validity (and the problem of cross-validity) in HCI we are losing sight of the point of HCI: to improve the quality of life of users, which will come about faster and more reliably through pursuing validity in the relatively abstract realm of research, publication and publication processes.

Acknowledgements

The author thanks David Mackay and Alan Blackwell, Cambridge University, for pointing out the error, the consideration of which triggered this paper. Jeremy Gow pointed out that MAUI was already powerful enough to detect the problem. Harold Thimbleby is a Royal Society-Wolfson Research Merit Award Holder, and gratefully acknowledges this support, which also supported the original research.

References

1. D. G. Altman, "Poor-quality medical research: What can journals do?" *Journal of the American Medical Association*, **287**(21):2765–2767, 2002.
2. F. Bacon, *Novum Oranum (The new organon or true directions concerning the interpretation of nature)*, 1620.
3. E. von Elm & M. Egger, "The scandal of poor epidemiological research," *British Medical Journal*, **329**:868–869, 2004.
4. R. P. Feynman, "Cargo Cult Science," in *Surely You're Joking Mr. Feynman!* R. Hutchings ed., Vintage, 1992.
5. M. Fleischmann & S. Pons, "Calorimetry of the Pd-D2O system: from simplicity via complications to simplicity," *Physics Letters A*, **176**:118–129, 1993.
6. G. Gay & H. Hembrooke, *Activity-centered design*, MIT Press, 2004.
7. W. D. Gray & M. C. Salzman, "Damaged merchandise? A review of experiments that compare usability evaluation methods," *Human-Computer Interaction*, **13**(3):203–261, 1998.
8. W. D. Gray & M. C. Salzman, "Repairing damaged merchandise: A rejoinder," *Human-Computer Interaction*, **13**(3):325–335, 1998.
9. J. Grudin, "Crossing the Divide," *ACM Transactions on Computer-Human Interaction*, **11**(1):1–25, 2004.
10. L. Mlodinow, *Some Time with Feynman*, Penguin Books, 2004.
11. J. Gow, H. Thimbleby & P. Cairns, "Misleading Behaviour in Interactive Systems," *Proceedings BCS HCI Conference*, **2**, edited by A. Dearden and L. Watts, Research Press International, pp33–36, 2004.
12. G. Lindgaard, "Is the notion of validity valid in HCI practice?" *Proceedings 7th International Conference on Work with Computing Systems*, pp94–98, 2004.

13. K. Popper, *The Logic of Scientific Discovery*, Routledge, 2002.
14. A. Sokal, "Transgressing the Boundaries: Toward a Transformative Hermeneutics of Quantum Gravity," *Social Text*, **46/47**:217-252, 1996.
15. H. Thimbleby, "User Interface Design with Matrix Algebra," *ACM Transactions on Computer-Human Interaction*, **11**(2):pp181–236, 2004.
16. H. Thimbleby, "Explaining Code for Publication," *Software — Practice & Experience*, **33**(10):975–1001, 2003.
17. H. Thimbleby, *Journal of Machine Learning Research, Times Higher Education Supplement*, 9 May, 2004.
18. H. Thimbleby, "Computer Algebra in User Interface Design Analysis," *Proceedings BCS HCI Conference*, **2**, edited by A. Dearden and L. Watts, Research Press International, pp121–124, 2004.
19. J. Waller, *Fabulous Science: Fact and Fiction in the History of Scientific Discovery*, Oxford University Press, 2004.
20. D. R. Wixon, "Evaluating usability methods: why the current literature fails the practitioner," *Interactions*, **10**(4):28-34, 2003.

A   The Error

Ironically the error in question occurs in the discussion of a safety related interactive device [15, p217]. The user interface of a commercial Fluke digital multimeter is being discussed. The meter (like many user interfaces) has modes that change the meaning of buttons: in different modes, buttons mean different things. In particular the Fluke multimeter has transient modes entered by pressing shift keys: these change the device mode briefly, which is then restored after the next key press.

It suffices to quote an extract from the original paper as published, along with its original error:

The Fluke meter has a shift button, which changes the meaning of other buttons if they are pressed immediately next. (It only changes the meaning of three buttons, including itself, all of which anyway have extra meanings if held down continuously; additionally, the shift button has a different, non-shift, meaning at switch on.) In general if S represents a shift button and A any button, we want SA to be the button matrix we choose to represent whatever "shifted A" means, and this should depend only on A.

For any button A that is unaffected by the shift, of course we choose $SA = A$. Since the shift button doubles the number of states, we can define it in the usual way as a partitioned matrix acting on a state vector (**unshifted-state : shifted-state**). Since (at least on the Fluke) the shifted mode does not persist (it is not a lockable shift), all buttons now have partitioned matrices in the following simple form

$$\left(\begin{array}{c:c} A_{\text{unshifted}} & 0 \\ \hdashline 0 & A_{\text{shifted}} \end{array} \right)$$

and

$$S = \left(\begin{array}{c:c} \mathbf{0} & I \\ \hdashline I & \mathbf{0} \end{array} \right)$$

which (correctly, for the Fluke) implies pressing $\boxed{\text{SHIFT}}$ twice leaves the meter unshifted (since the submatrices are all the same size and $SS = I$).

The error in the above description is that the matrix written as

$$\left(\begin{array}{c:c} A_{\text{unshifted}} & \mathbf{0} \\ \hdashline \mathbf{0} & A_{\text{shifted}} \end{array} \right)$$

should have been

$$\left(\begin{array}{c:c} A_{\text{unshifted}} & \mathbf{0} \\ \hdashline A_{\text{shifted}} & \mathbf{0} \end{array} \right)$$

This could be argued a trivial error for a scientific paper (a rate of 0.5% error reported per page), and one that is surrounded by context that makes the intention clear. However, had the same error been made in a real design, then the specified device would not behave as intended, perhaps catastrophically so.

That Mackay could spot the error is some encouragement that a designer, or a design team, could equally spot similar errors in an actual design process. How, then, might the error be detected — and are there more general lessons than the particular example?

For clarity, hereon we notate the correct matrix A and the erroneous matrix $\underline{A}$. The matrix, in either its correct or incorrect form, is clearly a composite of an unshifted and a shifted meaning. The differences between A and $\underline{A}$ appear in how the shifted meaning persists, or does not persist, as the button is pressed repeatedly by the user. $\underline{A}$ allows the shifted meaning to persist, which is incorrect.

We now present three very different ways of seeing this error. One is suitable for hand calculations; the next more suited to an automatic tool such as MAUI [11] (which can already detect this problem) or a computer algebra system [18]; finally, we show there is an informal approach to detect the error that would be open to any designer but (like all such approaches) suffers from the likelihood of false positive assessments.

A.1   A Straight Forward Calculation

The paper gives a recipe for constructing any matrix A from its shifted and unshifted meanings, A_{shifted} and $A_{\text{unshifted}}$. Since shift is not supposed to persist, for any two matrices A and B each constructed in the way suggested, the product AB should not mention B_{shifted}, since a shift before A could only affect A but not B.

If we follow the construction shown in the original paper, unfortunately B_{shifted} does appear in the product (it is highlighted by an arrow):

$$\underline{AB} = \left(\begin{array}{c:c} A_{\text{unshifted}} & 0 \\ \hdashline 0 & A_{\text{shifted}} \end{array} \right) \left(\begin{array}{c:c} B_{\text{unshifted}} & 0 \\ \hdashline 0 & B_{\text{shifted}} \end{array} \right)$$

$$= \left(\begin{array}{c:c} A_{\text{unshifted}}B_{\text{unshifted}} & 0 \\ \hdashline 0 & A_{\text{shifted}}B_{\text{shifted}} \end{array} \right)$$

Thus if A is shifted, B must be also, which is incorrect (though of course the whole matrix is wrong). Compare this result with the correct construction:

$$AB = \left(\begin{array}{c:c} A_{\text{unshifted}} & 0 \\ \hdashline A_{\text{shifted}} & 0 \end{array} \right) \left(\begin{array}{c:c} B_{\text{unshifted}} & 0 \\ \hdashline B_{\text{shifted}} & 0 \end{array} \right)$$

$$= \left(\begin{array}{c:c} A_{\text{unshifted}}B_{\text{unshifted}} & 0 \\ \hdashline A_{\text{shifted}}B_{\text{unshifted}} & 0 \end{array} \right)$$

Here, there is no B_{shifted} in the product anywhere; whether A is shifted or unshifted, the meaning of AB depends on $B_{\text{unshifted}}$ and not on B_{shifted} under any circumstances. This is what is meant by the shift not being persistent.

As an aside, it is interesting to note that we can examine the meaning of two consecutive key strokes without knowing what preceded them (or even the actual state of the device before they are pressed); indeed, in this case we know what AB means regardless of whether it follows S or not.

A.2   A Mode Based Calculation

The design tool MAUI [11], which Gow built for exploring properties of interactive systems specified by matrix algebra already has facilities for detecting this class of error. Here, we show how MAUI works.

It is important to remember that the mathematics is concealed by the tool. A designer using a suitable tool need not be as mathematically literate as the exposition here appears to suggest.

MAUI can find device properties automatically (such as the partial properties discussed above); relations between modes are just another case of the properties MAUI can handle. In particular, properties MAUI discovers about a device can be expressed in terms of modes and mode changes.

MAUI defines modes as sets of states. We would therefore define two modes, $\mathbf{s}$ and $\mathbf{u}$ representing the shifted and unshifted modes. The designer would be told that $\mathbf{u}\underline{A}$ remains in mode $\mathbf{u}$ but that $\mathbf{s}\underline{A}$ stays in $\mathbf{s}$. But $\mathbf{s}\underline{A}$ should have returned to mode $\mathbf{u}$!

Inside MAUI, this is how it is done: A mode is represented as a vector, such that for all states s in the mode M represented by $\mathbf{m}$, $\mathbf{m}_s = s \in M$. We define $\Box\mathbf{a} \sqsubseteq \mathbf{b} = \forall i\colon \mathbf{a}_i \Rightarrow \mathbf{b}_i$. It is now a routine calculation to show $\Box\mathbf{u}\underline{A} \sqsubseteq \mathbf{u}$ and $\Box\mathbf{s}\underline{A} \sqsubseteq \mathbf{s}$ (which is the error), whereas $\Box\mathbf{u}A \sqsubseteq \mathbf{u}$ and $\Box\mathbf{s}A \sqsubseteq \mathbf{u}$ (which is correct). Our notation is suggestive of counting states in a mode, and this is in fact what MAUI does.

A.3   Simulation

MAUI allows a device to be simulated (and many other tools can simulate devices specified by matrices or equivalent formalisms), and it is a simple matter for a designer to try out a simulated device out in order to satisfy themselves it behaves as intended.

The problem here is that any hand-driven simulation will likely miss errors — the designer might have been more worried over some other potential error, and omitted to test whether the shift key effect was persistent or not; or the designer might have found that the shift key works, but they have failed to check every possible combination of key presses. The state spaces of typical devices are enormous, and way beyond direct human assessment.

Though a simulation is realistic, a designer is really in no better a position than a user: just because the device appears correct in some or even in a majority of states, the designer is liable to believe the device correct on incomplete information. Worse, the areas of the device the designer explores carefully are likely to be areas of concern and hence are anyway the areas that have been more rigorously designed; problems may remain undiscovered in areas that no designer has paid much attention. For safety related devices, therefore, it is crucial that a tool-based or mathematical analysis is made. Indeed, if a designer 'plays' with a device simulation in MAUI and believes some property true, they can ask MAUI to confirm this or point out the conditions under which the property fails.

B   Discussion

In short, the paper [15] claimed a property (shifted meanings do not persist) and showed a matrix that failed the claimed property, as is evident by the straight forward calculations carried out above. In the design context, perhaps the matrix A or $\underline{A}$ would be proposed, and would then be checked against the desired property or properties. Simply, $\underline{A}$ would fail the test and would be eliminated from the design.

Had a similar design issue (or claim in a scientific paper) been treated using, say, transition diagrams, which are a superficially simpler formalism, it is unlikely that the design property could have been checked, let alone analysed so readily. Matrices have the clear advantage of being easy to calculate with. Indeed the calculations needed above were routine and easy to do by hand (they only involved 2×2 matrices — regardless of the complexity or sizes of the submatrices A_{shifted} and $A_{\text{unshifted}}$).

Arguably the algebraic formula $\square \mathsf{s} \underline{A} \sqsubseteq \mathsf{s}$ (or its straight forward translation into words: pressing the button a keeps the device in shifted mode) is a clearer representation of the error than the earlier result involving $\underline{AB}$, but the calculation using modes relies on being very clear about which states are in which modes, as well as doing a multiplication involving all states. Such calculations are better suited to a computer than a human!

In an ideal world, a real designer would probably use a design tool to handle or hide the details; understanding matrix multiplication and doing hand calculations would be largely and in some cases unnecessary. In a more reasonable, not so idealised world, the design task would probably be split between different people: the specification of design requirements (such as non-persistent shift meanings) would be formulated by mathematically competent designers once; then a design tool would be used to automatically check the required properties continued to hold as the design was developed or iterated — in this case, the development and continual modifications of the design could be managed by the tool without any reference to the underlying technical computations, matrix algebra or otherwise.

Model-Based Engineering of Widgets, User Applications and Servers Compliant with ARINC 661 Specification

Eric Barboni[1], Stéphane Conversy[1,2], David Navarre[1], and Philippe Palanque[1]

[1] LIIHS – IRIT, Université Paul Sabatier
118 route de Narbonne, 31062 Toulouse Cedex 4
{barboni, conversy, navarre, palanque}@irit.fr
http://liihs.irit.fr/{barboni,navarre,palanque}
[2] ENAC – DTI/SDER – Ecole Nationale de l'Aviation Civile
7, avenue Edouard Belin, 31055 Toulouse
conversy@enac.fr

Abstract. The purpose of ARINC 661 specification [1] is to define interfaces to a Cockpit Display System (CDS) used in any types of aircraft installations. ARINC 661 provides precise information for communication protocol between application (called User Applications) and user interface components (called widgets) as well as precise information about the widgets themselves. However, in ARINC 661, no information is given about the behaviour of these widgets and about the behaviour of an application made up of a set of such widgets. This paper presents the results of the application of a formal description technique to the various elements of ARINC 661 specification within an industrial project. This formal description technique called Interactive Cooperative Objects defines in a precise and non-ambiguous way all the elements of ARINC 661 specification. The application of the formal description techniques is shown on an interactive application called MPIA (Multi Purpose Interactive Application). Within this application, we present how ICO are used for describing interactive widgets, User Applications and User Interface servers (in charge of interaction techniques). The emphasis is put on the model-based management of the feel of the applications allowing rapid prototyping of the external presentation and the interaction techniques. Lastly, we present the CASE (Computer Aided Software Engineering) tool supporting the formal description technique and its new extensions in order to deal with large scale applications as the ones targeted at by ARINC 661 specification.

1 Introduction

Interactive applications embedded in cockpits are the current trend of evolution promoted by several aircraft manufacturer both in the field of civil and military systems [7, 10]. Embedding interactive application in civil and military cockpit is expected to provide significant benefits to the pilots by providing them with easier to use and more efficient applications increasing the communication bandwidth between pilots and systems. However, this technological enhancement comes along with

G. Doherty and A. Blandford (Eds.): DSVIS 2006, LNCS 4323, pp. 25–38, 2007.
© Springer-Verlag Berlin Heidelberg 2007

several problems that have to be taken into account with appropriate precautions. ARINC specification 661 (see next section), aims at providing a common ground for building interactive applications in the field of aeronautical industry. However, this standard only deals with part of the issues raised. The aim of this paper is to propose a formal description technique to be used as a complement to ARINC 661 for the specification, design, implementation and validation of interactive application.

The paper is structured as follows. Next section introduces ARINC 661 specification to define software interfaces for a Cockpit Display System. It presents informally the content of the specification but also its associated architecture that has to be followed in order to build ARINC-661-compliant interactive applications. Section 3 presents the ICO formalism, a formal description technique for the design of safety critical interactive applications. This description technique has already been applied in various domains including Air Traffic Control applications, multimodal military cockpits or multimodal satellite ground segments. Its applicability to cockpit display system and its compatibility with ARINC specification 661 is discussed and extensions that had to be added are also presented in section 4. Section 5 presents the use of the formal description technique on an interactive application called MPIA (Multi Purpose Interactive Application) currently available in some cockpits of regional aircrafts. Last section of the paper deals with conclusions and perspectives to this work.

2 ARINC 661 Specification

This section presents, in an informal way, the basic principles of ARINC 661 specification. The purpose of this section is to provide a description of the underlying mechanisms of ARINC 661 specification and more precisely how its content influences the behaviour and the software architecture of interactive applications embedded in interactive cockpits.

2.1 Purpose and Scope

The purpose of ARINC 661 specification (ARINC 661, 2002) is to define interfaces to a Cockpit Display System (CDS) used in interactive cockpits that are now under deployment by several aircraft manufacturers including Airbus, Boeing and Dassault.
The CDS provides graphical and interactive services to user applications (UA) within the flight deck environment. Basically, the interactive applications will be executed on Display Units (DU) and interaction with the pilots will take place through the use of Keyboard and graphical input devices like the Keyboard Cursor Control Unit (KCCU).

ARINC 661 dissociates, on one side, input and output devices (provided by avionics equipment manufacturers) and on the other side the user applications (designed by aircraft manufacturers). Consistency between these two parts is maintained through a communication protocol:

- Transmission of data to the CDS, which can be displayed to the flight deck crew.
- Reception of input (as events) from interactive items managed by the CDS.

In the field of interactive systems engineering, interactive software architectures such as Seeheim [14] or Arch [9] promote a separation of the interactive system in at least three components: presentation part (in charge of presenting information to and receiving input from the users), dialogue part (in charge of the behaviour of the system i.e. describing the available interface elements according to the current state of the application) and functional core (in charge of the non interactive functions of the system). The CDS part may be seen as the presentation part of the whole system, provided to crew members, and the set of UAs may be seen as the merge of both the dialogue and the functional core of this system.

2.2 User Interface Components in ARINC 661

The communication between the CDS and UAs is based on the identification of user interface components hereafter called widgets. ARINC 661 defines a set of 42 widgets that belong to 6 categories. Widgets may be any combination of "container", "graphical representation" of one or more data, "text string" representations, "interactive", dedicated to "map management" or may "dynamically move".

In ARINC 661, each widget is defined by:

- a set of states classified in four levels (visibility, inner state, ability, visual representation),
- a description in six parts (definition section, parameters table, creation structure table, event structure table, run-time modifiable parameter table, specific sections).

The main drawback of this description is the lack of description of the behaviour itself. Even if states are partially described, dynamic aspects such as state changes are informally described. As stated in ARINC 661 (section 1.0 introduction), the main paradigm is here based on this comment:

"A UA should not have any direct access to the visual representations. Therefore, visual presentations do not have to be defined within the ARINC 661 interface protocol. Only the ARINC 661 parameter effects on graphical representation should be described in the ARINC 661 interface. The style guide defined by the OEM should describe the "look and feel" and thus, provide necessary information to UAs for their HMI interface design."

An additional textual description called SRS (for Software Requirement Specification), informally defines the look and feel of a CDS (Cockpit Display System). This SRS is designed by each manufacturer of airline electronic equipment (we worked with a draft document provided by Thales Avionics). This kind of document describes both the appearance and the detailed expected behaviour of each graphical or interactive component.

2.3 Overview of Our Contribution to ARINC 661

One of the goals of the work presented in this paper is to define an architecture that clearly identifies each part of this architecture and their communication, as shown on Fig. 1. The aim of this architecture is also to clearly identify which components will be taken into account in the modelling process and which ones are taken into account in a different way by exploiting SVG facilities. The architecture has two main advantages:

1. Every component that has an inner behaviour (server, widgets, UA, and the connection between UA and widgets, e.g. the rendering and activation functions) is fully modelled using the ICO formal description technique.
2. The rendering part is delegated to a dedicated language and tool (such as SVG).

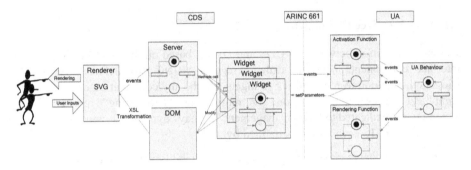

Fig. 1. Detailed architecture to support ARINC 661 specification

The following section recalls the basics of ICO notation and presents a new extension that has been required in order to be able to address all the modelling challenges put forward by interactive cockpit applications compliant with ARINC 661 specification, and then present the connection to SVG. Lastly, a real case study illustrates this architecture and how modelling all the elements of ARINC 661 specification are addressed using ICOs formal description technique.

3 ICO Modelling of ARINC 661 Components

We use the ICO formalism to describe formally the behaviour of the ARIC components. This section first briefly recalls the main features of the ICO formalism. We encourage the interested reader to look at [13, 11] for a complete presentation of the formal description technique and the environment supporting it. The second part is dedicated to the extensions that had to be defined in order to address the specificities of interactive applications compliant with ARINC 661 specifications.

3.1 Overview of the ICO Formalism

The Interactive Cooperative Objects (ICOs) formalism is a formal description technique dedicated to the specification of interactive systems [4, 11]. It uses concepts borrowed from the object-oriented approach to describe the structural or static aspects of systems, and uses high-level Petri nets [8] to describe their dynamic or behavioural aspects. ICOs are dedicated to the modelling and the implementation of event-driven interfaces, using several communicating objects to model the system, where both behaviour of objects and communication protocol between objects are described by Petri nets. The formalism made up of both the description technique for the communicating objects and the communication protocol is called the Cooperative Objects formalism (CO).

ICOs are used to provide a formal description of the dynamic behaviour of an interactive application. An ICO specification fully describes the potential interactions that users may have with the application. The specification encompasses both the "input" aspects of the interaction (i.e., how user actions impact on the inner state of the application, and which actions are enabled at any given time) and its "output" aspects (i.e., when and how the application displays information relevant to the user). Time-out transitions are special transitions that do not belong to the categories above.

An ICO specification is fully executable, which gives the possibility to prototype and test an application before it is fully implemented [12]. The specification can also be validated using analysis and proof tools developed within the Petri nets community and extended in order to take into account the specificities of the Petri net dialect used in the ICO formal description technique.

3.2 ICO Improvements

Two main issues have been raised while working with ARINC 661 specification that have not been encountered in previous work we have done in the field of interactive systems' specification and modeling.

- The first one is related to the management of rendering information in a more independent and structured way in order to be able to dissociate as much as possible the graphical appearance of interactive components from their behavior. This is one of the basics of interactive cockpit applications compliant with ARINC 661 specification as (as stated above) these two sides of the interactive cockpit applications are described in two different documents (communication protocol and abstract behavior in ARINC 661 specification while presentation and detailed behavior are described in the SRS (System Requirement Specifications)).
- The second one is related to the fact that ARINC 661 specification does not exploit current windows manager available in the operating system (as this is the case for Microsoft Windows applications for instance). On the opposite, the manufacturer in charge of developing the entire ARINC 661 architecture is also in charge of developing all the components in charge of the management of input devices, device drivers and to manage the graphical structure of the interactive widgets. In order to handle those aspects we have defined a denotational semantics (in terms of High-level Petri nets) of both the rendering and the activation functions. Beforehand, these functions were only partly defined (relying on the underlying

mechanisms provided by the window manager) and implemented using a particular java API thus making much more limited the verification aspects of theses aspects of the specification. Indeed, the work presented here addresses at the same level of formality, applications, widgets and user interface server (also called window manager). Besides, the connections and communications between these three parts are also formally described.

Next section presents in details the various mechanisms that have been defined in order to handle the low level management of input devices and focuses on one specific aspect called picking which correspond to the window manager activating of finding the interactive component that was the target of the user when an event has been produced. The case study in section 0 shows on a concrete example how those elements are combined for describing User Applications, Widgets and User Interface servers.

4 MPIA Case Study

MPIA is a User Application (UA) that aims at handling several flight parameters. It is made up of 3 pages (called WXR, GCAS and AIRCOND) between which a crew member is allowed to navigate using 3 buttons (as shown by Fig. 2). WXR page is in charge managing weather radar information; GCAS is in charge of the Ground Anti Collision System parameters while AIRCOND deals with settings of the air conditioning.

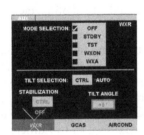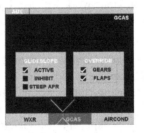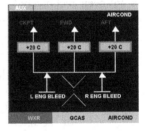

Fig. 2. Snapshots of the 3 pages of the UA MPIA

In this section, we present the modelling of a simple widget and its link to SVG rendering, then we briefly present the classical modelling of a user application to show the extension made to ICOs, and finally we present parts of the server. The purpose is not here to present the whole specification which is made up of about 40 models, but only to present brief extracts to show all bricks of the modelling.

4.1 Modelling ARINC 661 Interactive Widgets

The whole modelling process of ARINC 661 interactive components using ICO is fully described in [12]. The additional feature consists in using the rendering process described above, based on replacing the classical code-based rendering methods with rendering methods that modify the SVG Document Object Model. Rendering is the process of transforming a logical description (conceptual model) of an interactive component to a graphical representation (perceptual model). In previous similar works, we specified rendering with Java code, using the Java2D API., However, describing graphics with an imperative language is not an easy task, especially when one tries to match a particular look. Furthermore, the java code for graphics is embedded into the model, which makes it hard to change for another look. This is even more difficult when several components share a common part of the graphical representation, for instance when components must have a similar style and when this style has to be changed.

To overcome these two problems, we changed for an architecture that uses declarative descriptions of the graphical part and that supports transformations from conceptual models to graphical representations. These two elements exploit XML-based languages from the W3C: the SVG language for graphical representation, and the XSLT language for transformation. SVG is an xml-based vector graphics format: it describes graphical primitives in terms of analytical shapes and transformations. XSLT is an xml-based format that describes how to transform an xml description (the source) to another xml description (the target). An XSLT description is called a "stylesheet". Due to space constraints this work is not presented in the next section as we focus on the behavioural aspects of models.

4.2 Modelling User Applications

Modelling a user application using ICO is quite simple as ICO has already been used to model such kind of interactive applications. Indeed, UAs in the area of interactive cockpits correspond to classical WIMP interfaces,

As the detailed specification is not necessary to expose the modification of ICO, we only present an excerpt of the models that have been produced to build the MPIA application. This excerpt is the first page (WXR) of the application (left part of Fig. 2).

4.2.1 Behaviour

Fig. 3 shows the entire behaviour of page WXR which is made up of two non connected parts:

- The upper part aims at handling events from the 5 CheckButtons and the modification implied of the MODE_SELECTION that might be one of five possibilities (OFF, STDBY, TST, WXON, WXA). Value changes of token stored in place *Mode-Selection* are described in the transitions while variables on the incoming and outgoing arcs play the role of formal parameters of the transitions.
- The lower part concerns the handling of events from the 2 PicturePushButton and the EditBoxNumeric. Interacting with these buttons will change the state of the application.

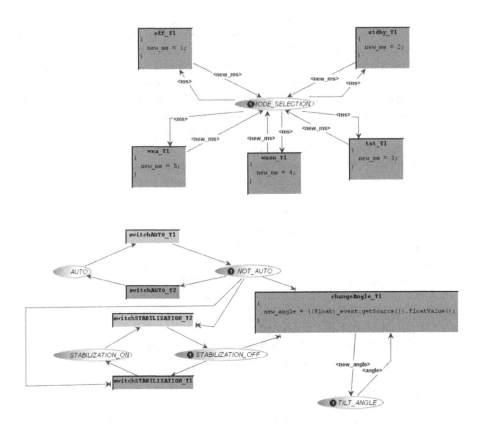

Fig. 3. Behaviour of the page WXR

4.2.2 Activation Function

Fig 4 shows an excerpt of the activation function for page WXR.

	Widget	Event	UserService	ActivationRendering
wxrOFFAdapter	off_CheckButton	A661_INNER_STATE_SELECT	off	setWXRModeSelectEnabled
wxrSTDBYAdapter	stdby_CheckButton	A661_INNER_STATE_SELECT	stdby	setWXRModeSelectEnabled
wxrTSTAdapter	tst_CheckButton	A661_INNER_STATE_SELECT	tst	setWXRModeSelectEnabled
wxrWXONAdapter	wxon_CheckButton	A661_INNER_STATE_SELECT	wxon	setWXRModeSelectEnabled
wxrWXAAdapter	wxa_CheckButton	A661_INNER_STATE_SELECT	wxa	setWXRModeSelectEnabled
autoAdapter	auto_PicturePushButton	A661_EVT_SELECTION	switchAUTO	setWXRTiltSelectionEnabled
stabAdapter	stab_PicturePushButton	A661_EVT_SELECTION	switchSTABILIZATION	setWXRTiltSelectionEnabled
tiltAngleAdapter	tiltAngle_EditBox	A661_STRING_CHANGE	changeAngle	setWXRTiltSelectionEnabled

Fig. 4. Activation Function of the page WXR

From this textual description, we can derive the ICO model shown on Fig. 5. The left part of this figure presents the full activation function, which is made up of as many sub Petri nets as there are lines in the textual activation function. The upper right hand side of the figure emphasises on of these sub Petri nets. It describes how the availability of the associated widget is modified according to some changes in the WXR behaviour. The lower right hand part of the Figure shows the general pattern associated to one line of the activation function: It describes the handling of the event raised par the corresponding widget, and how it is linked to an event handler in the WXR behaviour.

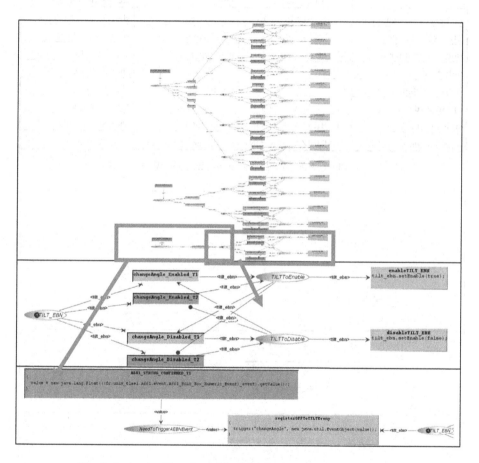

Fig. 5. Activation Function of the page WXR expressed in Petri nets

The use of Petri nets to model the activation function is made possible thanks to the event communication available in the ICO formalism. As this kind of communication is out of the scope of this paper, we do not present the models responsible in the registration of events-handlers needed to allow the communication between behaviour, activation function and widgets. More information about this mechanism can be found in [2].

4.2.3 Rendering Function

The modelling of the rendering function (shown on Fig. 6) into Petri nets (shown on Fig. 7) works the same way as for the activation function, i.e. for each line in the rendering function, there is a pattern to express that in Petri nets. This is why we do not detail more the translation.

	ObCSNode name	ObCS event	Rendering method
modeSelectionAdapter	MODE_SELECTION	token_enter <int m>	showModeSelection(m)
tiltAngleAdapter	TILT_ANGLE	token_enter <float a>	showTiltAngle(a)
initAutoAdapter	AUTO	marking_reset	showAuto(true)
autoAdapter	AUTO	token_enter	showAuto(true)
notAutoAdapter	AUTO	token_remove	showAuto(false)
initStabAdapter	STABILIZATION_ON	marking_reset	showStab(true)
stabAdapter	STABILIZATION_ON	token_enter	showStab(true)
notStabAdapter	STABILIZATION_ON	token_remove	showStab(false)

Fig. 6. Rendering Function of the page WXR

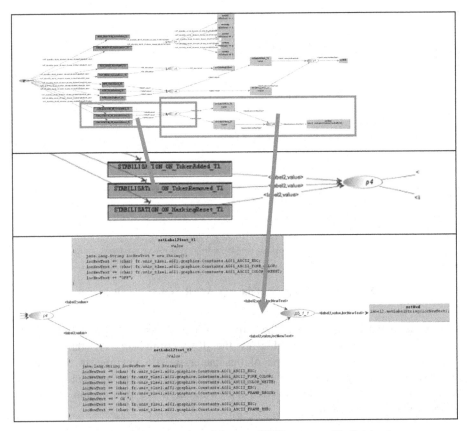

Fig. 7. Rendering Function of the page WXR expressed in Petri nets

4.3 Modelling User Interface Server

The user interface server manages the set of widgets and the hierarchy of widgets used in the User Applications. More precisely, the user interface server is responsible in handling:

- The creation of widgets
- The graphical cursors of both the pilot and his co-pilot
- The edition mode
- The mouse and keyboard events and dispatching it to the corresponding widgets
- The highlight and the focus mechanisms
- ...

As it handles many functionalities, the complete model of the sub-server (dedicated in handling widgets involved in the MPIA User Application) is complex and difficult to manipulate without an appropriate tool. As the detailed model is out of the scope of this paper, Fig. 8 only present an overview of the complete model.

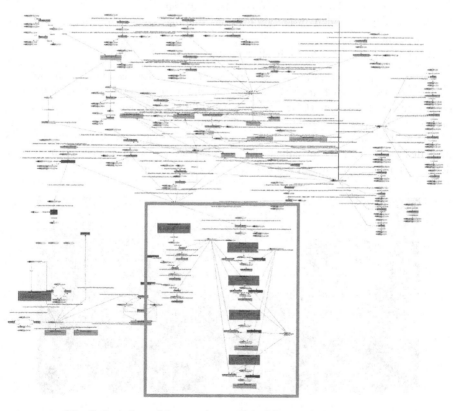

Fig. 8. Overview of the complete model of the user interface server

The rectangle at the bottom of Fig. 8 represents the part of the model of the server in charge of the interaction technique and input devices management. The rest of the model corresponds to the management of the widgets.

4.4   Modelling the Complete MPIA User Application

We do not present here the full model of the user application MPIA neither the one of the user interface server, but the formal description technique ICO has been used to model in a complete and non ambiguous way all the pages and the navigation between pages for such user application, and still produces low-sized and readable models. Modelling Activation functions and Rendering functions using Petri nets, legitimates the use of the table notation as a readable way to express the connection between the dialog and the presentation parts.

Another issue is that the models of the user application MPIA can both be connected to the modelled CDS or to an implemented CDS, using a special API, as it respects the ARINC 661 specification. As testing an implemented user application is still a problem that has to be solved, especially when the UA is connected to a real CDS, a model based approach may support testing at different levels:

1. Test a modelled user application on the modelled CDS.
2. Test the modelled user application on the CDS implemented by the manufacturer.
3. Code and test the user application on the implemented CDS.

The first step promotes a very iterative prototyping process where both the User Application and the CDS may be modified, as the second step allows user testing on the real interactive system (CDS), with classical prototyping facilities provided by the models expressed in ICO of the User Application.

The MPIA application has been fully modelled and can be executed on the CDS modelled using the ICO formalism. However, it has also been connected on a CDS developed on an experimental test bench as shown in Fig. 9.

Fig. 9. The MPIA application modelled using ICO connected to experimental CDS at THALES

5   Conclusions and Perspectives

This paper has presented the use of a formal description technique for describing interactive components in ARINC specification 661. Beyond that, we have shown that this formal description technique is also adequate for interactive applications embedding such interactive components. One of the advantages of using the ICO formal description technique is that it provides additional benefits with respect to other notations such as statecharts as proposed in [15]. Thanks to its Petri nets basis the ICO notations makes it possible to model behaviours featuring an infinite number of states (as states are modelled by a distribution of tokens in the places of the Petri nets). Another advantage of ICOs is that they allow designers to use verification techniques at design time as this has been presented in [3]. These verification techniques are of great help for certification purposes.

We are currently developing techniques for providing support to certification processes by allowing verification of compatibility between the behavioural description of the interactive application and task model describing nominal or unexpected pilots behaviour. Support is also provided through the verification of interactive system safety and liveness properties such as the fact that whatever state the system is in there is always at least one interactive element available.

Acknowledgements

The work presented in the paper is partly funded by DPAC (Direction des Programmes de l'Aviation Civile) under contract #00.70.624.00.470.75.96. Special thanks are due to our colleagues at THALES P. Cazaux and S. Marchal.

References

1. ARINC 661 specification: Cockpit Display System Interfaces To User Systems, Prepared by Airlines Electronic Engineering Committee, Published by AERONAUTICAL RADIO, INC, april 22, 2002.
2. Bastide R., Navarre D., Palanque P., Schyn A. & Dragicevic P. A Model-Based Approach for Real-Time Embedded Multimodal Systems in Military Aircrafts. Sixth International Conference on Multimodal Interfaces (ICMI'04) October 14-15, 2004 Pennsylvania State University, USA.
3. Bastide R., David Navarre & Philippe Palanque. Tool Support for Interactive Prototyping of Safety Critical Interactive Applications. In Encyclopedia of HCI, C. Gaoui (Ed.). ISBN: 1-59140-562-9. Hard Cover. Publisher: Idea Group Reference Pub Date: July 2005. Pages: 650.
4. Bastide R., Ph. Palanque A Petri Net Based Environment for the Design of Event-Driven Interfaces. 16th International Conference on Application and theory of Petri Nets (ATPN'95), LNCS, Springer Verlag, Torino, Italy, 20-22 June 1995.
5. Beaudoux O., 2005. XML Active Transformation (eXAcT): Transforming Documents within Interactive Systems. Proceedings of the 2005 ACM Symposium on Document Engineering (DocEng 2005), ACM Press, pages 146-148.

6. Blanch R., Michel Beaudouin-Lafon, Stéphane Conversy, Yannick Jestin, Thomas Baudel and Yun Peng Zhao. INDIGO : une architecture pour la conception d'applications graphiques interactives distribuées. In Proceedings of IHM 2005, pages 139-146, Toulouse - France, September 2005.

7. Faerber R. Vogl T. & Hartley D. Advanced Graphical User Interface for Next Generation Flight Management Systems. In proceedings of HCI Aero 2000, pp. 107-112.

8. Genrich H. J.. (1991). Predicate/Transition Nets, in K. Jensen and G. Rozenberg (Eds.), High-Level Petri Nets: Theory and Application. Springer Verlag, Berlin, pp. 3-43.

9. Gram C., Cockton G. (Editors). Design principles for interactive software. Chapman et Hall ed.1995.

10. Marrenbach J., Kraiss K-F. Advanced Flight Management System: A New Design and Evaluation Results. In proceedings of HCI Aero 2000, pp. 101-106.

11. Navarre D., Palanque, Philippe, Bastide, Rémi. A Tool-Supported Design Framework for Safety Critical Interactive Systems in Interacting with computers, Elsevier, Vol. 15/3, pp 309-328, 2003.

12. Navarre D., Philippe Palanque & Rémi Bastide. A Formal Description Technique for the Behavioural Description of Interactive Applications Compliant with ARINC 661 Specification. HCI-Aero'04 Toulouse, France, 29 September-1st October 2004.

13. Palanque P., R. Bastide. Petri nets with objects for specification, design and validation of user-driven interfaces. In proceedings of the third IFIP TC 13 conference on Human-Computer Interaction, Interact'90. Cambridge 27-31 August 1990 (UK).

14. Pfaff, G. E. (Hrsg.): User Interface Management Systems, Proceedings, Workshop on User Interface Management Systems, Seeheim,(1. - 3.11.1983); Springer Verlag 1983.

15. Sherry L., Polson P., Feary M. & Palmer E. When Does the MCDU Interface Work Well? Lessons Learned for the Design of New Flightdeck User-Interface. In proceedings of HCI Aero 2002, AAAI Press, pp. 180-186.

16. Souchon, N., Vanderdonckt, J., A Review of XML-Compliant User Interface Description Languages, Proc. of 10th Int. Conf. on Design, Specification, and Verification of Interactive Systems DSV-IS'2003 (Madeira, 4-6 June 2003), Jorge, J., Nunes, N.J., Falcao e Cunha, J. (Eds.), Lecture Notes in Computer Science, Vol. 2844, Springer-Verlag, Berlin, 2003, pp. 377-391.

17. UsiXML, http://www.usixml.org/?view=news.

18. Villard, L. and Layaïda, N. 2002. An incremental XSLT transformation processor for XML document manipulation. In Proceedings of the 11th international Conference on World Wide Web (Honolulu, Hawaii, USA, May 07 - 11, 2002). WWW '02. ACM Press, New York, NY, 474-485.

Usability Requirements for Improving the Infection Module of a Hospital Intensive Care Unit Information System

Mónica Sara Santos[1], João Falcão e Cunha[2], and Altamiro da Costa Pereira[3]

[1] Faculdade de Engenharia da Universidade do Porto / Escola Superior de Tecnologia da Saúde do Instituto Politécnico do Porto, Praça Coronel Pacheco, 15 4050-453 Porto, Portugal
Tel: +351 222061000; Fax: +351 225081390
mss@estsp.ipp.pt
[2] Faculdade de Engenharia da Universidade do Porto, Porto, Portugal
jfcunha@fe.up.pt
[3] Faculdade de Medicina da Universidade do Porto, Porto, Portugal
altamiro@med.up.pt

Abstract. The Intensive Care Unit (ICU) of Hospitals deals with patients in life critical conditions. The Intensive Care Information System (ICS) can therefore provide extremely important information to support medical doctors' (MDs) decisions. For instance, it is critical to manage well information about the evolution of a large amount of infections over time, about the antibiotics administered to each patient, and the impact on his/her life condition. Good quality information and interaction in such an extreme environment is therefore critical for helping MDs target well medicines to patients. This paper describes the initial stages of a project aiming at improving a real ICS, in particular from the interaction point of view, taking into account the stringent usability requirements from the MDs. Through a validated low definition prototype of the infection module of ICS, the paper proposes innovative active ways of providing suggestions to MDs on what actions to take.

Keywords: Human Computer Interaction, Requirements Engineering, Medical Information Systems.

1 Introduction

The Intensive Care Information System (ICS) used in four major hospitals in the North of Portugal is called *intensive.care*. It is being developed at the Biostatistics and Medical Informatics Service (SBIM) in the Medicine School of Universidade do Porto (FMUP) [1].

ICS' main functions are to register patients' admission and discharge notes, to register electronic clinical data such as patients' antecedents, diary, therapy data, procedures, diagnosis, complications and infection management, and to calculate ICU prognostic scoring indicators (see Fig. 1). These scoring techniques are used to obtain quantitative statements about the patients' health condition. They include APACHE II

G. Doherty and A. Blandford (Eds.): DSVIS 2006, LNCS 4323, pp. 39–51, 2007.
© Springer-Verlag Berlin Heidelberg 2007

(Acute Physiology and Chronic Health Evaluation System), SAPS II (Simplified Acute Physiology Score), SOFA (Sequential Organ Failure Assessment) and TISS-28 (Therapeutic Intervention Scoring System-28) [2]. TISS-28 is registered by Nurses, while all other indicators are registered by MDs.

Intensive.care is composed of several modules, which vary in complexity as there are some basic ones, such as the patients' admission and discharge notes, and others that are more complex, such as the infection or complications management.

Intensive.care works with large amounts of data and amongst its stakeholders are the ICU patients, people that are in a very critical health condition, and the ICU MDs for whom time is extremely valuable. So there is the need for very high quality data, good system performance and lack of errors.

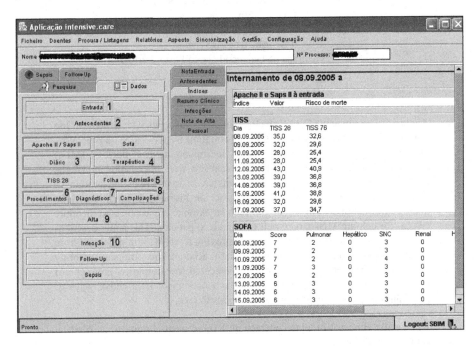

Fig. 1. Starting menu of *intensive.care* (on the left) where users can navigate through the existing modules (1 – admission; 2 – antecedents; 3 – diary; 4 – therapeutics; 5 admission chart; 6 – procedures; 7 – diagnosis; 8 – complications; 9 – release; 10 – infection). On the right there is an overview of prognostic scoring indicators' evolution for a patient, selected by the *Índices* option (central tabs).

Every hospital in Portugal has a central information system that manages patients' information. This system is called SONHO. *Intensive.care* connects to SONHO, automatically getting the patients' demographic data and storing it in the local patient record (whenever the person is already known in the hospital central system). Since every single public hospital in Portugal uses SONHO, *intensive.care* is prepared to easily being introduced into a new ICU, requiring nevertheless some customization.

Intensive.care has never had a Human Computer Interaction (HCI) development plan and has not been developed having usability as a main concern. Its development has always been focused on its functionality rather than its HCI characteristics. Therefore *intensive.care* has some notorious HCI problems and its users feel there are many things about it that could be improved. Moreover, there are some modules of *intensive.care* that have never been used, in particular because of their HCI problems.

Meetings with several *intensive.care* users, reported in the next sections, indicate that it is a successful application, but still with several problems. The current study has identified the modules that most need improvements and aims at defining overall requirements. Since there is an intention of implementing *intensive.care* in other ICUs, usability problems need to be addressed, so a formal HCI evaluation is being conducted in order to propose an improvement plan for *intensive.care*. This improvement plan will produce a document containing a set of usability requirements for the evolution of *intensive.care*.

Currently *intensive.care* is implemented in four hospitals in Portugal, but these units have started using it at different times. Since *intensive.care* has been gradually implemented in different units, it has different kinds of users when it comes to their experience with the application. The users range from those who have three years experience to those who have been using *intensive.care* for only a few months.

The next section presents the methodology of the overall study. Section 3 presents the preliminary results of the interviews with key stakeholders, which led to the choice of the infection module for a more focused HCI evaluation. In section 4 there is the definition of some requirements, supported by a prototype, for the improvement of the infection module. In the final sections there are the proposed future work and the conclusions.

2   Methodology

An HCI study and evaluation is being conducted in order to produce an HCI evolution plan for *intensive.care*. This evolution plan is based on a set of usability requirements that are being defined, based on the results from the application of well-known HCI techniques. At different stages of this evaluation, usability requirements will be specified and evaluated by *intensive.care*'s stakeholders.

The current project started with the study of the ICS tool and of the ICU information management problem. This was made to gain some knowledge about the system and the way it interacts with users' needs. There were some meetings with the development team, including the current project manager and the first project manager of *intensive.care*.

Several interviews were held with users, which can be divided into two sets. The first set was composed by three interviews to key users of *intensive.care* in three different hospitals. These interviews were intended to collect information about the most problematic issues about *intensive.care*. The main objective was to find areas from *intensive.care* that most users felt should be improved, and after that to focus the study in those areas.

After compiling the results of the interviews, there was a qualitative study that resulted in the establishment of the main module from *intensive.care* where the HCI evaluation would be centred. The focus for the evolution was set to be the infection module, as will be seen on section 3.

When the focus area was established, the second set of interviews took place. They happened in two hospitals with experts in infection in ICU. Since the evaluators have no medical background, these interviews aimed to understand the basis of infection, its implications and its management. Knowing work methods are not the same in every hospital, it seemed important to hear what MDs from two different hospitals had to say about infection itself and their needs for an infection module in their ICU software.

One of the hospitals where MDs were interviewed has *intensive.care* installed, so they are experienced with *intensive.care*. The other interviewed MD does not work with *intensive.care* at all, as it is not installed at his hospital. Since the current expectations about the improvement of the infection module are that it will suit every MD that deals with infection, it is important to elicit requirements from different MDs, even those who are used to working with other applications and not *intensive.care*. Only this way can a proposal be reached that will suit all users.

Intensive.care's users are mainly MDs and it is very difficult to elicit requirements from them, as they have such tight and unpredictable schedules. This happens because they work at ICUs and deal with critically ill patients that might need attention at any time [3].

Previous to the field observation, there was a quick visit to two ICUs in two different hospitals. This was intended to provide an overview of the environment and the existing machines in such units. Later, there was some field observations intended to understand the users' real difficulties with *intensive.care* in general and with the infection module in particular. As most of the times users do not really know what they want or even what they think about an interface, observing them is one of the best ways of finding that out [4]. "Data about people's actual behaviour should have precedence over people's claims of what they think they do" [5].

A prototype was used to create the first proposal for the evolution of the infection module. Since this is a preliminary requirements specification stage, a low-fidelity prototype was used, as these prototypes are cheap, simple and quick to create and modify [4], [6]. This prototype was evaluated and validated by some stakeholders, including two of the previously interviewed MDs who are experts in infection, and by several other MDs specialized in Intensive Care.

3 Analysis of Stakeholders' Preliminary Interviews' Results

After understanding the overall *intensive.care* current characteristics, including functionality and architecture, the study concentrated on understanding the evolution requirements of the main user stakeholders.

The interviews were semi-structured, having only few questions intended to obtain an overview of the current usage of *intensive.care* and its users' satisfaction [7]. The questions were:

1. For how long have you been using *intensive.care*?
2. What are its most important modules?
3. What are the most problematic modules?
4. What modules would you like to see improved?
5. What modules are never used and why?
6. What are your favourite modules?
7. Have you got any knowledge of or experience with similar systems?
8. Have you got any suggestion?

The interviewed users are MDs specialized in intensive care, with many years of experience in ICUs, who are the key users of *intensive.care* in their unit. They are also ICU managers, so they manage all the MDs in their unit and they have inside knowledge about their real usage of *intensive.care*.

One of the interviewed users has been using *intensive.care* since its beginning and is the main consultant for its further development. She works with it everyday and started using it even before every single patient's data in her ICU started being registered in *intensive.care*, which happened in January 2003. One of the other interviewed users has been using *intensive.care* since November 2003 and the remaining one since May 2005.

It is very interesting to have available users that have such different degrees of experience with *intensive.care*. More experienced users are expected to have more ideas of how *intensive.care* can evolve, because they have been using the system daily for a few years and have had the time to explore all of its potential. On the other hand, more recent users are expected to have a different perspective about *intensive.care*. This happens because as they have been using it only for a few months, they probably have only explored its basic functionality. Besides, their memory is fresher to remember their initial contact with the system and the difficulties they felt when first using it.

It is also interesting to have users from different ICUs because these units do not all have the same work methods. Given that, these users' usage of *intensive.care* is not exactly equal from an ICU to another.

After this first set of interviews, there were some coinciding responses about parts of *intensive.care* that should be improved.

In a general way its users enjoy working with *intensive.care* and feel the application eases their everyday work. Most ICU tasks are covered by *intensive.care*'s functionality set. But when it comes to the more complex tasks, such as infection and complications, users have some resistance in switching from the traditional paper reports to the electronic version presented in *intensive.care*. This happens both for cultural reasons and because of the difficulty for the development team to map the procedures in *intensive.care* exactly as they are made on paper. Also, for some of the most complex tasks there is the need for adjustment in work methods, in order to make *intensive.care* a simple and standard system.

Table 1. Overview of *intensive.care*'s modules usage in each hospital where *intensive.care* is installed. The check sign means the module is used in the respective hospital. The cross sign means the module is never used in the respective hospital.

	H1	H2	H3
Module 1 **Entrance, Admission, Antecedents and Release**	✓	✓	✓
Module 2 **Diary and Therapeutics**	✓	✓	✗
Module 3 **Prognostic Score Indicators**	✓	✓	✓
Module 4 **Procedures**	✓	✓	✗
Module 5 **Diagnosis**	✓	✓	✗
Module 6 **Complications**	✗	✗	✗
Module 7 **Infection**	✓	✗	✗

Table 1 reflects an overview of the usage of *intensive.care*'s modules in each of the three analysed ICU hospitals. We'll call these hospitals H1, H2 and H3. *intensive.care*'s modules are grouped here into modules, 1 to 7.

Patients' entrance, admission and release data, and prognostic scoring indicators are referred to as being easy to register, navigate and use.

When it comes to more intricate tasks, such as registering and managing of infections, complications, diagnosis, procedures and surgery, the users feel *intensive.care* does not provide the best solution, as these tasks are difficult to use in the system.

In a general way, most of the previously referred to complex tasks are registered in *intensive.care*, that is, users find these tasks should be improved, but still use them. When it comes to infection and complications, things change. The infection module is being used in only one of the hospitals, the one that has been using *intensive.care* for the longest time. The complications are not being registered in any other ICU. In all cases, users believe these modules are important and should be improved because they are difficult to use. One of the users who do not register infection data in *intensive.care* said, in the interview, that the infection process is complex and that in his opinion, in *intensive.care* it is particularly difficult to use.

When questioned about their favourite parts of *intensive.care* users referred to the prognostic scoring indicators functionality (see Fig. 2) and the interaction with SONHO. The prognostic scoring indicators functionality is said to be very easy and intuitive to use. It is also said to provide very useful information, as it gives a general perspective of the patients' health condition evolution since their arrival into the ICU. *intensive.care*'s interaction with SONHO is pointed out as being very helpful because when a new patient arrives into the ICU his demographic data is automatically imported from SONHO, which saves a lot of time and guarantees the integrity of this data.

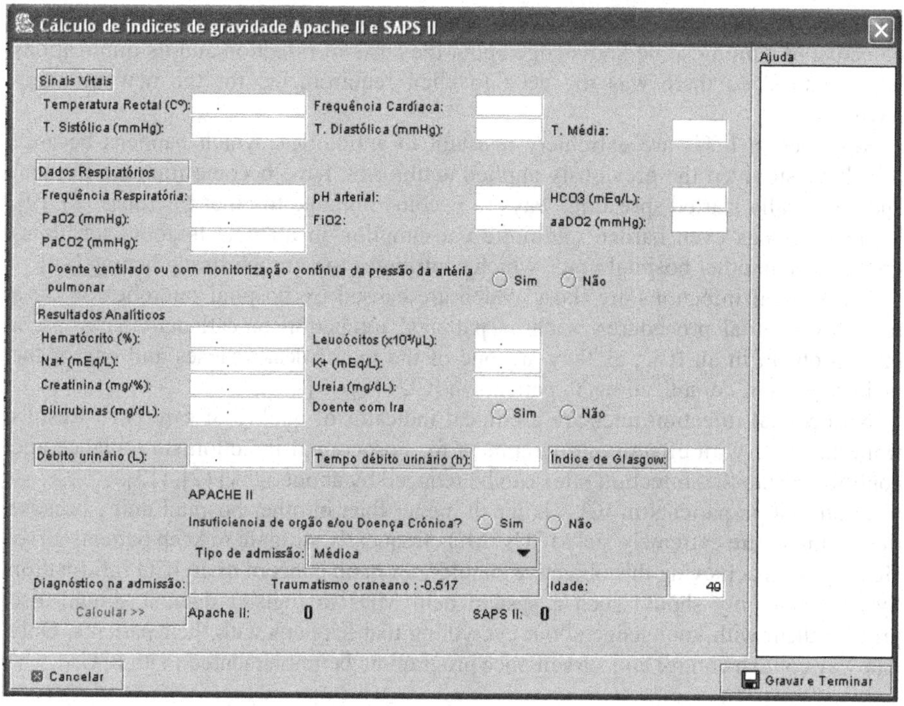

Fig. 2. The APACHE II /SAPS II prognostic scoring indicators module

From this preliminary analysis, we can gather that the usability requirements to be specified will cover some different areas of interaction.

Requirements related to the usability of *intensive.care*'s modules are being specified, as some ICU tasks are difficult to perform in *intensive.care*, and therefore do not have the acceptance they could have otherwise.

Requirements related to mobility might, too, be specified, as usually there are only two computer terminals with *intensive.care* in each ICU and a terminal in each MD's office. It might be interesting to have a mobility study to determine whether it would be reasonable to have mobile devices to register patients' data.

From the first set of interviews, a study focus was established. Due to its importance to the ICUs and its complexity, the infection module was selected to be the object of the current HCI evaluation. This is a complex module as infection is not a simple matter in intensive care. On the contrary, it is one of the main and more complicated issues in ICUs.

4   User Interface Requirements from the ICU for the New Infection Module

As referred to on the previous section, a study focus for this HCI evaluation was settled and the infection module was chosen to be the main object of study.

There were two interviews with MDs who are experts in infection in ICU, with the objective of gaining some knowledge about the basis of infection and its implications in patients. Also there was the need to elicit requirements for the new infection module.

Microbes in ICUs are extremely resistant to antibiotics, which happens because they have survived the previously applied antibiotics, have become immune to them and genetically started spreading ways to become immune to other microbes [8], [9]. To make things even harder, antibiotic consumption in an ICU is about ten times greater than in other hospital units, which contributes to microbe strengthening [10].

Nosocomial infections are those which are caused by hospital microbes or are a result of hospital procedures, such as patients' intubation or catheters. They are a main problem in an ICU, as they are one of the major death causes and one of the main sources of complications in patients in ICUs [8], [9].

Nosocomial infection rates are a clinical indicator of quality of care [11]. Results from hospitals with effective programmes for nosocomial infection surveillance and control indicate that infection rates can be reduced by about 32% [12], [13].

Death risk in patients in ICUs is much higher than in other hospital units, because these patients are extremely sick. ICUs' MDs frequently struggle to keep patients alive. Helping them achieving this objective should be a main concern of an ICU Information System. Not only should such a system help MDs to register data, it should also provide them with knowledge about everything that happens with their patients. Only that way could a control and surveillance programme be implemented in an ICU.

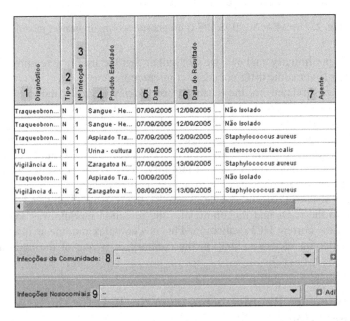

Fig. 3. Partial screen from the infection module in *intensive.care* (1 – diagnosis; 2 – type of infection: N for nosocomial or C for community-acquired; 3 – number of infection; 4 – analysed product: blood, urine, etc.; 5 – exam date; 6 – results date; 7 – microbe; 8 – community-acquired infections; 9 – nosocomial infections)

Intensive.care has an infection module that is being used in only one of the four hospitals that currently use the ICS tool (see Fig. 3). Users find it difficult and time-costly to use, so they prefer to use paper to register infection data. Taking into account what has been said before, this seems like an issue that needs to be addressed immediately, so a preliminary version of interaction requirements for this module was created.

A brief summary of the specified requirements will be presented next. A scale was used to classify each requirement. This scale is composed of three alphabetic values, L – Low, M – Medium and H – High, that will characterize each requirement in terms of its importance and its difficulty of implementation.

Table 2. Overview of the specified HCI requirements for the infection module

ID	Requirement	Imp.	Dif.
1	**Classification of microbes** – microbes should be classified according to their alert level, using colour coding; red for the ones defined as being the most problematic, orange for the ones defined as having an average alert level and green for those which are easy to control.	H	L
2	**Overview of the ICU** – a map of the ICU should be represented with colour coding for each bed, indicating alert levels according to patients' microbes.	H	M
3	**View of patients' in-days[1] in ICU** – there should be a graphical way to quickly identify the number of days each patient has been in the ICU.	H	L
4	**View of each patient's infections, harvested products[2] and antibiotics.**	H	H
5	**View of microbes' sensitivity** – for each isolated microbe in a patient's organism, there should be a list of the antibiotics that the microbe is sensitive and resistant to.	H	L
6	**Registering of product harvest** – each time there is a harvest of a product in a patient, it should be registered in *intensive.care* and automatically sent to the analysis laboratory; the id of the analysis should be stored in *intensive.care*.	H	H
7	**Registering of exam results** – for each harvested product there should be an exam result that should, automatically, be retrieved from the exams laboratories applications and inserted in *intensive.care*.	H	H

To evaluate and validate these requirements, a low-fidelity prototype was created in Microsoft PowerPoint (see Fig. 4) [6]. This prototype was analysed by some stakeholders, including two MDs who are experts in infection in ICU. After this evaluation, some changes were made to the initial prototype, so that it became much approximate to what users really need.

---

[1] In-days in the ICU are days patients remain hospitalized at the ICU.
[2] E.g.: blood, urine, gastric juice.

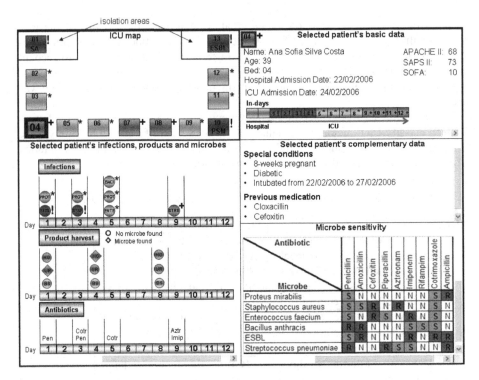

Fig. 4. Low-fidelity prototype for the patient screen of the new infection module. (! Represents the red colour; * represents orange and + represents green).

The use of colour provides a fundamental visual aid, so this prototype is based on colour-coding for quick identification of different situations. For the purpose of this paper, additional signs have been added to the prototype, because when printed in black and white, some colours are too similar to be distinguished one from another.

On the upper left part of the prototype (Fig. 4) there is a schematic drawing of the ICU. Beds are displayed as they are located in the real ICU, they have a number (the bed number) and a colour coding – red (!), orange (*) or green (+). If a bed is painted red it means the patient standing in it has an infection by a very hard to control microbe and might demand isolation and/or particular care. If a bed is orange, the infection is easier to control but still problematic. If it is green, then the patient has no infection, or has an infection by a microbe that is easy to control. Each bed is clickable to switch from a patient to another on this screen, as every other parts of the screen are related to the chosen patient. According to the ICU MDs, it is very important to have this global perspective of the unit, as patients' location is many times switched as determined by the alert levels.

All other parts of this screen are related to the chosen patient. The upper right part has patient's basic data as his/her name, age, admission dates in the hospital and in the ICU and the latest measure of the prognostic scoring indicators (APACHE II, SAPS II and SOFA). There is also a graphical view of the in-days, with in-days in the hospital not accounted and marked in light-blue. In this axis the evolution of the alert levels in the patient is represented with the same colours as explained before.

On the lower left part of the screen is a graphical view of three fundamental issues in infection in the ICU – infection, product harvest and antibiotics. The in-days are represented in the same way as explained before and for each day there might be the diagnosis of an infection by a microbe, product harvests, such as haemoglobin or bronchial secretions and the administration of antibiotics. Microbes, products and antibiotics are easily identifiable by abbreviations.

In the infections representation, microbes found are characterized by a colour, which is related to their alert level. Every time a new microbe is found, there is a new entry in the respective day.

The harvested products are represented by an abbreviation and a colour coding. Each product has a different colour code and is examined by the respective laboratory. The result of this exam might be a microbe isolation or a negative result. Many times – up to 60% of the times, even though the patient is infected, the results are negative, as microbes do not always survive through the complete product analysis process. In this prototype, if a microbe is isolated, the representation of the product becomes a rhombus; if not, it remains a circle. This way, by just looking at the screen, infected products are immediately identified.

This circles and rhombuses that represent infections and products are clickable for details, as are the days and the buttons tagged "Infections", "Product harvest" and "Antibiotics".

The last quadrant is split in two parts. The top is composed by the patient's complementary data, such as special conditions and previous medication, which is fundamental information for the MDs when choosing the antibiotics for each patient.

In the bottom there is the patient's microbes' sensitivity to antibiotics. This is represented by a grid, so the optimal combination of antibiotics can be chosen. Microbes are represented on the bottom left and antibiotics on the top. When crossing a microbe with an antibiotic, there is always a result: N – neutral, S – sensitive or R – resistant.

Whenever all the information in a part of the interface does not fit the screen, scrollbars are provided. In most of the cases they will not be necessary as usually patients stay in the ICU for about a week [9], and for that case, the window space is typically sufficient.

This prototype aims to provide a wider perspective of the ICU's current status and each patient's overview in terms of infection.

When a patient first arrives at an ICU he/she might have some infection symptoms and need to be immediately medicated, or else he/she might die. Even though several products are harvested and sent to the analysis laboratories, results from these analysis are never immediate and most of the times, they take a few days to arrive. So, MDs need to make a decision on which antibiotics to administer, based on some information about the patient and their own experience in ICU infection. This decision is based on several issues such as patient's background, previously taken antibiotics and symptoms, amongst many others.

A system like *intensive.care* should help MDs in their decision making, by not only showing them all the variables that should be thought about, but also having algorithms that could evaluate situations and provide advice about possible decisions.

This prototype is based on the display and introduction of information about the ICU and its patients. In the future there will also be a decision support system, which will help MDs on their decisions, based on the patients' variables and some artificial reasoning, which takes into account previous cases.

This addition is expected to reduce the amount of time MDs spend analysing all the variables about a single patient, by displaying patients' variables in a user-friendly way and making suggestions on the combination of antibiotics that should or could be administered to that patient. Wishfully it will help MDs save lives.

5   Future Work

Next, in this study, there will be an iteration over the current low-fidelity prototype, based on the inputs from several stakeholders. These stakeholders are both from the development team and from *intensive.care*'s users. Several MDs have evaluated and validated the prototype and gave their inputs for its improvement.

Afterwards a focus group will be conducted, that will gather several MDs from different ICUs. The results of this focus group are expected to be one of the most important contributors to the final requirements specification for the evolution of *intensive.care*, in particular in what concerns interaction. Joining together a group of MDs for a focus group might be problematic because of constraints such as medical emergencies or different work schedules [3]. However, such a brainstorming meeting is expected to collect much valuable information about *intensive.care*'s usability problems (and other problems), since MDs are experienced users and their debate of its problems might bring up some new important issues.

In the final stage of the evaluation, a high-fidelity prototype will be constructed to support the requirements specification and validation by *intensive.care*'s main stakeholders. This prototype will be functional and very similar to the new infection module final interface. Since it is such a complete and interactive prototype, users may evaluate and validate it more easily, as they can interact with it and simulate real actions [6], [4].

6   Conclusions

Intensive.care is a product that meets the majority of the ICU needs, but still has some unresolved usability problems that need to be addressed. There is a clear objective from SBIM to expand *intensive.care* to other ICUs in Portugal, but HCI problems need to be eliminated first.

One of the most problematic modules of *intensive.care* is the infection module, as it is hardly ever used, mainly due to its usability problems. Infections in ICU are a very serious problem because patients are critically ill and are prone to dying from several infections. MDs need to be fully supported by an ICS to be able to save more lives, by taking appropriate decisions on medicines and other treatments.

An easy to use infection module will aid MDs on their everyday tasks, by reducing the amount of time they spend in registering and analysing infection data, and providing them with advice on which decisions they could take when choosing antibiotics and other treatments.

Since *intensive.care* works in such an extreme environment, which deals with life and death in a daily basis, it is imperative that it provides good quality data and interaction, which will be the basis for all the decision support algorithms that might save lives. MDs need to be fully comfortable and confident while working with the system, so they can take full advantage of it.

The specification of HCI requirements and creation of prototypes based on these requirements is essential for user validation. At the end of this project a new infection module will be proposed to substitute the existing one. It is expected to be well accepted by *intensive.care*'s users, as it is being built with their help, based on their real needs. In the end, *intensive.care* will be a much more effective and pleasant application to work with, and therefore, a much more successful product.

Acknowledgements. The authors wish to thank Dr. António Carneiro, from Hospital de Santo António, Porto and Prof. António Sarmento, from Hospital Pedro Hispano, Matosinhos, for all their help, in particular in the requirements elicitation, prototype evaluation and validation phases.

References

1. Pereira, A.d.C. and T. Fonseca, *intensive.care Reference Manual*, SBIM, Editor. 2005.
2. Réanimation, S.F.d.A.e.d., *Scoring systems for ICU and surgical patients*. 2002.
3. Gosbee, J. and E. Ritchie, *Human-Computer Interaction and Medical Software Development*. Interactions (ACM), 1997. **nr.** 4(4): p. pag. 13-18.
4. Preece, J., Y. Rogers, and H. Sharp, *Interaction Design – beyond human-computer interaction*. 2002: John Wiley & Sons, Inc.
5. Nielsen, J., *Usability Engineering*. 1993: Morgan Kaufman.
6. Rudd, J., K. Stern, and S. Isensee, *Low vs. high-fidelity prototyping debate*. Interactions, 1996. 3(1): p. 76-85.
7. Ghiglione, R. and B. Matalon, *O Inquérito – Teoria e prática*. Third Edition ed. 1997: Celta.
8. Sarmento, A. and L. Lencastre, *Interview about Infection in ICU*. 2005.
9. Carneiro, A., *Interview about Infection in ICU*. 2006.
10. Metha, R.M. and M.S. Niederman, *Antibiotic Resistance in the Intensive Care Unit*. 2001.
11. Appelgren, P., et al. *Risk Factors for Nosocomial Intensive Care Infection: a Long-Term Prospective Analysis*. in *Acta Anaesthesiologica Scandinavica*. 2001.
12. Haley, R.W., et al., *The Efficacy Of Infection Surveillance And Control Programs In Preventing Nosocomial Infections In US Hospitals*. American Journal of Epidemiology, 1985. **121**(2): p. 182-205.
13. Misset, B., et al., *A Continuous Quality-Improvement Program Reduces Nosocomial Infection Rates in the ICU*. Intensive Care Med, 2004.

Interaction Walkthrough:
Evaluation of Safety Critical Interactive Systems

Harold Thimbleby

Department of Computer Science, Swansea University, Wales
h.thimbleby@swansea.ac.uk

Abstract. Usability evaluation methods are a battery of techniques for assessing the usability of interactive systems or of proposed interactive systems. This paper describes a new evaluation method, particularly appropriate for evaluating safety critical and high quality user interfaces. The method can also be used for informing HCI research. The method is applied when a specification is available of an interactive system, or when a system (or prototype) is working.

1 Introduction

Human computer interaction is the science and practice of effective interactive systems, most often involving people and computers. Usability, more specifically, is the theory and application of methods to improve the processes and products of interactive system design. Humans are an object of study (for example, to advance the science of psychology), and interaction is an object of study (for example, using usability evaluation methods); interaction can also be arranged to present users with controlled, novel situations, and hence generate phenomena that demand psychological accounts. The conventional view, then, is that evaluation of interactive systems focuses on the user.

Less obvious is that the computer (or embedded computer), not just the human, is a useful object of study in its own right. Despite interactive systems being fully defined by program, their behaviour is often not fully understood, particularly when coupled with human use.

One might make an analogy from the well-known story of the Tacoma Narrows bridge. Human sciences are very interested in the experience, behaviour and performance of humans, for instance, drivers who use bridges — indeed, drivers on the Tacoma Narrows bridge reported motion sickness that could perhaps have stimulated new research. On the other hand, one might think that the engineering of a finished bridge is not an interesting object for study; after all, it has been built from specifications, so its design and properties are surely known in principle. Unfortunately, the Tacoma Narrows bridge experienced catastrophic failure in 1940 due to wind-induced vibration [15]. In other words, its engineering was *not* fully understood, and moreover, unknown engineering issues had a direct impact on its usability.

This paper proposes and demonstrates a new 'usability evaluation method' but uniquely focussing on the device engineering rather than on the user. The

G. Doherty and A. Blandford (Eds.): DSVIS 2006, LNCS 4323, pp. 52–66, 2007.

benefits of this method are discussed, particularly for the safety critical domain. Analysis of the Tacoma Narrows bridge led to advances in dynamical systems, aerodynamics and so on; one may likewise hope that the methods proposed here for analysing interactive devices will lead in a similar way to advances in the theory and science of interactive devices.

1.1   Background

There are many usability evaluation methods, each appropriate to one or more stages of the design lifecycle. It is conventional to divide methods into three groups: test, inspection and inquiry. **Test methods** use representative users to work on typical tasks, and their performance is measured or otherwise assessed; testing requires a working system, or a prototype. **Inspection methods** instead use experts (typically HCI experts, but possibly software engineers or domain experts) to inspect a design; inspection can be done at any stage of design, from prototype to marketplace. **Inquiry methods** inquire into the users' preferences, desires, and behaviour, and try to establish the requirements of a design.

To this list should now be added **device methods**, such as this paper will describe below.

Conventional usability evaluation methods (UEMs) can be adjusted to need. For example think aloud can be used in at least three ways: introspection, normal think aloud, and cooperative evaluation. A UEM may be applied to the interactive system, the training material, the user manuals, or to the environment the user operates in. UEMs can be used in laboratories, in focus groups (perhaps with no system present), or in the wild. One can further run a UEM in anything from a purely informal way to an experimentally rigorous way — depending on whether one wants basic information to help a practical design, or whether one wants experimentally and statistically respectable information for, say, a scientific paper.

All UEMs are concerned primarily with the user experience, though they should be distinguished from user acceptance models [27], which are intended more to inform management or procurement questions than to improve design. On the other hand, *system* evaluation methods focus on the technical system design and are typically concerned with the reliability, integrity and safety of the system; such methods range from formal mathematical work (theorem proving, model checking) to informal procedures such as code walkthrough. There are many schools of software engineering (e.g., extreme programming, agile development), and many advocate different overall approaches. Nevertheless, software engineering methods assume the usability requirements are otherwise established, and evaluate conformance of the implemented system to its requirements.

UEMs are not without controversy. For example, Wixon [26] believes published papers on evaluations have failed the needs of usability professionals. Gray and Salzman [5,6] compared many experiments with UEMs and found the standards of experimental work questionable, in some cases leading to erroneous claims.

All evaluation methods take stands on the questions of sampling, satisficing, frequency, severity and realism. There are other issues: such as obtaining quantitative or qualitative data. Generally, interactive systems and their use are complex; a UEM cannot hope to sample all of a system or all of its and its users' space of interactive behaviour (nor all users and all user personalities, etc). UEMs therefore sample a restricted space of the design — typically therefore taking some arbitrary or trying, on the other hand, to take some statistically valid sample of the space. This is of course difficult to do for interfaces intended to be culturally sensitive, enlarging the space again. Furthermore, the results of a UEM may be sensitive to the people doing the evaluation; some studies show little overlap in results when undertaken by different assessors [11] — interestingly, this paper ([11]) expresses surprise at assessor sensitivity, but it is more likely a consequence of the difficulty of sampling a large, unknown space uniformly.

A UEM may uncover problems in a design (e.g., there is no undo), but may not know how frequently this problem arises in use; that is, many UEMs cannot distinguish between risk and hazard. A UEM may identify a potential problem, but not be clear how severe a problem it is for users. For example, a system may have no undo, which is a potential problem, but users may have other work arounds — the user interface without undo may then be usefully simpler than one with extra features.

The more effort put into using a UEM, in principle the higher quality results that can be expected; different UEMs have different cost/benefit curves, and one may thus choose a break-off point, once encountering diminishing returns on effort. However, there is no guarantee that if a UEM identifies a problem that it can be fixed, or worse, that fixing it does not introduce other problems (which of course, at the time of fixing will be unknown and unevaluated problems).

Finally, there may be questions about realism. A device may be evaluated in a laboratory, but the conditions of actual use may be very different — this is a particularly tricky question with safety critical devices, which may be very hard and often unethical to evaluate under realistic conditions of use (e.g., where the user is in a state of stress).

1.2   Wider Issues

Any review of UEMs, however brief, would not be complete without mentioning politics. Designs have many stakeholders, and UEMs generally attempt to promote the needs and values of users. These values may not be the values intended to be assessed or optimised by deploying the UEM. For example, in a safety critical environment, one may be more concerned with political fallout or public safety than the welfare of the actual operator, or one may be concerned with legal liability issues (hence, ironically, perhaps wanting an obfuscated design, so the user rather than the hardware seem to be at fault).

2   A UEM for Safety Critical Systems

We now introduce a new UEM, primarily intended for safety critical systems. It can of course be used for any interactive system, but the sorts of safety insight obtained in terms of effort may be too costly for other domains — though the UEM can be used on parts of systems with less effort, and may thus provide insight into those parts of the system at reduced cost.

We call the method Interaction Walkthrough (IW) and it may most conveniently be contrasted with Cognitive Walkthrough (CW) and Program Walkthrough (PW)[1] — it 'fills the gap' between these two approaches.

Cognitive Walkthrough (CW) is a psychological inspection method that can be used at any stage using a prototype or real system; it does not require a fully functioning prototype; it does not require the involvement of users. CW is based on a certain psychological learning theory, and assumes the user sets a goal to be accomplished with the system. The user searches the interface for currently available action to achieve their goal and selects the action that seems likely to make progress toward the goal. It is assumed the user performs the selected action and evaluates the system's feedback for evidence that progress is being made toward the goal.

Assessors start with a general description of who the users will be and what relevant knowledge they possess, as well as a specific description of representative tasks to be performed and a list of the actions required to complete each of these tasks with the interface being evaluated.

The assessors then step through the tasks, taking notes in a structured way: evaluating at each step how difficult it is for the user to identify and operate the element relevant to their current goals, and evaluating how clearly the system provides feedback to that action. Each such step is classified a success or failure.

To classify each step, CW takes into consideration the user's (assumed) thought processes that contribute to decision making, such as memory load and ability to reason.

CW has been described well in the literature (e.g., [25]), and need not be reviewed further here, except to note that CW has many variants (e.g., [16]). The gist is that a psychologically informed evaluation is based on the user's behaviour.

In contrast, Program Walkthrough (PW) evaluates a design based on the computer's behaviour. Instead of psychological models or theories and user tasks and goals, the PW assessor has programming language theory and walks through program code to work out what the computer would do. In a sense, then, CW and PW are duals.

In PW the programmer (more often working in a team) works through program code, to convince themselves that the program does what it is supposed to do, and that all paths are executed under the right conditions. Often a program walkthrough will result in improved testing regimes, and of course better debugged code. Usually, PW is seen as a quality control process rather than an

---

[1] In the context of this paper, the alternative name Code Walkthrough might be confused with CW as Cognitive Walkthrough!

evaluation method *per se*; the assumption is that there is an 'ideal' program, that the current one should aspire to. Various techniques, including PW, are recruited to move the current implementation towards the ideal 'bug free' program.

Neither CW nor PW are concerned with the *interaction* itself, in the following sense. In CW, the concern is on the user, and in PW the concern is on the execution paths of the program — which may well have little to do with the interaction. That is, interaction is a side effect of running a program. The program does input and output, with lots of stuff in-between, but the interaction appears to the user as continuous (except when the computation is slow). If one looks at a fragment of code, one has to work out what the input and output relation is. In the worst case, there is a non-computable step from doing PW to knowing what the interaction is.

Consider the following trivial-looking Java method, which is not even interactive in any interesting sense:

```
void star(long n)
{ while( n > 1 ) n = n%2 == 0? n/2: 3*n+1;
  System.out.println("*");
}
```

If the user provides a value for n, does the method print a star? The code fragment runs the Collatz problem, and whether it always prints a star is an unsolved question (though it *will* always print a star if n is a Java int). This example makes a clear, if abstract, demonstration that a program walkthrough cannot in principle fully determine what the user will see the program doing. Indeed, real programs are far more complex: they are concurrent, event driven, and their behaviour is dependent on internal state, and so on.

Instead, we need to start outside the program ...

3   Interaction Walkthrough, IW

Many interactive devices are developed in a process roughly conforming to ISO13407: a prototype is built, tested and then refined, and then the final system is built (which may have further refinements). Typically, the prototype is developed in an informal way, in some convenient prototyping tool, and then the final system is developed in a programming language that is efficient on the target hardware. Sometimes documentation and other training material will be written, based on the same prototype, and developed concurrently with the target system development.

Interaction Walkthrough works analogously, but with different goals. From a working system, whether a prototype or target system, another system is developed. Thus, a *parallel system* is developed from the interaction behaviour of the system being evaluated.

Developing the parallel system requires the assessor to ask numerous questions, and to go over in detail many of the original design decisions — and perhaps make some decisions explicit for the first time. To reprogram a system, the assessor needs to know whether features are instances of a common form, are different, or are identical ... and so on.

As the parallel system is built, the assessor will program in a new way, and therefore make independent decisions on the structure of the parallel program. The assessor makes notes of design questions and issues. Since the assessor is working independently of the original developers and programmers, new questions will be raised. For example: why are these two features *nearly* the same? Why weren't they programmed to be identical?

Inevitably, some (but by no means all) of the design issues raised by this phase of the IW will cover similar ground to a conventional heuristic evaluation [12] (e.g., noticing, if it is the case, that there is no undo).

The assessor will stop this phase of IW when either sufficient questions, or any 'killer' questions, have been raised, or when the rate of discovery has diminished and the rate of return is insufficient for the purposes of the evaluation. Generally, such discovery processes follow a Poisson distribution, and modelling the rate of discovery can inform a rational cut-off point [13].

Reprogramming a system or even a partial system, as required by IW, is not such a large undertaking as the original programming, since impossible and impractical features have already been eliminated. However reprogramming is still a considerable effort, and the assessor may choose to do a partial implementation, concentrating on certain features of interest. The assessor may use RAD tools, such as compiler-compilers, as well as *ad hoc* tools to both speed up the process and to ensure consistency.

Typically, it is not possible to determine exactly what the device's actual behaviour is merely by experimenting on it. The user manual and help material must also be used. Thus the assessor will discover discrepancies between the documentation and the target system. Moreover, the assessor will be using the user manual material with a keener eye than any user! Typically, user manuals have definitional problems that IW will expose.

At the end of the reimplementation phase of IW, the assessor has three products: a realistic simulation, a list of questions and/or critiques, and a deep understanding of the system (typically including a list of formal properties) — achieved more rapidly that other people on the design team. It is also worthwhile writing a *new* user manual for the simulation as well as documentation; writing manuals forces the assessor to work to a higher standard, and may also provide further insights into the design as a side-effect. It is also standard practice; if a safety critical device is being evaluated, the success of the evaluation should not depend on a particular member of staff.

Next the assessor involves users through cooperative evaluation [28]. Are the issues raised of significance to users in actual practice? Thus the list of questions and critiques is refined to a prioritised list.

The prioritised list can then be fed back into the iterative design process in the usual way. The IW implementation may also be iterated and made more realistic or more useful, for instance, for further cooperative evaluation.

3.1 Key Steps of IW

In summary, IW is an UEM based on the following steps:

1. Clean reverse engineering, generally ignoring non-interaction issues, using a device, its user manual and training material.

2. Development of an accurate simulation.

3. Recording design questions and queries, arising from Steps 1 & 2.

4. Review with domain experts using the original device and/or simulation.

Steps 1–3 iterate until 'showstopper' or 'killer queries' are found, or the rate of discovery becomes insufficient. The whole process may be iterated; for example, working with end users may reveal short-comings in the simulation.

3.2 Variations and Extensions

Once a simulation is available, it can be used for many purposes, such as training tests, collecting use data (which perhaps is too complex to collect from a real system), for random simulation, and so on. Other possibilities are to embed automatic UEMs [8] inside the system built for the IW exercise — many automated UEMs would interfere with the target system's operation, and so would be inappropriate to deploy without a different (in this case, IW) implementation. We do not consider these additional benefits strictly part of a UEM itself, but the 'added value' implies IW should be viewed as playing a wider part of the quality control and inquiry methods than merely finding certain types of usability problem.

An IW simulation can easily be built to generate a formal specification of the device in question, which can be used for model checking and other rigorous analyses. Indeed, if methods such as the Chinese Postman [2,22] are used for reverse engineering, they in any case require an explicit graph of the device. Figure 2 shows an automatically drawn transition diagram, drawn from the specification generated by the IW program; the transition network has been checked for strong connectivity (as it happens, by one of the internal checks in the program itself, although the analysis could have been done by external programs). For example, the connectivity analysis in this example makes one node automatically highlighted as not being in the main component of the graph — thus showing either the device has a problem, or (as is the case here) the reverse engineering of it is not complete.

3.3 Relation of IW to Software Engineering

In typical software engineering processes, there is a progression (e.g., the spiral model or waterfall) from requirements to product. IW creates a parallel path, which does not start from the explicit specifications used in standard refinement. Instead, the idea is effectively to 'rationally reconstruct' such specifications, insofar as they relate to user interaction, and to do so independently, without the implementation bias that would inevitably have crept into the original process.

Normal software engineering is concerned with validation and verification (V&V) of the product, with caveats that normally there are leaps of imagination connecting what can be formally established and what is actually implemented.For example, a model checking language like SMV does not lend itself to efficient implementation, so the target system is actually informally implemented, however rigorous its specification might have been. Instead, IW works from what has actually been implemented (not what should have been implemented), and works out its (interaction) specification, in fact, sufficient to reimplement some or all of its user interface. Thus it is likely that IW will bring rigour into interaction evaluation that, very likely, will have been omitted in the standard software development process.

4 Worked Example

As an exercise in IW, a Graseby 3400 syringe pump and its user manual [4] was reverse engineered as a Java program. This worked example raises interesting design questions that were uncovered by IW — and on the whole, ones that were very unlikely to have been uncovered by other UEMs — and hence this example illustrates IW well. The Graseby 3400 is an extremely popular and established product (hence of some interest to evaluate by a new method) but this paper does not assess the risks, if any, of the issues mentioned.

This IW exercise developed three products:

- A photorealistic simulation; see Figure 1. The simulation only shows LEDs and the behaviour of the LCD panel; it does not show syringe activity.

- An automatically generated specification, used in particular to draw a transition diagram (which in fact is animated as the Java simulation is used); see Figure 2. This was developed to ensure the completeness of the simulation for the purposes of IW. In fact, not all of the 3400 was simulated, as it is a complex device.

- A list of 38 detailed design questions. The list of questions was generated as the reverse engineering proceeded. The reverse engineering phase was stopped when the rate of new question generation slowed and the process appeared unproductive. As will be seen, compared to a typical UEM, the questions are very detailed and technical, although presenting the full list is not the purpose of this paper.

Twelve anaesthetists and an NHS Pump Trainer (the person who trains pump operators) were interviewed, based on the list of 38 design questions generated during the reverse engineering phase. For reasons of space in this paper, we do not review all questions here; the paper is introducing IW, not reviewing any particular device except insofar as it helps illustrate IW.

The IW assessor then worked with a consultant anaesthetist in a detailed cooperative evaluation of the 3400, undertaken during a routine 3 hour operation.

Fig. 1. Screen shot of the Graseby simulation in bolus mode, with the 'start' LED flashing, indicating that the device is infusing. The image was made by holding the Graseby 3400 over a scanner.

Two incidents during the operation had been anticipated by some of the design questions. We now briefly summarise the design questions, then briefly summarise the use (in this case, clinical) perspective.

– The user manual states that the numeric keys are set up like a calculator. In fact, numbers have a slightly different syntax to an ordinary calculator, notably: (*i*) there is a *silent* timeout; (*ii*) decimal points zero the decimal fraction (whereas on a calculator, pressing the decimal point does not lose significant digits). See Table 1.

– Inaccurate entry of numeric data produces no error warnings (no beeps) and might (potentially) lead to adverse effects; see Table 1 for a summary.

– Numeric entry has a CANCEL button (which would be called AC or CE on a calculator), but there is no undo.

– The bolus feature has no explicit method of exit, but has a 10 second timeout. There are, however, 'spare' soft keys which might have been used for explicitly exiting bolus mode.

– Although there is a CANCEL button, there is no consistent escape from any mode.

The last case in Table 1 deserves further explanation. Conventional calculators do not ignore underflow unless a number already has more than (typically) 8 significant figures; in particular entering 0.009 would be handled correctly on all conventional calculators. Instead, the Graseby has a fixed number of decimal digits (1 or 2 depending on the mode), and always ignores underflow. As designed: underflow should be avoided by first choosing the correct units. For example, if the anæsthetist wants to enter 0.009mg/ml, they should instead (*as the device is designed*) enter 9µg/ml. This is an example of a design question, revealed by IW, which can then be presented to users, to see whether it is an actual (in this case, clinical) issue.

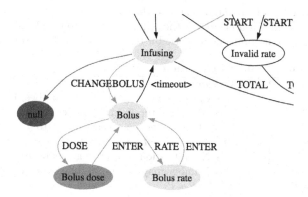

Fig. 2. Partial screen shot of the Graseby transition diagram, drawn by Dot. The diagram is updated after each user action, and it is coloured: the current state is green; transitions that have been tested are green; states that have been visited are yellow; undefined states and transitions are red — note that the simulation does not yet define the actions for changing the infusion rate.

In a typical UEM these issues would easily be overlooked; in IW, they need examining closely otherwise a program cannot be written.

During the operation, the consultant anæsthetist entered the patient's weight incorrectly, as 8kg rather than 80kg.This was caused by a decimal point error.

The patient was infused continuously with Remifentanil, and, because of the length of the operation, the syringe needed to be changed. After the delay caused by a syringe change, the anæsthetist used the bolus feature, however he assumed switching the 3400 off and on again was the only way to get out of bolus mode and resume the infusion — switching off and on would of course have caused a further delay. He tried leaving the bolus mode by pressing various buttons, but of course this activity merely postponed the effect of the timeout which would have exited the bolus mode.

Neither of these incidents had any clinical significance (and they were not reported); in fact, they were quite routine issues. The anæsthetist noticed both, and had work-arounds. Nevertheless redesign of the 3400, along the lines anticipated in the IW, would have avoided both incidents. *Interestingly, such a redesign would not require any changes to any training material or the user manual; fixing the cases considered here would just make erroneous use simpler.*

In the larger context of improving the design, an open question is *how* the anæsthetist noticed his errors. For instance, an eye tracking experiment would help establish the relative effects of the LCD display's feedback to the tactile feedback of button pressing. Would improving the sound feedback help (in an already noisy operating theatre)? These are certainly worthwhile questions to investigate further, beyond the scope of IW, but questions raised by the process of IW.

Table 1. Partial list of potential issues to do with number entry. Column 2 shows the number displayed if a user presses the sequence of buttons indicated in Column 1 (provided there were no previous numeric buttons pressed in the current state).

Key sequence	Effect	Comment
9999.42	999.42	*Numeric overflow loses digits*
		• Causes no error report (e.g., no beep)
		• Does not stop fraction entry
		• The number may seem correct to a quick glance
1.[pause]9	9.00	*Timeouts reset number entry*
		• No indication to user (e.g., no beep)
		• Number may be bigger than expected
111.[pause]9	9.00	*Timeouts reset number entry*
		• No indication to user (e.g., no beep)
		• Number may be smaller than expected
1.2.3	1.30	*Repeated decimals lose digits*
		• No indication to user (e.g., no beep)
0.009	0.00	*Numeric underflow is not rounded*
		• No indication to user (e.g., no beep)

5   Other Examples

Several devices have previously been evaluated in methods approximating IW: microwave cooker [17]; video recorder [18]; fax [19]; mobile phone [20]; ticket machine [21]; calculator [23].

One might thus argue that IW (or an approximation thereof) gave or supported useful HCI design insights, of sufficient standard to contribute to these refereed publications.

There are *numerous* papers in the literature promoting new UEM or HCI methods using examples that are based on reverse engineered systems, that is, they are interpretable as 'hindsight-IW' case studies; however, these papers generally wish to make the claim that their methods should be used from specifications, not from reverse engineering, which may have been forced on them because their method was invented after the example product was build, or because the relevant form of specification was not available. The Palanque and Paternò edited book [14] is a case in point: it applies many formal HCI methods to existing browsers and browser features. For IW, the reverse engineering is integral to the process; it *adds* value, as explained above; whereas for most of these papers reverse engineering was used only incidentally, to ensure the proposed method could manage realistic cases (a detailed argument for this point of view is made in [24]).

6   Further Work

There are several ways to develop the work proposed here.

The simulation was written in Java, but a more structured framework would be extremely beneficial (e.g., in VEG, Z, SMV etc), particularly for providing direct support for reverse engineering and output of specification texts for further analysis in standard tools; on the other hand, the Java included code for checking, generating Dot diagrams, and the Chinese Postman — in an ideal world, these would be features in interactive development frameworks.

To what extent are the insights of IW the investigator's insights, as opposed to insights derived from the IW process? The IW process should be tested and used with more analysts. Having a structured framework (as proposed above) would make IW more accessible to more people.

The recording of design queries should be integrated into the IW framework. Currently, the issues and questions were simply recorded in a textfile (for the worked example in this paper, we used LaTeX) and in comments in the Java program, but there was no tool-based management of them. In particular there was no explicit connection between the list of problems and the state space of the device — for example, had there been, diagrams like Figure 2 could be very helpfully annotated with actual and suspected problems.

7   Conclusions

As pointed out by Paul Cairns, IW is a programmer's version of Grounded Theory. Grounded Theory is, briefly, an inductive approach to build social theories grounded in systematically analysed empirical data [3]. In IW, the 'theory' is the resultant program (or, more precisely, the program is an implementation of the theory), and the empirical data is derived not from social data but from program behaviour.

There are six key reasons why IW reveals useful evaluation information that was unlikely to have been known without it:

1. The assessor is discovering a new specification by reverse engineering. This is more useful than re-examining the original specification (if there is one!) because the original specification and program inevitably contain traces of their development and the sequence of design decisions. For a user of the final system, the design rationale and its working out is irrelevant: the user is interested in the working product. Thus the IW assessor works from that product, and constructs a clean specification, without the 'historical taints' that CW would be enmeshed with.

2. Second, IW starts with a system that works. Many UEM inspection — CW amongst them — can work from prototypes, even non-functional prototypes such as story boards, which very likely will not have worked out details of how the real system is going to work, creating the problem Holmquist calls *cargo cult design* [7]. In safety critical areas it is crucial that the details get evaluated and that nothing crucial is left to the imagination of the evaluators, who may be tempted to gloss details that have not been worked out for a prototype.

3. A third reason for the effectiveness of IW is that the assessor can choose any programming language or approach to construct the simulation — thus

allowing them to work in a much more suitable programming environment than perhaps the implementors of the actual target system were able to. For example, the implementors of the target system may have had to use assembler or PIC code, whereas the IW assessor can use Java, SMV [9,10], or Promela — or any special purpose GUI languages, such as VEG [1] — as they wish. Using a 'nice' language with powerful abstraction features, particularly one with model checking, appropriate for the interactive simulation will highlight inconsistencies in the target design in a way that cannot be done on the target system.

4. Fourth, the simulation can embed arbitrary test, diagnostic and debugging information to help the assessor. For example, it can generate transition diagrams, diagnostic logs, and so forth: to help the assessor assess how much of the device has been simulated and tested, but also to give formal insight into the design, for instance to check properties. Algorithms such as the Chinese Postman [2,22] can be used to ensure a complete coverage of the state space is achieved.

5. Fifth, the assessor can use a full range of modern model checking and theorem proving techniques to check the interface against desirable interaction properties. Loer and Harrison give persuasive examples [9,10] of the effectiveness of this approach — indeed, their work is essentially IW, as they had to reverse engineer systems (though their approach is suited to early use in software production, on the assumption that formal specifications are available), and their systems do not have the performance to be production systems.

6. Finally, the *real* success of any UEM lies in its recommendations being adopted either in the product being evaluated or in some future product (or perhaps in persuasive argument in published papers — which will, in turn, affect future products). IW has the advantage over other UEMs that it is driven by reverse engineering software, and therefore is already half-way towards offering ideas that can contribute to changing the *software* of the product, such as how to refactor it. Other UEMs risk making suggestions that are superficially appealing (even based on empirical evidence) but which are too hard to implement and are therefore resisted by the very people who must make the intended changes.

Arguably, the greatest use of IW would be the software engineering insights it provides a system developer. Rather than rely on UEMs to identify usability problems that then need fixing, surely it is better to adopt a system development process that avoids as many problems as possible? To do so requires using suitable quality and quality assurance processes, which of course are often skipped under the pressures of industrial design. An IW process exploits best software engineering practice to build an accurate simulation of the system being evaluated; it is likely that the IW assessor is an expert programmer, and therefore brings to their evaluation practices that might be applied in normal design. If so, then IW can be an agent of change in improving work practice to avoid usability problems in *future* devices by encouraging the use of better processes. Indeed, in a typical industrial environment, identifying problems with today's product, which has already shipped, is of less interest than improving future products by learning from problems with today's product.

Further work that would be desirable is to compare the efficiency (significant problems identified per unit effort) of IW with other methods, as well as the organisational impact of IW (e.g., process improvements) against the impact of other methods.

Acknowledgements. Harold Thimbleby is a Royal Society-Wolfson Research Merit Award Holder, and gratefully acknowledges this support. Paul Cairns (UCL) pointed out the useful analogy between IW and GT. Michael Harrison (Newcastle) and Matt Jones (Swansea) both provided many useful comments on the approach.

References

1. J. Berstel, S. Crepsi Reghizzi, G. Roussel & P. San Pietro, "A scalable formal method for design and automatic checking of user interfaces," *ACM Transactions on Software Engineerng and Methodology*, **14**(2):123-167, 2005.
2. W-H. Chen, "Test Sequence Generation from the Protocol Data Portion Based on the Selecting Chinese Postman Problem," *Information Processing Letters*, **65**(5):261–268, 1998.
3. B. G. Glaser & A. L. Strauss, *The Discovery of Grounded Theory: Strategies for Qualitative Research*, Chicago, 1967.
4. Graseby Medical Ltd., *Graseby 3400 Syringe Pump: Instruction Manual*, 2002.
5. W. D. Gray & M. C. Salzman, "Damaged merchandise? A review of experiments that compare usability evaluation methods," *Human-Computer Interaction*, **13**(3):203–261, 1998.
6. W. D. Gray & M. C. Salzman, "Repairing damaged merchandise: A rejoinder," *Human-Computer Interaction*, **13**(3):325–335, 1998.
7. Holmquist, L. E., "Prototyping: Generating ideas or cargo cult designs?" *ACM Interactions*, **12**(2):48–54, 2005.
8. M. Y. Ivory & M. A. Hearst, "The state of the art in automating usability evaluation of user interfaces," *ACM Computing Surveys*, **33**(4):470–516, 2001.
9. Loer, K. & Harrison, M., "Formal interactive systems analysis and usability inspection methods: Two incompatible worlds?, *Proceedings of the Interactive Systems. Design, Specification and Verification. 7th International Workshop*, DSV-IS 2000, Palanque, P. & Paternò, F. (eds) Lecture Notes in Computer Science, **1946**, 169–190, Springer-Verlag 2001.
10. Loer, K. & Harrison, M., "Towards usable and relevant model checking techniques for the analysis of dependable interactive systems," *Proceedings of the 17th IEEE International Conference on Automated Systems Engineering: ASE 2002*, Emmerich, W. & Wile, D. (eds), 223–226, 2002.
11. R. Molich, M. R. Ede, K. Kaasgaard & B. Karyukin, "Comparative usability evaluation", *Behaviour & Information Technology*, **23**(1):65–74, 2004.
12. J. Nielsen, *Usability engineering*, Academic Press, 1993.

13. J. Nielsen & T. K. Landauer, "A mathematical model of the finding of usability problems," *ACM SIGCHI conference on Human factors in computing systems*, 206–213, 1993.
14. Palanque, P. & Paternò, F., eds, *Formal Methods in Human Computer Interaction*, London, Springer-Verlag, 1997.
15. H. Petroski, *To Engineer is Human: The Role of Failure in Successful Design*, Vintage Books, 1992.
16. D. E. Rowley & D. G. Rhoades, "The Cognitive Jogthrough: A Fast-Paced User Interface Evaluation Procedure." *ACM CHI'92 Proceedings*, 389–395, 1992.
17. H. Thimbleby & I. H. Witten, "User Modelling as Machine Identification: New Design Methods for HCI," *Advances in Human Computer Interaction*, **IV**, D. Hix & H. R. Hartson, eds, 58–86, Ablex, 1993.
18. H. Thimbleby & with M. A. Addison, "Intelligent Adaptive Assistance and Its Automatic Generation," *Interacting with Computers*, **8**(1):51–68, 1996.
19. H. Thimbleby, "Specification-led Design for Interface Simulation, Collecting Use-data, Interactive Help, Writing Manuals, Analysis, Comparing Alternative Designs, etc," *Personal Technologies*, **4**(2):241–254, 1999.
20. H. Thimbleby, "Analysis and Simulation of User Interfaces," *Human Computer Interaction 2000*, BCS Conference on Human-Computer Interaction, S. McDonald, Y. Waern & G. Cockton, eds., **XIV**, 221–237, 2000.
21. H. Thimbleby, A. Blandford, P. Cairns, P. Curzon and M. Jones, "User Interface Design as Systems Design," *Proceedings People and Computers*, **XVI**, X. Faulkner, J. Finlay & F. Détienne, eds., 281–301, Springer, 2002.
22. H. Thimbleby, "The Directed Chinese Postman Problem," *Software — Practice & Experience*, **33**(11):1081–1096, 2003.
23. H. Thimbleby, "Computer Algebra in User Interface Design Analysis," *Proceedings BCS HCI Conference*, **2**, edited by A. Dearden and L. Watts, Research Press International, pp121–124, 2004.
24. H. Thimbleby, "User Interface Design with Matrix Algebra," *ACM Transactions on Computer-Human Interaction*, **11**(2):181–236, 2004.
25. C. Wharton, J. Rieman, C. Lewis & P. Polson, "The Cognitive Walkthrough Method: A Practictioner's Guide," in J. Nielsen & R. L. Mack, eds, *Usability Inspection Methods*, John Wiley and Sons, 1994.
26. D. R. Wixon, "Evaluating usability methods: why the current literature fails the practitioner," *Interactions*, **10**(4):28-34, 2003.
27. V. Venkatesh, M. G. Morris, G. B. Davis & F. D. Davis, "User acceptance of information technology: Toward a unified view," *MIS Quarterly*, **27**(3):425–478, 2003.
28. P. C. Wright & A. F. Monk, "The use of think-aloud evaluation methods in design," *ACM SIGCHI Bulletin*, **23**(1):55–57, 1991.

Collaborative Social Structures and Task Modelling Integration

Victor M.R. Penichet[1], Fabio Paternò[2], J.A. Gallud[1], and Maria D. Lozano[1]

[1] I3A-UCLM, Av. España s/n, 02007 Albacete, España
{victor.penichet, jose.gallud, maria.lozano}@uclm.es
[2] ISTI-CNR, via G.Moruzzi 1, 56100 Pisa, Italy
fabio.paterno@isti.cnr.it

Abstract. Interdisciplinary work groups have proved to be one of the best practices (in terms of efficiency) in modern organizations. Large applications have many different users who can play different roles with responsibilities and rights depending on such roles. There are so many roles, groups, relationships among them, tasks, and collaborations, that it is very difficult to develop an application without gathering all this information in a proper way. This paper describes a modelling approach supported by a graphical notation, which makes the representation of such information easier to analyse and manage. The goal is to provide a complete and integrated approach to model collaborative interactive systems.

1 Introduction

Software applications are often used by a large number of user groups who have different features and functions. The availability of high-speed network connections has contributed to increasing the number of these applications, where many different types of users participate in a temporally and geographically distributed way.

Such a variety of users, features, tasks, objectives, etc. have to be taken into account carefully when developing large applications. Designers should be provided with techniques and tools to gather all this information, which must be considered to develop multi-user collaborative systems.

This paper presents a modelling approach for collaborative systems to better understand the organization of the different users, the existing collaborations among them, and the individual tasks they perform. Such an approach is based on the role that users play in the system (the role view).

The organizational structure of the users of the system that will be deployed and the relationships among such users are modelled by means of two diagrams: the Organizational Structure Diagram (OSD) and the Collaborative Diagram (CD), respectively. The OSD models such a user structure: groups to which users belong, the roles they play, etc. Several CDs provide a model of the collaborations among users depending on the role they play or the groups to which they belong.

G. Doherty and A. Blandford (Eds.): DSVIS 2006, LNCS 4323, pp. 67–80, 2007.

The third diagram making up the role view is the Task Diagram (TD). There is a TD for each role in the system, and it specifies the tasks that a user with such a role performs.

The organizational structure, collaborative relationships, and tasks a user performs are modelled thanks to three graphical representations.

Instead of developing a new graphical notation for the TD, we have adopted an existing one. CTT [10] has been selected for this purpose because it is already widely accepted and consolidated. This paper also presents the integration between the OSD and CD diagrams with CTT. These three diagrams provide designers with an easy way to gather useful information on a system.

The rest of the paper is organized as follows. Section 2 discusses related work. Section 3 briefly describes the proposed role view to design and analyse collaborative systems. Section 4 is devoted to the integration between the adopted task diagram (CTT) with the rest of the diagrams in the role view. Section 5 presents an example to show the applicability of the proposal. Lastly, Section 6 concludes the work with some final remarks.

2 Related Work

Some coordination and communication problems appear when many users interact with the same system. A system that assists distributed developers in maintaining mutual awareness is presented in [6]. Our proposal is oriented to analysts and designers who develop applications where many users, probably geographically distributed, collaborate with each other. Software developed taking into account the user's organization and collaborations is generally much more usable.

The number of users in collaborative systems and their different features and functions raise specific issues and there is a need to provide designers with specific techniques and methods to model such systems.

In [2], a conceptual model is proposed to characterize groupware [3, 4, 5, 7] systems. This model describes objects and operations on such objects, dynamic aspects, and the interface between the system and the users, and amongst users. This characterization describes a groupware system from its users' point of view. Our approach describes the system from the role point of view, because we want to take advantage of the abstraction of features and functions that roles provide. We also propose a graphical notation to represent the roles, collaborations, etc. in a collaborative system.

Role modelling is used in [12] as an enabling technology for framework design and integration. Class diagrams with some role constraints, which are constraints on object collaborations, are used in such modelling technique. We propose to specify the organizational structure of system users , that is, how roles are grouped and related.

Role modelling is used as a mechanism for separation of concerns to increase the understandability and reusability of business process models [1]. In some modelling techniques for developing groupware systems [10, 11, 14], role or actor concepts are also considered when modelling the existing collaboration among the users of a system. We propose a notation that provides designers with a flexible way to represent social structures and interactions. It is a view of the system that facilitates the design and the analysis of the users' collaborations and provides a way of classifying, organizing, and representing the roles and the groups to which the users will belong.

Such methods use these concepts to ease comprehension of the system, and to allow designers to know who does what, or what kind of features or functions a particular user performs. In our work, it is also possible to represent the organizational structure of the system to be built. After modelling the organizational structure of the users, we suggest a graphical notation to represent the person-computer-person interactions, which provides an easy-to-grasp view of the existing collaborations among such users.

We use the ConcurTaskTrees (CTT) notation to model individual tasks instead of a new notation. Therefore, a mapping between different notations is necessary, which is a common technique to achieve a more complete model of a system (e.g. [9]).

3 The Role View

The *Role View* provides a way to model collaborative systems, and accordingly, provides designers with another way to analyse them. The main focus of the Role View is on the actors, the organizational structure, and the relationships among them.

This view is described by means of three diagrams: *Organizational Structure Diagram* (OSD), *Collaborative Diagram* (CD), and *Task Diagram* (TD).

The concepts we use to model collaborative applications by means of the OSD and CD diagrams, as well as the diagrams themselves, are explained in the following subsections, while for the TD, the existing CTT [10] graphical representation has been adopted. A more extensive example of the notation and the way of modelling collaborative systems through the Role View has been introduced in section 5.

3.1 Basic Concepts

We use some concepts in our approach that are going to be briefly explained in this sub-section. Regarding organization, we use three concepts that we call *organizational items*: *actor*, *role*, and *group,* which are described in Table 1. Other concepts are used to express relationships and collaborations between the different classifiers: *instantiation*, *aggregation*, and *cooperative interaction* (Table 2).

3.2 Organizational Structure Diagram (OSD)

It is possible to model the organizational structure of the users by means of *actors*, *roles*, and *instantiation relationships*, *groups*, and *aggregation relationships*. The main advantage to modelling such structure is the possibility of classifying, organizing, and representing the users of the system.

Table 1. Organizational items

Organizational items	Description	Notation
Group	A *group* is a set of *roles* that need to interact together and to collaborate in order to reach a common objective. Common objectives would not be reachable without such collaboration.	GROUP_1
Role	A *role* is a set of *actors* that share the same characteristics and perform the same tasks	ROLE_1
Actor	An *actor* is an element able to perform a task. We could consider an *actor* as an instance of a *role*.	
User	A *user* is a person who interacts with the system, thus s/he is an *actor*. Some other things (not users) could be actors.	

Table 2. Organizational relationships

Relationship	Description	Notation
Instantiation (structure)	Between a *role* and an *actor* playing such role there is an *instantiation relationship*, that is to say, this actor is an instance of that role.	
Aggregation (structure)	An *aggregation relationship* is an existing association between the whole and its parts.	
Cooperative Interaction (collaboration)	A *cooperative interaction* means a cooperative task among several *actors*, *roles*, or *groups* in order to reach a common objective.	Task_role_1 Cooperative_task Task_role_2

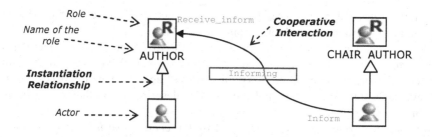

Fig. 1. Instantiation relationships between a role and an actor and cooperative interactions

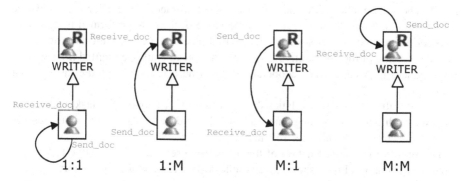

Fig. 2. The four fundamental cooperative relationships

Moreover, it allows designers to gain a much more structured, simple and real view of the role organization and the groups to which the users will belong. It will be the basis for designing user collaborations.

Once the organizational structure of the system users is represented (in terms of group, role, actor, and aggregation), the collaborations existing between the organizational items are established, which describe the different cooperative tasks performed. These tasks are represented in the CD, which is explained in Section 3.3.

The *Instantiation relationship* between role and actor provides a way to represent a role and an actor playing this role in the same diagram. Fig. 1 shows an example of *Instantiation relationship*. It links two organizational items: a role and an actor. This relation means that the source icon is an instance of the destination icon, that is to say, an actor performs such a role. Then, this figure represents a set of actors with the same features and the same functions, and an instance of such a set.

3.3 Collaborative Diagram (CD)

Once the structure of the organization is represented by the OSD, one of the main advantages is the possibility of modelling the collaborations among actors belonging to different roles and groups. The idea is not to model users' interaction, but to model the interaction between users through computers and networks.

When structuring the whole system according to different primary objectives, a CD is made for each objective. Each CD will explain the existing interaction between the organizational items (groups, roles, actors) that are necessary to achieve such objectives. The whole set of CDs describes all collaboration in the system.

Interaction among actors is symbolized by the *cooperative interaction* relationship, a solid black arrow in the diagram. Such relationships are cooperative tasks, which are performed by several actors within the system.

Solid black arrows representing cooperative tasks have three labels as shown in Fig. 1. The source label is the name of the task performed by the actor who starts the cooperation, and the destination label is the name of the task performed by the actor who cooperates with the first one. The squared label situated in the centre of the arrow is the name of the cooperative task. The arrowhead could be omitted if necessary, for instance, in a concurrent cooperative task where the order of the tasks is not important.

A cooperative interaction relationship representing a cooperative task also has an intrinsic cardinality at the beginning and at the end. This cardinality indicates the number of actors performing the role tasks.

The source and the destination of the arrow representing a cooperative task determine the cardinality. Fig. 2 shows an example with every possible cardinality.

4   Integration of the Role View and ConcurTaskTrees

Tasks models are a useful tool to analyze and design applications from the point of view of the users who are going to interact with such applications.

The role view that we propose provides a new perspective to the designers. Users are organized in roles and related groups. The result of these relationships between roles and groups is what we define as *organizational structure* of the users of an application which is graphically represented in the OSD (see section 3).

Traditionally, in order to discover a way to fix large problems, they are divided into simpler sub-problems which can be modelled separately. We propose the CDs to identify and model the collaborations between users in every sub-problems (see section 3). Different organizational items from the OSD are related in the CDs to represent such collaborations.

Therefore, this method to design collaborative systems allows designers, first, to *identify and analyse the organizational structure* of the system users, and then, it also provides a way to *model the collaborations among the users of such system*.

Mapping different notations is a technique already used to obtain a complete model of the system. For example, [9] shows a mapping approach between ConcurTaskTrees and UML [13] to include one of the most widely used notation for task modelling into the Unified Modelling Language.

The *role view* is composed of three different diagrams as it was mentioned before: OSD, CD, and TD. OSD and CD were detailed in Section 3, while for the TD, the existing CTT graphical representation has been adopted. The organizational items and relationships integration within the CTT notation is explained in the next sub-sections. Such integration is necessary to achieve a coherent model of the system.

4.1 Group and Aggregation Relationship

Group and aggregation concepts do not have a direct mapping from the OSDs and CDs to the CTT notation. They are concepts used to classify the roles that the users of the system are going to play.

An OSD represents the set of all the users of the system. These users play roles, and such roles belong to one or more groups. A user, by himself, cannot directly belong to any group.

The group concept was defined in Section 3 as a set of *roles* whose actors need to interact together and to collaborate in order to reach a common objective. Hereby, this common objective could be one of these sub-problems in which the main problem is decomposed to make it simpler to manage, as mentioned in the introduction of this section.

Each sub-problem is modelled by means of a CD and several TDs. The CD represents the existing collaborations among some organizational items of the OSD, while there is a TD, which is represented by the CTT graphical notation, for each role that participates in the sub-problem.

4.2 Role

The *role* organizational item of the Role View (see Table 1) is the one which has the most direct correspondence in the CTT task model, because the role concept is also considered in the CTT notation in the same way.

In a CTT cooperative model, every role has an associated task diagram with all the tasks that are performed by such role. That is, if there is a role item in the Role View, there will be an associated CTT task diagram for this role, which shows all the tasks performed by a user playing such role.

4.3 Actor and Instantiation Relationship

Actor and instantiation relationship concepts do not have a direct mapping between the OSD and the TD. User interactions with the system and collaborations between users with different roles are considered in CTT. However, collaborations among users with the same role are not taken into account. Therefore, the introduction of these concepts provides a way to represent such collaborations.

Actors introduce a new concurrent situation in the typical CTT models because of this type of collaboration. Fig. 4 and Fig. 5 show the representation of two actors with the same role who are collaborating with each other. This kind of collaboration is further explained in the following sub-section.

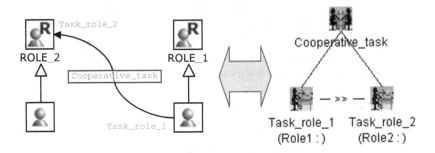

Fig. 3. The basic correspondence between the CD and TD diagrams

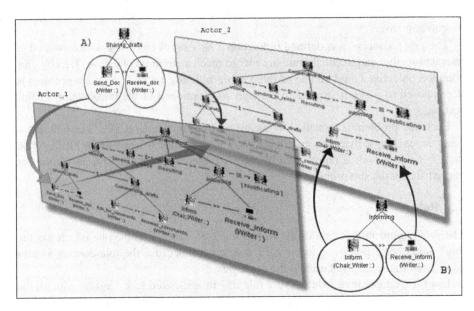

Fig. 4. Interaction between actors and roles

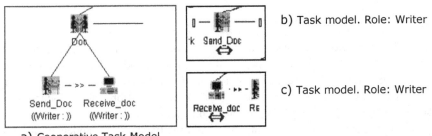

Fig. 5. Collaboration between actors with the same role

4.4 Cooperative Interaction Relationship

Cooperative interaction relationships between the organizational items of a CD have a direct mapping in the TD.

Every role within CTT has an associated task diagram as mentioned before, but there is also a cooperative part to structure the cooperative tasks, which are decomposed until tasks performed by a single user are reached [10]. These single user tasks also appear in the corresponding role task diagram as connected tasks (see Fig. 5).

The right part in Fig. 3 shows a *cooperative task* represented in CTT. The left part in Fig. 3 shows *cooperative interaction relationship* between two roles in a CD. As shown, the mapping of *cooperative task, task role*, and *role* concepts between the two diagrams is a simple matter.

Each diagram shows a different view of the system, hence some information appears in one but not in the other. In a CD, every *cooperative interaction relationship* has an intrinsic cardinality at the beginning and at the end, which indicates the number of actors performing the role tasks. This aspect is not shown in the TD. On the other hand, a TD has some other elements that are not in the CD such as: (1) the *CTT task category* of each task performed by each role, that is, if they are *interaction, application*, or *user* tasks; and (2) the *CTT temporal operator* necessary to link the two role tasks which will constitute the cooperative one, that is, if it is an *enabling, enabling with information passing, etc.* operator.

Considering that CDs represent actors and roles in the same diagram, two sorts of collaborations could occur: collaborations among users with different roles, and collaborations among users with the same role. Up to now, CTT has focused on relationships among users in a system playing different roles (Fig. 4). The notation we propose in this paper (see Fig. 3) allows designers to model relationships among users playing the same role as well (Fig. 4).

Collaborations among users with the same role can be appreciated more clearly in CDs. Although the CTT notation could represent this semantic by writing the same role name in the individual role tasks below the cooperative one (Fig. 4), for the sake of clarity, we have added double brackets and arrows, as shown in Fig. 5.

5   Example

We show a simple example of an application for internal publication of documents in an organization in order to better explain the approach proposed.

5.1 Brief Problem Description

Some employees elaborate together documents to be published in their organization. There is interaction among them in order to get a candidate document to be published. A supervisor (writers' chair) can send a document to be revised by other members of the organization. The candidate document is received by a reviewers' chair who decides what kind of review to apply. There are two possibilities: (AAO) all at once, where all the reviewers receive the candidate document at the same time and the chair waits for their answers to continue; and (OAA) one after another, where the chair selects an order for review. In the latter case, if any reviewer decides that the candidate document is not ready to be published, then is not necessary to continue with the process. If the candidate document is finally published, then the authors will be informed. Published documents can also be read by readers: a group of people who can only read and comment documents, not modify them.

5.2 Designing the Collaborative System

When designing a collaborative system, our approach uses the three diagrams introduced in this work. Such diagrams provide designers with a way to gather information about the organizational structure of the users of the system (OSD), relationships among them (CD), and the tasks they are going to perform (TD).

The diagram in Fig. 6 shows the OSD of the example considered. Such diagram represents the organizational structure of the users of the application for internal publication of documents. The first decision is to make a logical division of the users into two groups: those who are able to modify, create, etc. (internal), and those who only have the possibility of viewing the products generated by the members of the first group (external). The "external" group is only composed of users playing the "reader" role.

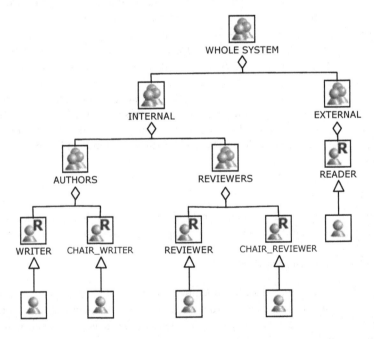

Fig. 6. Organizational Structure Diagram (OSD) of the example

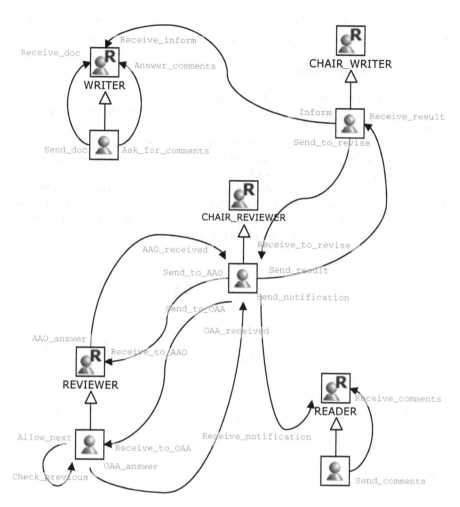

Fig. 7. Actor interactions in the internal publication system example: Role View. Note that the name of the cooperative tasks have been omitted for the sake of simplicity.

The "authors" group is made up of roles with writing features, whereas the "reviewers" group is composed of roles with document editing features.

Once the organizational structure of the users has been represented by means of the OSD, a CD is generated for each main objective in the problem. As the problem we are studying in this example is not very large, all its collaborations will be represented in the same CD. Such diagram is shown in Fig. 7.

Lastly, a TD is specified by using the CTT notation for each role in the system. Fig. 8 shows the cooperative model, while Fig. 9 shows an example of a TD which represents every individual task that a user playing the role "Chair_reviewer" could perform. That is, an actor playing such role also has to perform the tasks "Select_doc", "Read_doc",

"User_decision", "Select_AAO_or_OAA", "Answer_analysis", among other tasks in addition to those tasks that will be connected to constitute a cooperative one.

5.3 Analysis of a Collaborative System

The graphical notation presented in this paper could also be used to analyse an existing collaborative application in order to improve the way in which users work together to achieve common objectives.

Groups and roles can be represented and organized in an OSD to study if the current organizational structure of the users of the system is the best or, on the contrary, could be improved by restructuring such organization.

Likewise, CDs facilitate the study of the cooperative tasks performed in the system. As our proposed graphical notation provides analysts with additional information about collaborations among users, and such information is represented in an intuitive and easy way, then it is possible to analyse whether collaborations are adequate, or they should be redesigned in some other way.

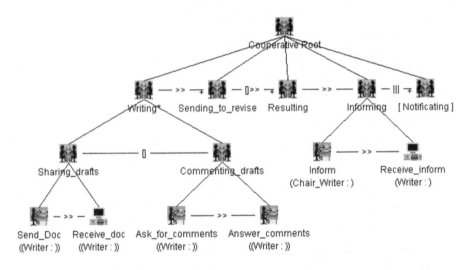

Fig. 8. Actor interactions in the internal publication system example: Task View

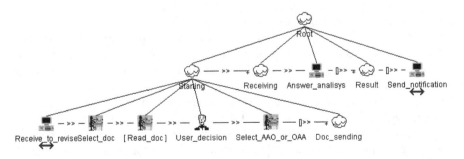

Fig. 9. Role task diagram example: "Chair_reviewer"

For instance, when the "Chair_reviewer" knows the result of the review, a notification is sent to the "Chair_writer", and then the "Chair_writer" informs authors of the document about the decision. By analyzing the diagram, analysts could detect that a "Chair_reviewer" could inform actors with the role "Writer" directly, which would avoid an unnecessary step

6 Conclusions

A new modelling approach for collaborative systems has been presented in this paper. By means of the proposed graphical notation, the organizational structure of the users of the system is specified on the basis of the roles they play and the groups to which they belong.

Likewise, this approach provides designers with a way of representing cooperative relationships that users must perform to achieve a common objective. Organizational structure and collaborations among users are easily and intuitively represented by way of an OSD and one or several CDs.

We have adopted ConcurTaskTrees to represent individual tasks that each user performs because it is one of the more widely accepted notations in task modelling. Therefore, an integration of the organizational and collaboration models and CTT is also presented in this work.

Representing tasks, collaborations, and the organizational structure of the users of a system not only makes its design easier, but also facilitates the study and the analysis of existing systems to propose a new re-design if necessary.

Acknowledgements

We would like to thank the European ADVISES TMR for funding this work, which was also supported by the Spanish CYCIT project TIN2004-08000-C03-01 and the grant PCC-05-005-1 from JCCM.

References

1. Caetano, A., Silva, A. R., and Tribolet, J. 2005. *Using roles and business objects to model and understand business processes.* In Proceedings of the 2005 ACM Symposium on Applied Computing.L. M. Liebrock, Ed. SAC '05. ACM Press, New York, NY, 1308-1313
2. Ellis, C., Wainer, J.: *A Conceptual Model of Groupware,* in Proceeding of CSCW'94, 1994, p. 79-88, ACM Press.
3. Greenberg, S.: *The 1988 conference on computer-supported cooperative work: Trip report.* ACM SIGCHI Bulletin, 21(1), pp. 49-55, July 1989.
4. Greif, I.; *Computer-Supported Cooperative Work: A Book of Readings.* Morgan Kaufmann, San Mateo CA, 1988.
5. Grudin, J. *CSCW: History and Focus.* University of California. IEEE Computer, 27, 5, 19-26. 1994

6. Gutwin, C.; Schneider, K.; Penner, R.; Paquette, D.; *Supporting Group Awareness in Distributed Software Development*. EHCI/DSVIS 2004, 9th IFIP Working Conference on Engineering for Human-Computer Interaction, Tremsbuttel Castle, Hamburg, Germany, July 11-13, 2004, 14 pages. Also to be published in Lecture Notes in Computer Science, Springer-Verlag, Berlin, 2004

7. Johansen, R. (1988): *Groupware: Computer support for business teams*. New York: The Free Press.

8. Mori, G., Paternò, F. ,Santoro, C. "CTTE: Support for Developing and Analysing Task Models for Interactive System Design", IEEE Transactions on Software Engineering, pp.797-813, August 2002 (Vol. 28, No. 8), IEEE Press.

9. Nóbrega, L., Nunes, N., Coelho, H.; *Mapping ConcurTaskTrees into UML 2.0*, 12th International Workshop on Design, Specification, and Verification of Interactive System (DSV-IS'2005), July 13–15, 2005, Newcastle upon Tyne, England, Springer-Verlag, 2005

10. Paterno', F.; *Model-based Design and Evaluation of Interactive Applications*. F.Paternò, Springer Verlag, November 1999, ISBN 1-85233-155-0

11. Pinelle, D., Gutwin, C., Greenberg, S.: *Task analysis for groupware usability evaluation: Modeling shared-workspace tasks with the mechanics of collaboration*. ACM Transactions on Computer-Human Interaction (TOCHI) Volume 10 , Issue 4, Pages: 281 - 311. (2003) ISSN:1073-0516

12. Riehle D, Gross T.; *Role model based framework design and integration*. Proceedings of OOPSLA '98. ACM Press, 1998; 117-133

13. Rumbaugh, J.; Jacobson, I.; Booch, G.: *The Unified Modeling Language. Reference Manual*. Addison-Wesley. 1999

14. Van der Veer, G. C.; Van Welie, M. 2000. Task based groupware design: Putting theory into practice. In Proceedings of the 2000 Symposium on Designing Interactive Systems. New York, ACM Press, 326–337.

Towards Model-Driven Development of Staged Participatory Multimedia Events

Jan Van den Bergh, Steven Huypens, and Karin Coninx

Hasselt University – transnationale Universiteit Limburg
Expertise Centre for Digital Media – Institute for BroadBand Technology
Wetenschapspark 2
3590 Diepenbeek
Belgium
{jan.vandenbergh,steven.huypens,karin.coninx}@uhasselt.be

Abstract. The industry nowadays is showing an increasing interest towards an extended interactive television experience, called participation television. This increasing interactivity brings the creation of such television events closer to the creation of regular software as we know it for personal computers and mobile devices. In this paper we report on our work in model-driven development of one kind of such interactive television shows, staged participatory multimedia events. More specifically, this work reports on the domain-specific language we created to model these events and the generation of abstract prototypes. These interactive prototypes are built using web-languages and can be used to perform early evaluation.

1   Introduction

In recent years the entertainment industry has known an increasing focus on interactive and social programmings. The traditional passive, lay back television medium is getting more interactive to compete with other popular interactive entertainment devices. Every day more television shows allow user interaction in one way or another, e.g. well-known TV-games are being extended to get a new social dimension[1].

Participation television is the kind of interactive television with the highest degree of public involvement. The watchers are no longer constrained to merely passive viewing or anonymous participation, but they can become part of the show if they want to. This can be accomplished by not only using a remote control and keyboard for interaction, but by adding devices such as microphones and webcams to create input for the show and by using cross-medial aspects; e.g. users can view or interact using their remote control and television set, their PC or even their mobile phone.

The creation of participation television shows is complex, not only regarding the social, creative and managerial aspects, but the software needed for those shows is becoming very complex and more similar to traditional software engineering projects compared to the production of traditional broadcast television shows. Within the IWT project Participate, we extend existing software engineering techniques for the creation of interactive desktop applications so they can be applied to participation television.

---

[1] http://research.edm.uhasselt.be/kris/research/projects/telebuddies/

G. Doherty and A. Blandford (Eds.): DSVIS 2006, LNCS 4323, pp. 81–94, 2007.
© Springer-Verlag Berlin Heidelberg 2007

In this paper, we report on our results obtained by combining a model-based development approach in combination with prototypes in the earliest phases of development. We show that it is possible to combine high-level models to generate interactive abstract prototypes of participation television formats.

We will start the remainder of this paper by shortly discussing some related work within the model-based community and how participation television formats are designed and realised, followed by the introduction of our approach and modeling notation for high-level participation television specification. This is followed by a discussion of how we use current standards from the World Wide Web Consortium (W3C) to construct interactive abstract prototypes. Finally, we explain how we generate the interactive abstract prototypes from the high-level specification and draw some conclusions.

2 Related Work

At the moment several tools (from companies such as Aircode, Alticast, Sofia, iTVBox and Cardinal) are commercially available for the development of interactive television applications. These tools provide a graphical environment enabling a non-technical user to easily create simple iDTV software or websites. They require no technical knowledge like Java, MHP or DVB-HTML [6] from the designer and thus ease the creation of iDTV. Most of them also offer an emulator which enables the author to preview the result of his work on his own PC, rather than deploying his output to a set-top box.

These environments are however too limited for the development of participation television. They are mostly centered to designing the graphical layout of various pages and the addition of some common iDTV modules and components. There is no support to add the interaction components needed for the participation of the viewer in a television show.

A number of tools have been created that allow early prototyping based on models. Canonsketch [2] is a tool that provides synchronized models at different levels; at the highest level, a UML class diagram is used to represent the structure of a single dialogue using the notation proposed in [10]. The Canonical Abstract Prototypes notation (CAP) [4] allows to describe the functionality offered by a user interface at an abstract level using a limited set of icons that are linked to specific areas of the screen. At the most concrete level, a preview using HTML is provided.

Elkoutbi et al. [7] use UML diagrams to define user interfaces at an abstract level using annotated collaboration diagrams and class diagrams from which statechart diagrams can be generated. Based on these statecharts, complete functional prototypes are generated. The approach is concentrating on form-based user interfaces for a single user. The specifications that are used as input, however, have to be rigorously defined in comparison to what we want to accomplish.

Pleuss [12] proposes a methodology that uses UML to model multimedia applications. A code generator for Flash supporting his methodology is under development.

Several model-based approaches for the development of user interfaces are taking into account some form of context-sensitiveness. The TERESA-tool [11,9] allows the semi-automatic creation of multi-platform user interfaces (mostly targeted to the web) starting from a task model. Another task-based method is described by Clerckx et al. [3], who provide tool support that enables derivation of a context-sensitive dialog model from a context-aware task-model. In combination with a presentation model, the tool is able to generate context-aware prototypes.

Other approaches, such as Damask [8] for low-fidelity prototyping use a purely informal sketch-based interface. Damask uses models, originating from the model-based design community, in the backend but does not expose the designer to these models to enable consistent prototyping of multi-device user interfaces. Damask allows interactive testing of the sketched interfaces, but models cannot be reused.

3   Staged Participatory Multimedia Events

Broadband end users currently witness an evolution towards ubiquitous entertainment being delivered over their High-Speed Internet (HSI) line. As such the broadband pipe is used to deliver complete experiences to the home. Unfortunately, this enables the home-based users only to consume more professional content (Hollywood movies on demand) and to get some low level interaction with the broadcast television: time shifted viewing, voting, etc.

The goal of Staged Participatory Multimedia Events (SPME) is therefore to actively engage end-users and turn them into true participators, thus providing a stage for users to participate in challenging interactive television applications that do not exist today. Several devices like microphones and webcams will be used in these formats to enable the different participators with true interactivity. In the future, this will lead to television shows with thousands of active participants, where complex software is needed to cope with these new formats.

In the remainder of this paper we will use an auction as an example of a SPME. The auction SPME could start when a regular auction is being broadcast and at least one of the viewers has offered an item for sale. When enough interested viewers are registered, an auctioneer can decide to start the auction. After a short welcome message, he introduces the seller to the interested viewers. The seller then has the opportunity to promote the item, after which the auction starts. Any of the registered viewers can then make a bid on the item or ask questions to its seller. When a satisfactory price is reached, the auction is concluded. The control flow specification and a prototype implementation of this scenario are shown in Fig. 1.

It is clear that creating such an interactive show requires establishing and creating a complicated software infrastructure. It is our intent to facilitate the creation of such shows by offering a set of models from which the necessary code, targeting a set of pre-build networked components, can be generated. These models should abstract away a lot of the details and complexity of such infrastructure. In our approach this abstraction is reached by using layered models. The models at the highest level of abstraction do not have a direct relationship with the software infrastructure but relate to the structure of a SPME and the structure of the user interface that the participants of the SPME interact with on their television set. These high-level models can be used without the lower level details to enable early design evaluation using generated prototypes. These models and prototypes are discussed into more detail in the following sections.

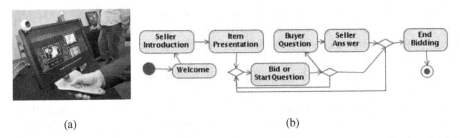

(a)   (b)

Fig. 1. The auctionTV scenario: (a) a high-fidelity prototype implementation ©Alcatel (with permission), (b) control flow specification

4   Specification Language

We created a domain-specific modeling language that uses abstractions familiar to those involved in the creation of participation television. We chose to define a domain-specific language instead of traditional models used in model-based user interface design or software engineering because this allows us to create a language that uses concepts familiar to the target audience, creators of a SPME, and still can be translated into the required software concepts. The attentive reader will notice that the content of some models used in model-based design of user interfaces, such as dialog model, user model and presentation model, is combined in new models in the domain-specific language.

In this paper we will limit ourselves to those language parts relevant for the creation of the first high-level models. The first part is the general flow of the show. It is specified in the scenario model, which is built around the concept of *scenes* or *template instances* and is discussed in section 4.1. The second, and last, relevant part describes the screen composition for the different roles that are involved within a scene or template as is explained in section 4.2. Before discussing these two models, we start with the necessary definitions for the used terminology.

Definition 1. *A* template *is a reusable behavioral artifact containing a flow of actions in which a specified number of participants having different roles can be involved. A template can receive data as input and output parameters.*

Definition 2. *A* scene *is an instance of a template. The value of all input parameters of a scene needs to be specified either explicitly in the model or implicitly through derivation from output parameters of another scene in the scenario diagram.*

4.1   Scenario Model

The scenario model describes the structure of a SPME using scenes (see definition 2). The overall layout of the diagram is based upon the graphical language used to program LEGO mindstorms[2] . The language also features a horizontal bar, the *heading*, at the top that serves as a starting point for one or more parallel flows[3]. The flow of a program

---

[2] http://mindstorms.lego.com/
[3] Our current tool support does not take parallel flows into account.

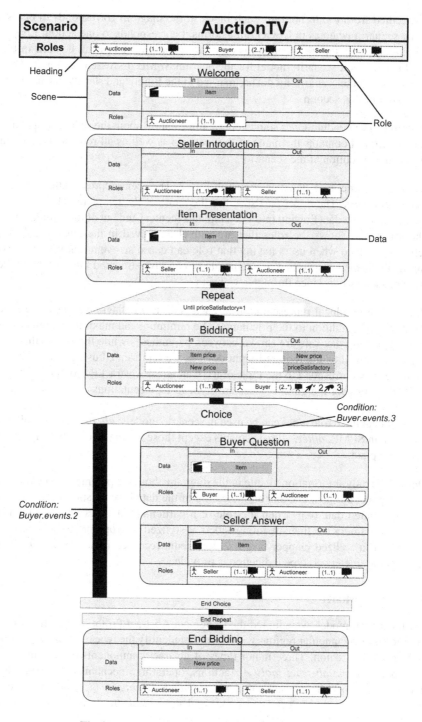

Fig. 2. An annotated example of a scenario diagram

is specified from top to bottom. Each block in the diagram corresponds to one scene of the scenario whereas in LEGO mindstorms it corresponds to one action. Loops and conditional behavior are specified using two separate blocks as can be seen in Figure 2, which shows a scenario model for the auction SPME discussed section 3. The different parts of the scenario-model are marked in the Figure and shortly discussed in the remainder of this section.

Heading. The heading gives some generic information about the scenario, specified in that diagram. It contains the name of the scenario as well as all roles that are required to start the execution of the scenario.

Scenes. A scene is depicted as shown in Fig. 2. The scene representation consists of three main areas. The upper part specifies the name of the template, while the middle part specifies the data flowing into the templates (center) and out of the template (right). The lower part shows the roles that are actively involved in the template. A role is actively involved when users having that role can cause an event that triggers or ends part of the behavior specified in a template or can give streamed input to the modeled system, such as live-video through a webcam.

Roles. The graphical representation of each role in the diagram shows role-specific information in addition to the role name. The minimum and maximum number of participants having that role are shown between parentheses while the events that can be triggered as well as the required input devices are represented using icons. The icons for the events correspond to the tools of the Canonical Abstract Prototype notation [4], while the icons for the input devices are stylized representations of a camera 🎥 and a microphone 🎤 .

Two predefined role types can be used in scenario models: *all*, representing all participants of an SPME, *other*, all participants except those having roles explicitly specified in the template.

Data. The only information visible in the diagram about the parameters and the results of a template, are its name and an indication of the data type. A stick-Figure is shown for role-related data (e.g. when the role of a participant changes within a template), a stylized camera for live streaming video, a stylized microphone for live streaming sound, and a stylized clapper board 🎬 for media recorded in advance. For all other types of parameters no type indication is provided.

4.2 Screen Model

For the screen model, we adopted the Canonical Abstract Prototype notation [4]. This notation uses rectangular regions with icons that identify the type of abstract component that spans this region. Three major types of abstract components exist with different subtypes: *generic abstract tools* ↗ (actions, operators, mechanisms or controls that can be used to operate on materials), *generic abstract material* □ (containers, content, information, data that is operated upon) and *generic abstract active material* ⬚ (a combination of both other types).

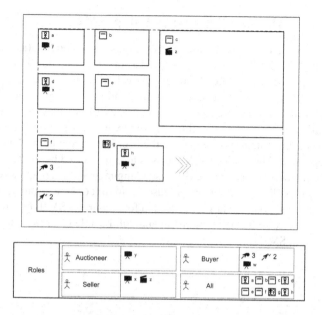

Fig. 3. An example of a screen model

Our notation is shown in Fig. 3. The differences with the Canonical Abstract Prototype notation are driven by the difference in targets. The standard Canonical Abstract Prototype notation is used to give designers an overview of the functionality that is to be shown to a user on a screen or in a window on a screen. Depending on the designer's creativity, the final screen layout can be entirely different.

The screen model, however, is intended to design user interfaces that target entire television screens. A single model can describe the different screen compositions that are used within one or more templates. Therefore each icon is combined with a character that identifies the component. Each character-icon combination appears within both the screen layout and the role section establishing the connection between the participants and the abstract components he can observe. Multiple character-icon combinations can be placed within one region with each combination visible to participants with a different role. We also introduced two new icons to identify user interface components that show a participant (participant element 🖾) or a collection of participants of which zero or more can be emphasized (active participant collection 🖾). A concrete example of the latter type of user interface component can be seen in the lower right corner of Fig. 3.

Because involvement of the participants is an important aspect of a SPME, icons referring to the origin of multimedia materials are added to the icons in CAP-notation [4]. The sources can be either live multimedia streams 🎥 or recorded multimedia 📷 . The sources are linked to users with a certain role with means identical to the ones used to link user interface components with participants with a certain role.

5   Interactive Abstract Prototypes Using XML

The dynamic abstract prototypes are expressed using a combination of XHTML, XForms [5] and CSS. XHTML merely serves as a container for embedding the dynamic abstract prototype. XForms and CSS are respectively used for expressing the structure of the dynamic abstract prototype and the styling and positioning of the abstract components. This combination was chosen because the tools to display these specifications are freely available and the specifications are relatively easy to read. Furthermore, the style and layout, the structure of the show, the user interface and the runtime data are all cleanly separated. The choice for XForms is also motivated by the fact that it is designed to be embedded in another XML-based language and is completely declarative (including event handling). This enables reuse for more concrete prototypes, for which the XForms-structure could be largely reused in for example a SMIL [1] document. XS-miles[4] is being ported to the MHP platform and will be able to show content expressed using XForms and SMIL .

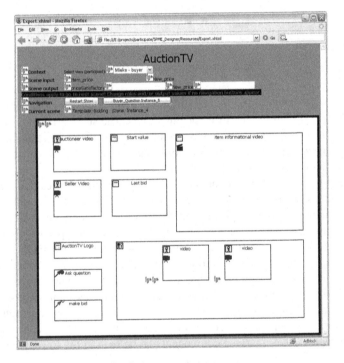

Fig. 4. An example prototype

An example of a prototype corresponding with the *Bidding* template in the scenario in Fig. 2 and the screen layout in Fig. 3 is shown in Fig. 4. It shows a typical screen during *prototype simulation*. The upper part contains controls for navigating through the abstract prototype. At the top left one can select a participant with a certain role. In

---

[4] http://www.xsmiles.org

this case the participant is Mieke and has the role "bidder". At the next row, the values of all parameters of the current template are shown. The next line similarly shows input fields for the corresponding output, followed by triggers for navigating through the abstract prototype, including a trigger for restarting a simulation and triggers for all transitions to other scenes that are possible in the active context (selected participant and parameter values). The last line of the top part displays the current template and scene. The rest of the screen shows the actual prototype using the CAP notation. User interface components in the abstract prototype can show a tooltip when hovering over them giving concrete information about its function. The tooltip for the abstract component *Ask Question* in Fig. 4 shows a button, *Question*, that triggers a transition to the corresponding scene.

The remainder of this section provides more detail about how XForms and CSS are combined to create the dynamic abstract prototypes. The overall structure of a document describing a prototype is shown in Fig. 5. The document consists of three major parts: (1) simulation related data, including the participants of the simulated show, scenario structure and the applicable constraints, (2) the prototype manipulation controls and (3) the description of the user interfaces associated with the templates.

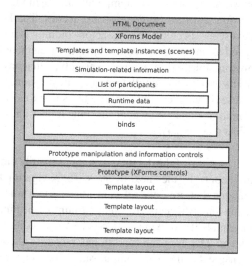

Fig. 5. The document structure of a prototype document

Templates and scenes. The template structure is coded into XForms instances and is shown in Listing 1.1. It lists all templates in the same order as they appear in the scenario model described in section 4. Each template has a name and all corresponding scenes appearing in the scenario are described in nested tags. Each scene also has a name and a next scene specification. Notice that the elements *instances* and *next* are used because the XForms processor requires an element to only contain one type of sub-element in order to iterate over them.

Listing 1.1. DTD for template and scenes structure

```
<!ELEMENT scenario (template+)>
  <!ATTLIST scenario name CDATA #REQUIRED>
<!ELEMENT template (instances)>
  <!ATTLIST template name CDATA #REQUIRED>
<!ELEMENT instances (inst+)>
<!ELEMENT inst (next?,params?)>
  <!ATTLIST inst name CDATA #REQUIRED>
<!ELEMENT next (option+)> <!ELEMENT option EMPTY>
  <!ATTLIST option templ CDATA #REQUIRED>
  <!ATTLIST option inst CDATA #REQUIRED>
  <!ATTLIST option conditional CDATA #REQUIRED>
<!ELEMENT params (param+)>
<!ELEMENT param (#PCDATA)>
  <!ATTLIST param name CDATA #REQUIRED>
  <!ATTLIST param input (true|false) #REQUIRED>
```

Choices and iterations are not directly coded into the templates although each instance can have multiple following templates, instead all possible next templates following a specific scene are mentioned. The template *Bidding* in Fig. 2, for example, can have both *Buyer Question* and *End Bidding* as next scenes. The Figure however only shows *Question* as next scene, because no satisfactory bidding is reached yet. Note that also *Bidding* is not listed as an option because a navigation element to the currently active page can be confusing. Furthermore, this is a prototype that has no link to program logic. When the current user in the simulation is no buyer, none of the next options would be shown, because only buyers can trigger a transition to another scene. A warning (on black background) is displayed whenever some transitions could be hidden due to unsatisfied constraints (see Fig. 4).

Bind expressions. This section of the document contains mainly bind-tags that indicate relevancy of navigation controls (the "next triggers" for navigating to other scenes), or user interface components that are only relevant for a certain role. The generation of bind-expressions for the "next-triggers" results in a number of bind tags for unconditional transitions that equals the maximum number of unconditional transitions for a single scene and in one bind tag for each conditional transition. Additional bind expressions are provided to ensure that input and output values for scenes are always displayed correctly.

Simulation related information. All simulation-related data, is also encoded using an XForms instance. The show related information contains all runtime information about the show and a list of participants (with name, role and other related data such as media streams). The runtime information includes the information about the currently active participant, the currently active scene and tags that can be referenced to by controls that are shown conditionally (such as the possible transitions to another template). Among these tags there is one tag for each bind related to a "next trigger". The relevance, combined with a CSS rule indicating that disabled XML-elements should not be displayed, allows hiding of all irrelevant items.

User interface specification. The user interface specification is entirely contained within one XForms group (from now on referred to as *group*), representing the screen. This group contains a set of groups, one for each template. These groups are shown one at a time, depending on the currently active scene as described in the XForms model.

Each group contains XForms controls for each user interface component in the screen model. When controls are only visible to a certain role, they are only made relevant to this role, and consequently only shown to the relevant users. Additional information is shown when hoovering over the controls in the CAP-notation (using an ephemeral XForms message). The FormsPlayer plugin for Internet Explorer allows embedding XForms controls in hints (displayed in most browsers as tooltips) Fig. 4. This enables using XForms outputs, combined with appropriate CSS-rules to show the CAP-notation of the components in the html-page and to show low-level user interface components in tooltips for establishing real user interaction. In this way, the abstraction can be used to spark creativity, while keeping the interactivity of low-level controls.

6   Generating Dynamic Abstract Prototypes

The prototypes can be automatically generated from the models specified in section 4. We will shortly discuss the main aspects of this algorithm in this section: the generation of the templates and template instances section in the XForms model, the generation of a list of participants, and the generation of the prototype's user interface.

Templates and template instances. For each scene in the scenario, the template is added. When a scene is followed by a choice-construct, all possible next scenes are added as options to the list of scenes that can follow the current scene except when the next scene is the current scene. The generation of the scenes is illustrated in Fig. 6

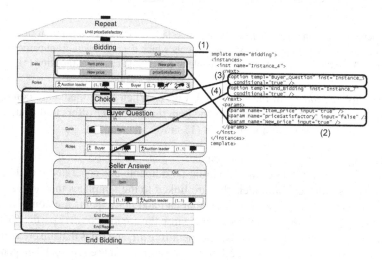

Fig. 6. Generation of the templates and scenes: (1) template generation, (2) parameter generation, (3) and (4) generation of next options

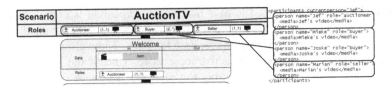

Fig. 7. Generation of the participants

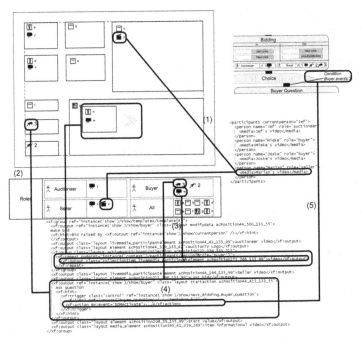

Fig. 8. Generation of the participants and user interface controls: (1) generation of media links for participants, (2) generation of repeated elements which contain media from participants with role *buyer* (3), and (4) trigger that is only visible to buyers and causes a transition (5)

for the template *bidding* of the scenario in Fig. 2. When other media are connected to participants with a certain role, such as the item that the *seller* offers to the auction, can be derived from the screen model. Fig. 8 (1) shows an example.

Participants. The initial list of participants is generated based on the roles present in the scenario heading, while the remaining participants are generated based upon the roles present in the screen models that are linked to the templates that are used in the scenario model. In this case, only roles that can add participants are considered. This means that the following role-types cannot cause the creation of new participants: roles that are already represented in the list, the meta-role *all*, and roles that are created during the scenario (i.e. they are mentioned as output of one or more scenes.) The generation of the participants can be done completely using the heading (see Fig. 7, because all roles are actively participating).

User interface. Most of the user interface generation process is straight-forward; for each abstract user interface component in a screen model, an output-control is generated with the appropriate style and position in CSS. Some triggers can cause a transition between scenes. Fig. 2 shows how this is marked in the scenario. The event-labels and the roles that can cause these events are used as a constraint on the transitions leaving the choice statement. In this case, a XForms trigger has to be generated that causes the transition (see Fig. 8 (4) and (5) for an example.)

7   Discussion and Conclusions

We presented an approach to make early evaluation of a special kind of participation television, staged participatory multimedia events (SPME), possible through the automated creation of abstract prototypes from a limited set of models, defined in a domain-specific modeling language. The modeling language has been succesfully used to express a limited set of participation television scenarios. We believe that despite the abstractness of both the models and the prototype, they are able to express the participation aspect using the icons that were added to the Canonical Abstract Prototype (CAP) [4] notation. Further work will show whether all icons in the original CAP notation are relevant to participation television and whether additional icons are required.

It is our firm believe that using this kind of high-level models through tools allows an effective approach to quickly get a good grip on the required functionality of such an application. We have created proof-of-concept tool support, based on MS Visio and the corresponding SDK, for the notation and prototype generation. The models shown in Fig. 2 and Fig. 3 were created using this tool support in less than half a day including filling in a limited amount of previously unspecified details. These models included enough information to derive a running abstract prototype from those specifications. Despite the fact that our experience is still very limited, we believe that our approach can be used to verify whether all required functionality is being thought of and to create some preliminary results, which do not have to be thrown away, very quickly.

The use of abstraction has the advantage that one is not tempted to spend a lot of time in perfecting details in the early stages of design. The disadvantage is that the resulting abstract prototypes do not have the feel of a more concrete prototype and thus one cannot get feedback about the feel from users. Replacing the CSS-background images with concrete images provides more concrete information when necessary.

The abstract prototypes can now be completely generated from the presented models. We are planning to do some more tests with the defined model types and will extend our model generation approach to incorporate additional models that can provide us with more details about the timing and the user interactions. We will also investigate the generation of more concrete and higher-fidelity prototypes from the presented models complemented with lower-level details and a model providing more information about the interactions from participants with the SPME infrastructure within a scene.

Acknowledgements. This research was performed in the context of the IWT project Participate of Alcatel Bell. Part of the research at the Expertise Centre for Digital Media is funded by the ERDF (European Regional Development Fund), the Flemish Government and the Flemish Interdisciplinary institute for Broadband Technology (IBBT).

References

1. Dick Bulterman, Guido Grassel, Jack Jansen, Antti Koivisto, Nabil Layaïda, Thierry Michel, Sjoerd Mullender, and Daniel Zucker. Synchronized multimedia integration language (smil 2.1). http://www.w3.org/TR/2005/REC-SMIL2-20051213/, December 13 2005.
2. Pedro F. Campos and Nuno J. Nunes. Canonsketch: a user-centered tool for canonical abstract prototyping. In *Proceedings of EHCI-DSVIS 2004*, volume 3425 of *LNCS*, pages 146–163. Springer, 2005.
3. Tim Clerckx, Frederik Winters, and Karin Coninx. Tool support for designing context-sensitive user interfaces using a model-based approach. In *Proceedings of TaMoDia 2005*, pages 11–18, Gdansk, Poland, September 26–27 2005.
4. Larry L. Constantine. Canonical abstract prototypes for abstract visual and interaction design. In *Proceedings of DSV-IS 2003*, number 2844 in LNCS, pages 1 – 15, Funchal, Madeira Island, Portugal, June 11-13 2003. Springer.
5. Micah Dubinko, Leigh L. Klotz, Roland Merrick, and T. V. Raman. Xforms 1.0. W3C, World Wide Web, http://www.w3.org/TR/2003/REC-xforms-20031014/, 2003.
6. DVB. Multimedia home platform. http://www.mhp.org/, 2006.
7. Mohammed Elkoutbi, Ismaïl Khriss, and Rudolf Keller. Automated prototyping of user interfaces based on uml scenarios. *Automated Software Engineering*, 13(1):5–40, January 2006.
8. James Lin and James A. Landay. Damask: A tool for early-stage design and prototyping of multi-device user interfaces. In *8th Internation Conference on Distributed Multimedia Systems (International Workshop on Visual Computing 2002)*, pages 573–580, San Francisco, CA, USA, September 26–28 2002.
9. Giulio Mori, Fabio Paternò, and Carmen Santoro. Design and development of multidevice user interfaces through multiple logical descriptions. *IEEE Transactions on Sofware Engineering*, 30(8):507–520, August 2004.
10. Nuno Jardim Nunes and João Falcão e Cunha. Towards a uml profile for interaction design: the wisdom approach. In *Proceedings of UML 2000*, volume 1939 of *LNCS*, pages 101–116. Springer, October 2000.
11. Fabio Paternò. Towards a uml for interactive systems. In *Proceedings of EHCI 2001*, pages 7–18. Springer-Verlag, May11–13 2001.
12. Andreas Pleuss. Mml: A language for modeling interactive multimedia applications. In *Proceedings of Symposium on Multimedia*, pages 465–473, December12–14 2005.

Integrating Support for Usability Evaluation into High Level Interaction Descriptions with NiMMiT

Karin Coninx, Erwin Cuppens, Joan De Boeck, and Chris Raymaekers

Hasselt University, Expertise Centre for Digital Media (EDM)
and transnationale Universiteit Limburg
Wetenschapspark 2, B-3590 Diepenbeek, Belgium
{karin.coninx, erwin.cuppens, joan.deboeck, chris.raymaekers}@uhasselt.be

Abstract. Nowadays, the claim that a human-computer interface is user friendly, must be supported by a formal usability experiment. Due to its inherent complexity, this is particularly true when developing a multimodal interface. For such a rich user interface, there is a lack of support for automated testing and observing, so in preparation of its formal evaluation a lot of time is spent to adapt the programming code itself. Based on NiMMiT, which is a high-level notation to describe and automatically execute multimodal interaction techniques, we propose in this paper an easy way for the interaction designer to collect and log data related to the user experiment. Inserting 'probes' and 'filters' in NiMMiT interaction diagrams is indeed more efficient than editing the code of the interaction technique itself. We will clarify our approach as applied during a concrete user experiment.

1 Introduction

When developing computer applications, a lot of time is spent designing the user interface. This is especially true when designing (3D) multimodal interfaces. As there are still a lot of uncertainties when designing this kind of interfaces, a new application typically has to be evaluated by means of a user experiment. In our former work we proposed NiMMiT [1], a high level notation to describe interaction techniques in multimodal environments. By describing the user interaction on a high level diagram, an application framework can automatically execute the interaction technique. This has as advantage that the designer can quickly test and tune the interface, by just drawing a diagram, in stead of writing code. The diagram is then serialized into an XML syntax, allowing the application to execute the described interaction technique.

In this paper we show how an extension to NiMMiT can be used for debugging and collecting data from a user experiment. Previous usability evaluations required quite some coding effort to capture the required data. Our proposed approach allows a designer not only to develop the interaction at a high level, but also to carry out the evaluation with a minimum of coding.

G. Doherty and A. Blandford (Eds.): DSVIS 2006, LNCS 4323, pp. 95–108, 2007.
© Springer-Verlag Berlin Heidelberg 2007

In a first section, we shortly describe the basic principles of NiMMiT. Thereafter we explain how diagrams can be debugged and measured using 'probes' and 'filters'. Next we show our approach using a concrete example, in which we conducted a real user experiment with the proposed framework. This section first elaborates on the interaction technique and the NiMMiT diagrams. Thereafter we illustrate how the probes and filters are used in practice, and in the end we discuss the concrete experiment in order to evaluate our approach. We finish this paper with our conclusions.

The related work, by which our research has been inspired, will be covered in the relevant sections throughout this paper.

2   Interaction Modelling in NiMMiT

2.1   NiMMiT Primitives

NiMMiT ('Notation for MultiModal interaction Techniqes') is a diagram based notation intended to describe multimodal interaction between a human and a computer, with the intention to automatically execute the designed diagrams. NiMMiT shares some similarities with Petri-nets [2] and UML Activity Diagrams [3], but it is designed to support the special needs for multimodal interaction. In the remainder of this section, we shortly describe the primitives of our notation. For a more detailed description, we refer to [1].

In NiMMiT, interaction with the computer is seen as *event-driven*: users initiate an (inter)action by their behaviour, which invokes events into the system. These events can be triggered by different modalities, such as speech recognition, an action with a pointing device, or a gesture. Interaction is also *state-driven*, which means that not in all cases the system responds to all events. The response to an event, can bring the interaction in a next phase, responding to other events. Being *data-driven* is another important property of the notation. It is possible that data needs to be shared between several states of the interaction. For example, a subtask of the interaction can provide data, which has to be used in a later phase of the interaction (e.g. touching an object to push it). Finally, an interaction technique can consist of several smaller building blocks, which can be considered as interaction techniques themselves. Therefore, *hierarchical reuse* should be possible within the notation.

Taking the aforementioned considerations into account, NiMMiT defines the following basic primitives: states, events, task chains, tasks, labels and state transitions.

State: A state is depicted as a circle. The interaction technique starts in the start-state, and ends with the end-state. A state defines a set of events to which the system responds.

Event: An event is generated by the framework, based upon the user's input. A combination of events can be multimodal, containing actions such as speech recognition, gestures, pointer device events and button clicks. A single event or a specific combination always triggers the execution of a task chain.

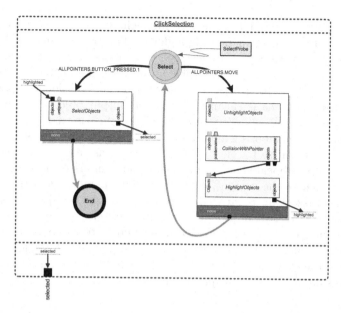

Fig. 1. NiMMiT Diagram of a Click Selection Interaction

Task Chain: A task chain is a linear succession of tasks, which will be executed one after the other.

Task: A task is a basic building block of the actual execution of the interaction technique. Typically, tasks access or alter the internal state of the application. E.g. when running in a typical 3D environment, a task can be 'collision detection', 'moving objects', 'playing audio feedback', ... Tasks can be predefined by the system, but designers can define their own custom tasks, as well. All tasks can have input and output ports, on which they receive or send parameters or result values. Input ports are required or optional, indicated by a black or a grey input port respectively.

Labels: As data can be shared throughout a diagram, NiMMiT needs a system to (temporarily) store values. This is done in 'labels', which can be seen as high-level variables.

State Transitions: Finally, when a task chain has been executed completely, a state transition moves the diagram into the next state. A choice between multiple state transitions is also possible, based upon the value of a certain label.

2.2 Example

Figure 1 shows a simple NiMMiT diagram which describes a click-selection in 3D. More complicated examples are shown in section 4 in order to illustrate our approach to use NiMMiT for a user experiment.

The NiMMiT diagram, shown in the picture, begins in the start-state, here named 'Select'. When one of the pointers moves, the event invokes the right-hand task chain. Here, in a first task, all the highlighted objects are reset, and the empty list is stored in the label 'highlighted'. The task chain is built in this way because in general, tasks are designed to be more generic. Considering the 'UnhighlightObjects' task, it can receive an optional parameter to unhighlight just *some* of the highlighted objects. In the second task, collision with the pointer and the entire 3D scene is calculated, and the output objects are sent to the 'HighlightObjects' task, which off course highlights the passed objects. The result is again stored in the label 'highlighted'. After the last task successfully finishes, the schema moves on to the next state, which in this case is the 'Select'-state again. This loop is repeated each time one of the pointers is moved.

As soon as one of the buttons, connected to the pointing devices, is pressed, the left-hand task chain is invoked. Here the highlighted objects now become selected, and the selected objects are put into the 'selected' label. This label is sent to the output port of the interaction technique, ready to be used in other subsequent interactions. However, if no object is highlighted at the time of the button press, the execution of the task chain will fail because the 'SelectObjects' task requires an object as input parameter.

3   Adding Support for Usability Evaluation to NiMMiT

In our former work, and throughout our current research, we have experienced the benefits of NiMMiT. In this section we show how NiMMiT can also be used to collect measurement data from a user's experiment in order to formally evaluate the designed interaction technique. This is done with minimal or no adaptation of the original diagram, through the use of probes, filters and listeners. Previous usability testing required quite some adaptations to the application code, in order to log the necessary data for our statistical analysis. Ivory and Hearst state that adding automation to usability evaluation has many potential benefits, as time efficiency and cost reduction [4].

3.1   Probes

A probe can be seen as a measurement tool that is connected at a certain place in a NiMMiT diagram, like an electrician placing a voltmeter on an electric circuit. Probes can be placed at different places in the diagram: at a state, a task chain, a task or at an input/output port of a task. An example is given in figure 1, in which a probe is connected to the 'Select'-state. The probe returns relevant data about the place where it is connected to, in a structured way:

State: probes contain all events that occur while the state is active.
Task Chain: probes contain the activation event(s) of the task chain, its status (executed, interrupted or failed), and the value of the label indicating the correct state transition.
Task: probes indicate whether or not the execution of the task succeeded.
Port: probes contain the value of the port to which they are connected.

Each loop, the data of all probes of the diagram is returned. If a probe is connected to a place which was not active in the current phase of the interaction, it returns empty. In this way, NiMMiT's probes are a useful tool to debug an interaction technique. For instance, by placing a probe on all states of a diagram, one can evaluate the correct order of the states or check for the events that are recognized. By placing a probe on an output port of a task, the output of the task can be verified. This can lead to a significant reduction of the time necessary to find logical errors in a diagram.

3.2   Filters

In order to collect data for a formal evaluation of an interaction technique, the direct output of a probe is not suitable. Therefore, we have defined the concept of *filters*. A filter can be seen as a meta-probe: a probe which listens to the values of one or more probes. As filters are probes themselves, filters can be connected to other filters as well. A filter can rearrange or summarize the data from the probes it is connected to, but it can also just wait until legal data arrives for the first time, and then start, stop or pause an internal timer. The latter approach can be used for measuring the time spent between two states of the interaction. Although the output necessary for a user experiment can be versatile, very often the same patterns return, such as summarizing a distance, counting the elapsed time or logging success or not. For these patterns, NiMMiT contains a standard set of commonly used filters. Of course, experienced users can still develop custom filters according to their special needs. As filters can be connected to several probes, even across diagrams, they are not visualized in a NiMMiT diagram.

3.3   Listeners

Filters and probes do not provide any output; they only collect and structure data. By connecting a listener to a probe or a filter, the output can be redirected to the desired output medium. By default, there are listeners that can write data directly to a file, to a text window, or even send it onto the network to an external computer which can be dedicated to handle, store or visualize the collected data. As with the filters, experienced developers can write their own listeners, if necessary. Listeners have no representation in the NiMMiT diagram, in order not to complicate the notation.

3.4   Leveraging Evaluation to the Diagram Level

The idea of probes, filters and listeners is not new. Our approach is somewhat similar to the *'Logging Services Project'* of the Apache Software Foundation [5]. In this project several APIs are defined that allow the developer to control which log statements are output. The APIs have three main components: loggers, appenders and layouts. These three types of components work together to enable developers to log messages according to message type and level, and to control at runtime how these messages are formatted and where they are reported.

Compared to NiMMiT, loggers can be mapped onto probes and appenders can be mapped onto listeners. Filters are defined in NiMMiT to offer more flexibility to the evaluation process, because several calculations can be automated and captured through these filters. The main value of our contribution, however is the fact that probes and filters can be connected using graphical notations, which avoids the need to write a lot of code for the capturing of data, which still is necessary in e.g. the *'Logging Services Project'*.

3.5   Situating NiMMiT with Respect to Usability Evaluation

Previous usability evaluations required quite some adaptation to the existing code in order to capture the data. The objective of this paper is to partially automate the capturing with a minimum of coding, by using probes, filters and listeners that are integrated into NiMMiT.

This automated evaluation fits into the taxonomy suggested by Ivory and Hearst. In their taxonomy, they emphasize the role of automation and group usability evaluation along four dimensions [4]:

Method Class: Usability Evaluation is classified into five method classes: testing, inspection, inquiry, analytical and simulation.

Method Type: Because of the wide range of evaluation methods within each of the method classes, they are grouped into related method types. These types typically describe how evaluation is performed.

Automation Type: The automation type specifies which aspect of the usability evaluation method is automated: none, capture, analysis or critique.

Effort Level: The effort level indicates the human effort required for the method execution.

Figure 2 shows how the NiMMiT evaluation system fits into the suggested taxonomy by indicating the values of the different parameters. .

Fig. 2. Evaluation in NiMMiT according to the taxonomy of Ivory and Hearst

4   Case Study: The Object-In-Hand Metaphor

In this paragraph, we elaborate in detail on a concrete interaction technique which has been evaluated by a user experiment. Both the interaction technique, as well as gathering the information for the evaluation are implemented using the NiMMiT notation, probes and filters. In the first subsection we describe the interaction technique and shortly clarify the diagrams. Next we show how the probes and filters are placed in order to capture relevant data. Finally, although not the main focus of this paper, we briefly show the results of the experiment itself.

4.1 The Metaphor

The interaction technique, used as a proof of concept in this paper, is based on the *Object-In-Hand Metaphor*, designed in the context of our former work. This metaphor addresses the problem of accessing an object in a 3D world, by using a proprioceptive gesture [6]. We refer the interested reader to [7] for more details upon this metaphor. In what follows, we will shortly point out the main properties: by bringing the user's non-dominant hand close to the dominant hand, the selected object is pulled out of its context and brought to a central position. The non-dominant hand, which is 'holding' the virtual object, creates a frame of reference for the dominant hand, as in real life [8]. The user can then manipulate the object with the dominant hand, while the force feedback provided by the PHANToM device, improves the naturalness. When the non-dominant hand is released, the object returns to its original position.

In the scope of the research presented in this paper, we have improved the metaphor with the insights of the results of our former work in which we evaluated the performance of a selection task using the dominant and the non-dominant hand [9]. As the original *Object-In-Hand Metaphor* shifts the problem towards the selection [7], an integrated solution for the selection task was necessary. Therefore, before pulling the object out of its context, we propose to select the object using the aperture selection technique [10]. This is done by keeping the thumb and the index of the non-dominant hand to each other. Using this gesture the aperture (a semi-transparent circle floating onto the projection plane) is activated. By moving the hand in space, the desired object can be activated. When closing the non-dominant hand into a fist, the selection is made permanent. Now the object can be brought into position with the aforementioned proprioceptive gesture.

4.2 Diagrams

In this section, we briefly describe the three diagrams which define the entire interaction, starting with figure 3, in which the topmost layer of the interaction is described. In the first state, 'Hand Open', the diagram listens to two events: 'hand-close gesture' and 'aperture gesture'. When the first gesture occurs (when making a fist with the non-dominant hand), there is a state transition to the 'Hand Close'-state. When the 'aperture gesture' occurs (closing index and thumb), the selection-task (shown in figure 4) is executed. After the selection finishes, we move back to either the 'Hand Open' or the 'Hand Close'-state, depending on the 'handOpen' label, which is the output of the 'ApertureSelection' task.

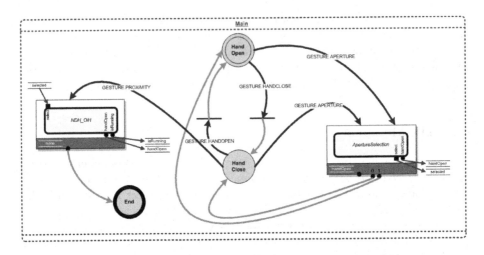

Fig. 3. Topmost-Level NiMMiT Diagram of the Object-In-Hand Metaphor

When in the 'Hand Close' state, the 'grabbing' of the object is activated by the 'Proximity' gesture. After this task chain finishes, the interaction technique ends, and we can start the next measurement.

Figure 4 shows the hierarchical NiMMiT diagram for the 'Aperture Selection'. Immediately after the start-state, we initialize the interaction and deselect all selected objects (if any). Thereafter, we arrive in the 'Select'-state. While moving, the leftmost task chain moves the aperture and calculates a possible collision with the objects in the world. The object that intersects with the aperture is stored in the label 'highlighted'. Still in the 'Select'-state, we can close or open our hand. When the hand is opened, the selection is cancelled, and hence we unhighlight and de-initialize the selection interaction. When the hand is closed, the selection is confirmed, and the object is selected. While the hand is opened or closed, the label 'handOpen' is respectively set to true or false. This value is sent to the output port, in order to allow the top-level diagram to make a transition to the appropriate state.

Finally, figure 5 shows the diagram which controls the non-dominant hand. As soon a the diagram is activated, an 'idle'-event is recognised, activating the top-left task chain. This chain animates the object to a central position and sets some control labels. After that, we arrive in the OiH-state. Here we listen to a 'move'-event, a 'handopen gesture' or a 'moveaway gesture'. When the hand is moved, the bottom left task chain moves the selected object according to the movements of the hand. When opening the hand, we arrive in the 'Suspend OiH'-state, after setting the 'handOpen' control variable. This state is basically the same as the 'OiH'-state except for the fact that it does not listen to the 'move'-event. Both the 'OiH' and the 'Suspend OiH'-state activate the bottom right task chain when the non-dominant hand is moved away. In this task chain, the object is moved back to its original position, which has been saved in a label in the very first task chain.

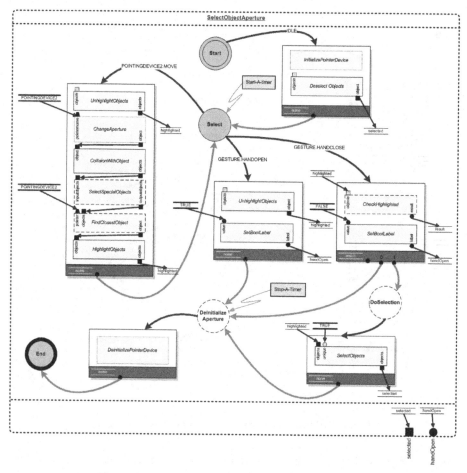

Fig. 4. NiMMiT Diagram of the Aperture Selection

After an object has been selected, and the NiMMiT diagram of the non-dominant hand is running, the user can manipulate the object with the dominant hand. The interaction of the dominant hand is also controlled by a NiMMiT diagram. However, as it plays a less important role in the user experiment we conducted, we will not to elaborate on this diagram.

4.3   Probing and Filtering

As described in section 3, in stead of adapting the low-level code implementation, we can place probes, filters and listeners in the diagrams for the evaluation of the Object-In-Hand metaphor. In this particular case, two parts of the interaction have to be monitored: we want to measure the time and correctness of both the selection part and the object manipulation part of the interaction.

As can be seen from figure 4, there are two probes placed in the selection diagram: one probe, *'Start-A-Timer'* is connected to the 'Select' state. The second

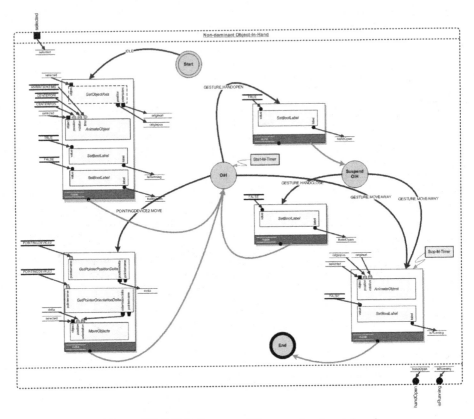

Fig. 5. NiMMiT Diagram of the non-dominant hand

probe, *'Stop-A-Timer'*, is connected to the 'Deinitialize Aperture' state. The probes return the state name and the list of events currently active, as soon as the state is active. When the state is inactive, the probes return an empty value.

The same is true for measuring the manipulation part of the interaction. To achieve this, two probes are placed in de diagram depicted in figure 5. The *'Start-M-Timer'*-probe is placed in the 'OiH'-state. The *'Stop-M-Timer'* is connected to the task chain responsible for restoring the object to its initial position. The latter probe returns the task chain's name and the calling event once the 'moveaway gesture' occurs.

The timing of the interaction is measured by using the filters, connected to the probes as shown in figure 6. A predefined 'TimeFilter' is connected to *'Start-A-Timer'* and *'Stop-A-Timer'*(fig 4). This filter starts a timer when the first probe contains its first valid data, and it stops measuring as soon as the second probe has a valid output. The same approach is applied to the probes *'Start-M-Timer'* and *'Stop-M-Timer'*(fig 5).

To test the correctness of both the selection and the manipulation, a custom filter has been created. One filter is connected to the TimeFilter of the selection diagram, the other to the TimeFilter of the manipulation diagram. Both 'cor-

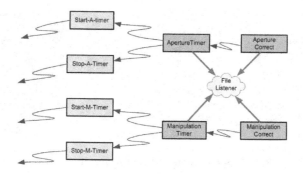

Fig. 6. Outline of the probes and filters used in the user experiment

rectness filters' wait until the connected TimeFilter has a valid output. This is true as soon as the diagram reaches the end-probe and the TimeFilter outputs its value. At that time, the 'correctness filter' executes a small piece of custom code, checking if the correct object has been selected or the correct manipulation has been performed. Depending on the result, the filter sets its output to true or false.

To output the results, we connected a file-listener to the filters. This listener, as described in section 3.3, sends the output of the registered probes and filters to a specified file. This tab-separated-file can easily be imported into a spreadsheet or database in order to do the necessary statistical analysis of the results. An outline of the relation between the probes and filters, as they are used in the experiment, is depicted in figure 6.

4.4   Setup of the User Experiment

Although not the main topic of this contribution, we find it important to shortly clarify the practical test we conducted as a proof of concept of our approach. As stated before, the aim of the test is to evaluate the performance of the aperture selection in combination with the Object-In-Hand metaphor, with respect to the scene complexity, but in the scope of this paper, its goal is mainly to illustrate the usefulness of our approach.

Twelve volunteer colleagues, all between the age of 23 and 45, eight males and four females, were asked to participate in the test. All subjects were right handed so that they could fit our right-handed setup. After reading the instructions, each user had to select and manipulate a given object in six scenes, increasing in complexity. The first three scenes were for practicing purposes, the last three were taken into account for the test. As can be seen from figure 7, the first scene only contains one box, the second scene contains a box in the middle of other boxes. In the last scene, the box is halved in size, put on a table and accompanied by a cylinder on each side. For each scene, the time spent to select the object and the time necessary to change the texture were logged, together with correctness of the actions' outcome. After the users completed the test, they were asked to fill out a little inquiry, to poll for their subjective impressions.

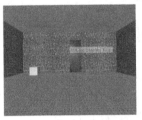
1 Scene 4

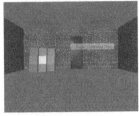
2 Scene 5

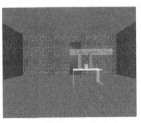
3 Scene 6

Fig. 7. Screenshots of three scenes in the test

To recognize the gestures of the non-dominant hand, our subjects wore a modified pinch-glove equipped with a magnetic tracker. The user's dominant hand operates a PHANToM force feedback device to manipulate the objects in the world. On the basis of the PHANToM is another tracker to measure the distance between both hands. The postures of the hand are recognized by the contactors of the pinch-glove: by closing the thumb and the index, contact is made and the aperture gesture is recognized. By closing the entire hand, another contact is made to recognize the fist posture.

After selecting the object using the aperture selection technique, and bringing it in a central position, the texture of the frontmost face had to be changed by selecting the face and choosing a texture from the menu. The manipulation of the object is carried out with the PHANToM device, while 'holding' the object with the left hand.

4.5   Results and Discussion

As described in section 4.3, the output of the probes and filters is saved into a tab separated text file. That file, containing the completion times and the success for each part of the task, has been imported into a database to easily select the desired results.

Table 1. Results of the user experiment

(a) Average time per scene.

	Scene	Time (ms)	Stdev
Selection	Scene 4	3764	1511
	Scene 5	4631	1348
	Scene 6	4437	983
	Total	4304	1287
Manip	Scene 4	17620	11113
	Scene 5	14808	7635
	Scene 6	17074	8358
	Total	16484	8996

(b) Number of errors per scene

	Scene	#Correct	#Error
Selection	Scene 4	14	3
	Scene 5	15	10
	Scene 6	20	5
	Total	49	18
Manip	Scene 4	12	2
	Scene 5	12	3
	Scene 6	11	4
	Total	35	9

Table 1(a) shows the average time over all correct trials of all users, for both the selection and the manipulation. Table 1(b) shows the number of correct actions in respect to the number of errors.

Although we expected scene 6 to be the most difficult for the selection, the objective results show that scene 5 causes more troubles. However, when we compare the values statistically using ANOVA, there is no significance: even between scene 4 and scene 5 (the lowest and the highest value), we receive a p-value of 0,11. If we look at the number of errors of the selection, it is true that scene 5 performs worse than the other, but the chi-square value between scene 4 and 5 is only 0,08, while the overall chi-square of the entire matrix is 0,17.

The same is true for the manipulation part of the interaction. We expected scene 6 to perform worst, because of the smaller object, but when applying ANOVA, even between scene 5 and scene 6, the p-value is as high as 0,50. Moreover, a chi-square test to find significance in the number of errors provides us with values between 0,40 and 0,70.

After the subjects completed their test, they were asked to fill out a subjective questionnaire. From the results, we could learn that most subjects were neutral or slightly positive about the interaction technique. Not surprising, is that most subjects agree that the interaction is rather tiresome in terms of holding the hand unsupported in the air in order to select or hold and manipulate the object.

In summary, we can conclude that the complexity of the scene has no significant influence on the performance of the selection, nor has a smaller object an influence on this particular manipulation task. Moreover we learned that one of the drawbacks of the tested interaction technique is the fatigue caused by holding the arms in the air. To improve the interaction, we will have to look for a solution to support the user's arms, although this is not obvious, since the PHANToM force feedback limits the possible positions.

5   Conclusions

In this paper, we have shown how probes, filters and listeners are used in NiM-MiT, a high-level notation to describe multimodal interaction, to provide a flexible and efficient way for collecting data from a user experiment. With the proposed approach, the data can be gathered without having to adapt the code of the application to be evaluated. We illustrated this by conducting a practical experiment, in which the Object-In-Hand metaphor in combination with aperture selection was tested with respect to the complexity of the scene. As shown in the paper, this partially automated user experiment provided us with the necessary data to draw formal conclusions about the evaluated interface.

Acknowledgments

Part of the research at EDM is funded by ERDF (European Regional Development Fund), the Flemish Government and the Flemish Interdisciplinary institute for Broadband technology (IBBT).

NiMMiT has been developed within the VR-DeMo project (IWT 030284), which is directly funded by the IWT, a Flemish subsidy organization. The authors also want to thank Tom De Weyer and Lode Vanacken for their valuable contributions with the implementation.

References

1. Vanacken, D., De Boeck, J., Raymaekers, C., Coninx, K.: NiMMiT: A notation for modeling multimodal interaction techniques. In: Proceedings of the International Conference on Computer Graphics Theory and Applications (GRAPP06), Setbal, Portugal (2006)
2. Palanque, P., Bastide, R.: Petri net based design of user-driven interfaces using the interactive cooperative objects formalism. In: Interactive Systems: Design, Specification, and Verification, Springer-Verlag (1994) 383–400
3. Ambler, S.: Object Primer, The Agile Model-Driven Development with UML 2.0. Cambridge University Press (2004)
4. Ivory, M.Y., Hearst, M.A.: The state of the art in automating usability evaluation of user interfaces. ACM Computing Surveys **33** (2001) 470–516
5. Apache Software Foundation: Logging services project @ apache. http://logging. apache.org (2006)
6. Mine, M.R., Brooks, F.P.: Moving objects in space: Exploiting proprioception in virtual environment interaction. In: Proceedings of the SIGGRAPH 1997 annual conference on Computer graphics, Los Angeles, CA, USA (1997)
7. De Boeck, J., Cuppens, E., De Weyer, T., Raymaekers, C., Coninx, K.: Multi-sensory interaction metaphors with haptics and proprioception in virtual environments. In: Proceedings of the third ACM Nordic Conference on Human-Computer Interaction (NordiCHI 2004), Tampere, FI (2004)
8. Guiard, Y.: Asymmetric division of labor in human skilled bimanual action: The kinematic chain as a model. In: Journal of Motor Behaviour. Volume 19. (1997) 486–517
9. De Boeck, J., De Weyer, T., Raymaekers, C., Coninx, K.: Using the non-dominant hand for selection in 3D. In: Proceedings of the first IEEE Symposium on 3D User Interfaces 2006, Alexandria, Virginia, US (2006)
10. Forsberg, A., Herndon, K., Zeleznik, R.: Aperture based selection for immersive virtual environment. In: Proceedings of UIST96. (1996) 95–96

An Investigation into the Validation of Formalised Cognitive Dimensions

Chris Roast and Babak Khazaei

Culture and Computing Research Centre,
Faculty of Arts, Computing, Engineering and Science
Sheffield Hallam University
Sheffield, S1 1WB, United Kingdom
c.r.roast@shu.ac.uk

Abstract. The cognitive dimensions framework is a conceptual framework aimed at characterising features of interactive systems that are strongly influential upon their effective use. As such the framework facilitates the critical assessment and design of a wide variety of information artifacts. Although the framework has proved to be of considerable interest to researchers and practitioners, there has been little research examining how easily the dimensions used by it can be consistently applied. The work reported in this paper addresses this problem by examining an approach to the systematic application of dimensions and assessing its success empirically. The findings demonstrate a relatively successful approach to validating the systematic application of some concepts found in the cognitive dimensions framework.

Keywords: Cognitive Dimensions Framework, Theory validation, Empirical methods.

1 Background

The cognitive dimensions framework ([1-3]) has been developed as a simple informal, broad-brush method for evaluating information artefacts such as: notations, computer applications, and everyday devices. The essence of its approach is simple, a number of 'cognitive dimensions' are described that are properties jointly of the 'notation' and of the environment in which it is used. For instance, the dimension of 'viscosity', loosely defined as 'resistance to change', is used to characterise the ease or otherwise with which an environment and a notation allow modifications to be made. The power of the dimensions framework arises from the claim that it provides a generic basis for examining qualities that are core to the effectiveness of information artefacts. For instance, 'viscosity' as a concept can be identified in a variety of information artefact uses. Hence, the effort involved in (re-)organising ones' email folders, sub-folders and email rules can be viewed and the effort involved in, say, marking-up literary texts for automated processing both can be seen as viscous in character. Although these two examples are distinct their common characterisation enables experience within one case to be transferred to another, and so facilitating improved, and

G. Doherty and A. Blandford (Eds.): DSVIS 2006, LNCS 4323, pp. 109–122, 2007.

alternative, design possibilities. Inter-relations between dimensions have also been illustrated within the framework, for instance, in general the availability of abstraction mechanisms can relate to viscosity. An abstraction mechanism can often be used to reduce the effort that characterises high viscosity. Thus for email management the codification of relevant abstractions may be explored as a means of improving the process (as with, say, gmail). In the case of email re-organisation, the recognition of types of email, such as, request, acknowledgement, dissemination and even spam, may help reduce the effort involved in their management. In the case of literary mark-up, the very abstractions often embodied by logical mark-up may be explicitly supported within a tool or environment.

Unlike many frameworks associated with interface assessment and evaluation, cognitive dimensions are not intended to map out necessary improvements in a design. The framework recognises that for different problems and activities, different dimensions may be more or less relevant. The dimensions indicate the related factors that should not be ignored in design of an information artifact. Hence, whether or not a particular dimension should be minimised at the expense of another is a decision that can only be made with detailed knowledge of a particular design context. However, it is evident that for certain activities, to be successfully pursued, particular values of certain dimensions are appropriate: thus, high viscosity is not a problem for search activities, but it can be a considerable problem for modification activities.

The concepts on which the dimensions are based have received broad interest within a variety of domains where the uptake and complexity of notations and artefacts has been seen as a bottleneck in their effective exploitation. There are examples of applying the dimensions to various information artefacts, in particular: interactive systems [4], programming languages (textual and visual) [2], programming paradigms [5] and [6], design notations and specification languages [7] and [8]. In addition, various methodological techniques and tools have been developed to support their use, see [9-12].

The aim of this paper is to show that it is possible to develop formal definitions of concepts drawn from cognitive dimensions and most importantly validate the definitions with relatively a simple empirical setting.

2 Cognitive Dimensions and Their Uptake

The dimensions and the framework have on the whole been loosely defined. Green's original definitions [1] consisted of a thumbnail description followed by an example or two and this has been the style continued in later papers, such as in [2] and [3]. In particular some have argued that an informal nature means they are more readily accessible to practitioners. The ideas can be employed flexibly without demanding that procedural or semantic constraints are adhered to.

Despite this it is evident that inexperienced users of the dimensions may fail to understand what is meant by some of the concepts, and that the dimension framework can be difficult to apply in a consistent or reliable fashion. For instance, if the information artifact is complex, practitioners can be unsure as to whether dimensions have been examined to a similar level throughout. Different analysts bring a different emphasis to applying the dimensions and find it hard to systematically distinguish between them, especially when focusing upon features and behaviours of a particular artefact. For some purposes this subjective character of the dimensions may not be a significant concern, especially if the dimensions are being employed to motivate innovative design alternatives [13]. However within the context of researching the framework and its use, ambiguities and un-certainties limit comparative assessments of artifacts and their versions, and the inter-relations between dimensions suggested by the framework.

Blandford et al [14] and Connell et al [15] provide another approach to employing cognitive dimensions in design. In this case the dimensions provide a basis for the automated analysis of a system that can be employed with only a limited account of the features and characteristics of the target system. Although the work reported below is also concerned with the automated cognitive dimensional analysis, it is motivated by the exploration of cognitive dimension definitions and their character as opposed to explicitly enabling analysis to be conducted within the context of specific design activities and case studies. Hence the definitions explored below are aimed at underpinning the type of conceptual tools that may be available for analysts and designers. The approach we take is to employ these formal definitions in the automated analysis of small scale simulated systems. With this we are able to experiment, contrasting our expectations about the cognitive dimensional character of a simulated system with those provided by following formal definitions. Experimentation with alternative definitions can also support the process of pinpointing a more objective characterisation of the cognitive dimensions and their properties.

3   What We Are Doing in This Paper

With any tool there are questions that can be asked regarding whether or not it serves its intended purpose, and for cognitive dimensions this is no different. For instance, we could ask whether or not a dimension concept, such as viscosity, is valid in terms of the examples cited and the inter-relationships it has with other dimensions. Similarly as a framework we could examine its adequacy, such as whether or not design flaws that we would like it to capture can be located within the framework, or whether another dimension is required to capture important examples.

In general the validation of a tool or model involves having to bridge between its analytic domain and the empirical world in which it is intended to be valid and in which evidence is normally found. The very character of the analytic domain can complicate this process, as the analysis concepts may not have strong foundations in an empirical context. The cognitive dimensions concepts that are the focus of this work suffer from this problem. The main concepts used by the dimensions are characterised largely by means of examples and illustrations. Take for example the concept of 'viscosity': it is described in terms of the difficulty or effort when a user changes some feature or property of an interactive system, alternatively it can be viewed in terms of the systems resistance to some changes and not others. Although examples can help illustrate what 'viscosity' might be like, it is difficult to know if it is particular to types of change, objective or subjective "measures" of effort, or whether it should be viewed as absolute or relative to a specific system, activity and so forth.

The tool that performs the automated analysis is called CiDa - given a simulated system (expressed as a state based system) and a formal definition of possible user goals and actions, CiDa performs model checking for a set of propositions about dimension properties of a system. Fig 1 outlines the relationships of interest: a simulated target system is available to both users and CiDa (in a form that it can analyse); the analysis of this system is provided by CiDa for users; and the value of such an analysis comes from the fact that the user is able to relate the output to their own experience with, and understanding of, the simulated system. Through experience and experimentation with the system the informal validation of the properties output by CiDa can be attempted by users.

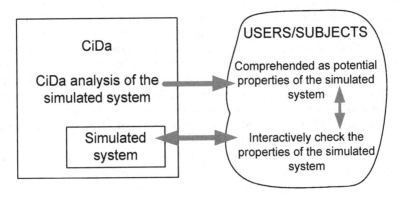

Fig. 1. The types of questions being asked of CiDa

Since CiDa provides an automated analysis it offers the advantages of being systematic and consistent in its analysis. Thus within the dimension properties defined and the potential user goals CiDa places no specific emphasis on any one dimension property or user goal, over any other.

However the effective use of CiDa for validation presupposes that the output of such an analysis can be understood and that users can satisfy themselves that it is correct. Hence in Fig 1 the block arrows should ideally represent non-problematic activities: (i) getting from CiDa output to an understanding of its output, (ii) users being able to relate CiDa output to how it is possible to interact and experiment with the simulated system finding the evidence for that output in system that is simulated, and (iii) engaging interactively with the system relating experience with the system back to their understanding of CiDa outputs. In order to assist with this process the experimental design was chosen to be one in which the simulated system was of limited scale and was represented to subjects in a "lightweight" domain setting.

4   An Overview of CiDa and Some Definitions

CiDa is a prototype model checking tool built to support theory development specifically for the cognitive dimensions framework. Although dimension formalisation have been posited [16], [5] and [6], their thorough examination and exploration is complex and can be unconvincing for practitioners. CiDa provides a model checking facility so that given proposed dimension definitions, a target system can be analysed exhaustively generating a list of dimension instances evident in the target system. The outcomes are independent of analyst expectations, bias or interests, and thus provide an objective comparable account of the dimensional features of the target system for the proposed dimension definitions. This has been of value enabling the "space" of dimensions to be explored [17] and also for proposed definitions to be enhanced. CiDa operates with a set of dimension definitions based mainly on temporal logic expressions, a target system definition (as a state transition system), and a bridge between the two described in terms of the possible user goals that each state of the target system may fulfill. Each definition characterises the patterns of potential goal satisfaction and actions that match the dimension of interest. Below we briefly describe the three dimensions characterisations employed in the study described.

Knock-on viscosity. Although we have informally referred to 'viscosity' in the introduction, researchers in the area have found it valuable to distinguish two types of viscosity, 'knock-on' and 'repetitive' [18]. The first of these is the one examined here, it refers to the complexity, or effort, resulting from the user of a system having to make changes that have unwanted side-effects which must then be put right. This effect can be found when, say, inserting a new section in a word processed document, and having to subsequently update section number references so that the references are once again correct. Characterising this, there are two goals (a) to add a new section, and (b) to have all section references correct, there is also the action that creates the new section (act). The user's difficulty occurs when (b) has been met and now (a) has to be met as well, because adding a new section may disrupt the existing ordering. This pattern is characterised in general as follows:

In every state that can be reached:
   I, goal (b) is met and goal (a) is not,
   *then applying **act** achieves goal (a) and negates goal (b)*

Premature Commitment. The dimension of premature commitment concerns the order in which goals can be fulfilled. Informally premature commitment occurs when a specific order of activity is demanded by a system that is in some sense inappropriate or unnecessarily constraining from the perspective of the user. More formally we employ the following concept of premature commitment based on that of [17], it is defined as a relation between two goals (a) and (b), and an action (act), such that:

1. *Every behaviour leads to the goal (a) involves the action **act** and the other goal (b) becoming true*
2. *Initially neither (a) or (b) are satisfied*
3. *The system behaviours ensure that (a) never necessarily entails (b) and (b) never necessarily entails (a)*

Secondary Notation. Besides definitions for knock-on viscosity and premature commitment CiDa also has a definition for the dimension of 'secondary notation'. The concept of secondary notation is that the user has a degree of freedom that enables additional alternative information to be recorded and manipulated. Within CiDa the definition of secondary notation is based upon assessing the lack of constraints that enable goals to be jointly satisfied. Fewer constraints mean that there are more potential goal combinations available to the user to employ as the basis for secondary notations.

For a primary goal (a) and a set of secondary goals (SG), the level of potential secondary notation is determined by the number of goals in SG that are formally independent of satisfying (a).

5   Experiment-Assessing the CiDa Analysis

We now describe the study conducted using the prototype CiDa tool to examine whether CiDa output can be employed in empirical assessment and whether CiDa output concurs with subjects' judgments. In order to address the potential difficulties of interpretation with such a study, the following experimental guides were followed:

- CiDa output should be presented as statements that are simple and consistent in style
- The target system complexity should be low, so that subjects can in effect become experts with limited effort
- The target system domain should have familiar elements to lower the complexity of developing an understanding of it
- The target system domain should be lightweight and not strongly goal oriented so that subjects do not feel challenged by it, do not suppose that their responses are being judged, and do not presume a specific use of the system.
- Subjects are encouraged to consider the details of multiple system behaviours. This is to be encouraged by asking them to make comparative assessments of different example systems.

Five example target systems were developed and simulated for CiDa analysis. To allow for cross-system comparisons each provided the same functionality (i.e. the reachable state space) but differed in terms of their interactive behaviour. Hence, we were able to compare the differing systems and examine if differences were apparent in the CiDa analysis of each.

5.1   The Example Systems

The target systems used for the study were based upon the idea of simple easily explored interactive tool for manipulating the appearance of a comic-book cartoon face. The comic-book face tools are sufficiently lightweight that novice users could easily familiarise themselves with them, and would not be unduly challenged by the domain. In addition, the graphical and direct nature of the cartoon face tools means that a realistic simulation of each design could be easily generated. All in all five alternative designs were considered, each allowed the same face configurations to be obtained, and each differed in terms of the action sequences needed to obtain face configurations.

The **state space** consists of a range of combinations of boolean attributes: awake, unshaven, listening-to-music and talking/singing (see Fig 2). The five **user actions** altered the state attributes in various ways. In this guise the specific actions had no cartoon face related meaning, so arbitrary symbols with no characterisation were used (see Fig 3). It was felt the range of alternative actions and states was sufficiently limited that no authoritative explanation of the actions would be necessary for participants in the study.

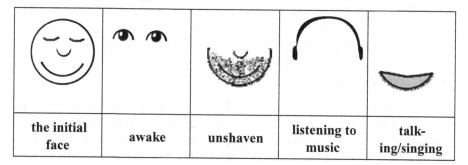

Fig. 2. The cartoon face tool with the attributes that can be present or absent

Fig. 3. Action buttons used to control the cartoon face

The potential user goals for this example system are listed below. The first two goals match single state attributes, the third is the explicit combination of two attributes and the last two allude to specific combinations of facial attributes.

Possible user goal - Corresponding cartoon-face attributes
Awake - Awake attribute present
Unshaven - Unshaven attribute present
Awake and clean shaven - Both awake **and** clean shaven attributes present
Listening late at night - headphones on present **and** unshaven present
Singing along - headphones on present **and** mouth open present

The appendix gives details of just one of the cartoon-face tools, "Design 1", the other designs (2 through to 5) are similar but differ in their action pre-conditions. All five designs are formally defined and individually analysable by CiDa. They can also be used to simulate their corresponding version of the cartoon-face tool. It should be noted that the designs were developed to not embody a specific coherent interpretation of the actions and their effects. On the contrary, the designs were intended to limit the degree to which subjects may confidently guess at particular behaviours. Fig 4 shows an example of two of the designs in differing states, paired as used in the study.

Fig. 4. A pair of the interactive cartoon face tools as used in the reported study

5.2 Experimental Design

The experiment was designed to allow subjects to engage in assessing statements about the nature of the cartoon face tools. Each subject was given the task of experimenting with two of the designs and comparatively judging which design fulfilled specific dimension related statements about them. It was envisaged that providing each subject with two designs would facilitate the more accurate identification of distinctive properties and behaviours, and thus assist in their task. The statements were drawn from the cognitive dimensions instances identified in the CiDa analysis of the same set of designs. The statements were presented as written propositions largely following a template form of expression for each dimension. Below are three example statements corresponding to the three dimensions analysed:

1. If you make him so that he's not listening late (using the blue eye button), he will not be singing.
   This corresponds to an instance of knock-on viscosity, making him not listen results in him not singing. Hence, if one was trying to achieve both of these, one might be frustrated by this unnecessary constraint.
2. When trying to make him chatty, you cannot avoid him being just shaved (when using the eye button).
   This corresponds to an instance of premature commitment; he has to be shaved prior to chatting. Although there is nothing preventing him being unshaved and chatting.
3. You can make him unshaven and at the same time both listen to music and chat, or one or the other or neither.
   This corresponds to an instance of secondary notation, there is sufficient flexibility in the system for the face to be unshaven while either chatting and/or listening.

To reduce the number of statements that subjects would have to assess, only a few of the possible dimension instances from CiDa's output were considered. The statements used were, where possible, ones that could be used to differentiate between the five designs used in the study. In addition, to avoid possible difficulties with comprehension, statements with relatively complex negative constructs were not used on the

Table 1. Specific cartoon-tool statements associated with knock-on viscosity related to example designs

Knock-on viscosity statements	Design				
	1	2	3	4	5
If you make him awake (using the blue eye button) he will be shaved	Y			Y	
If you make him unshaven (using the red X button) he will be listening late	Y	Y		Y	
If you make him sleep (using the zigzag button) he will be clean shaved		Y	Y		Y
If you make him so that he's not listening late (using the blue eye button), he will not be singing	Y	Y	Y	Y	Y
If you make him clean shaven (using the zigzag button) he will not be singing	Y	Y	Y	Y	Y

Table 2. Specific cartoon tool statements associated with premature commitment related to example designs

Premature Commitment statements	Design				
	1	2	3	4	5
When trying to make him unshaven, you cannot avoid him being shaved (when the blue eye is used)	Y			Y	
When trying to make him chatty, you cannot avoid him being just shaved (when using the blue eye button)	Y				

basis that they were likely to be more confusing and complex for subjects to assess. This resulted in a total of 12 statements for subjects to consider (see tables 1, 2 and 3).

Each subject was asked to experiment with randomly-allocated pairs of designs for the cartoon face tool with a view to becoming familiar with them and identifying differences between them. Fig 4 shows a pair of designs together as a subject may have seen on their screen. Following the familiarisation, the subjects were given the 12 statements on a paper questionnaire and asked to assess which was valid for which of the two designs using a five level confidence scale, ranging from definitely not valid through to definitely valid.

A total of 25 subjects took part in the study; all had just commenced a second year undergraduate introductory human-computer interaction option, and none had received any instruction regarding the cognitive dimensions framework. Familiarisation with the example system lasted up to ten minutes. The subjects then spent around 25 minutes answering questions set. Throughout the period they were free to experiment with the two tool designs allotted to them.

Table 3. Specific cartoon tool statements associated with secondary notation potential related to example designs

Potential notation flexibility statements	Design				
	1	2	3	4	5
You can make him unshaven and at the same time both listen to music and chat, or one or the other or neither	Y	Y	Y	Y	Y
You can make him unshaven and the same time awake or asleep		Y	Y		Y
You can make him unshaven and at the same time both listen to music and be awake or one or the other or neither			Y		Y
You can make him singing along and at the same time have his eyes open or closed				Y	Y
You can make him not listen late and at the same time both be unshaven and be awake, or either or neither			Y		Y

5.3 Results

Informally it was clear from the subjects' reactions to the study that not all the questions were easily answered, this was mainly evidenced from the group as a whole taking longer than planned and individuals requiring reassurance regarding details, such as whether or not their tool designs embodied different interactive behaviour. In some cases a difficulty in understanding the statements used was indicated by answers with the confidence value 3 ('Don't Know') and occasionally by their failure to answer. Missing values were assigned a rating of 3 in the analysis.

The first question in the analysis must therefore be whether some of the cognitive dimensions appeared to be harder to comprehend than others. Table 4. summarises the comparison between question types.

The frequency of answering with a 3, or leaving the question unanswered, varied little between question types, indicating that each type was equally easy (or hard) to understand. Analysis of variance showed no significant differences between question types ($F_{1,45} = 0.953$), no interaction between question type and design ($F_{4,45} = 0.337$), and no significant difference between design types ($F_{4,45} = 0.179$). In general the overall low degree of indecision is a good indicator of the subjects' confidence in comprehending the questions used.

In the experiment each subject explored two designs with a view to encouraging the comparative assessment of the specific designs. A secondary element of assessing comprehension is the level of discrimination by subjects between the designs they examined. The average proportion of question responses in which subjects differentiated between designs is 0.19 and this does not differ greatly between question types: secondary notation 0.23; premature commitment 0.2; and knock-on viscosity 0.15. This further evidences a consistent level of comprehension of the questions.

Table 4. Mean proportion of questions answered with a "3" or left unanswered. Figures in parentheses show standard deviations. N=50 in each cell.

Question type	Mean (sd)
secondary notation	0.108 (0.1576)
knock-on viscosity	0.100 (0.1237)
premature commitment	0.140 (0.2680)

The responses were analysed as a two-factor experiment, with repeated measures across the three question types (knock-on viscosity, premature commitment, and secondary notation) and independent groups across Designs 1 though to 5. Subjects' responses were classified as either conforming with the CiDa analysis, contrary to the CiDa analyis or neutral. Table 5 summarises subject agreement with respect to question type and indicates the significance of χ^2 tests on confirming and non-confirming responses (ignoring the neutral responses).

Table 5. Classified responses for each type of question over all designs

Question type	Conforming	Not conforming	Significance	Neutral responses
secondary notation	151	75	$p < 0.001$	17
knock-on viscosity	139	86	$p < 0.001$	21
premature commitment	46	40	$p = .52$	7
Total	336	201	$p < 0.001$	45

The degree of agreement between subjects responses and CiDa analyses is positive and significant for two of the question types, secondary notations and knock-on viscosity. The responses to the premature commitment questions show no significant level of agreement with the CiDa analyses.

The differences in agreement between question types may be influenced by the differing level of experience and experimentation required by subjects to address particular questions. The statements associated with knock-on viscosity are more focused upon causal relations and, as a result, accurately answering them may require considerable investigation on the part of the subject. The statements associated with secondary notation potential are more declarative in character, and are less focused upon details requiring exhaustive exploration. By contrast the premature commitment type questions demand a more thorough examination of a design, implying that the subject should engage in "trying" to achieve a specific goal. This appears to be evidenced by premature commitment question type having the highest proportion of neutral responses (see table 4).

Thus although the techniques for validating CiDa output appear appropriate for secondary notation and knock-on viscosity, for premature commitment alternatives are needed, such as: offering subjects more time, re-phrasing the question templates used, etc..

6 Conclusions

In general, the results support the primary focus of interest, that of validating the model of the cognitive dimensions embodied in the CiDa analysis tool. The study demonstrated that employing the available domain of the graphical tools was beneficial in ensuring it was conceptually manageable for novice users, and that the method of enabling them to contrast distinct tools helped encourage their exploration. By contrast, the use of relatively dry and verbose statements relating to instances of CiDa output appears to have made the task set quite demanding. Overall, the study goes someway towards dealing with the inherent complexity of validating the effectiveness and effective use of broad-brush conceptual frameworks such as cognitive dimensions. In addition, although in some design settings formally defined properties may be viewed as unnecessarily precise, the work demonstrates that those definitions examined provide largely valid assessments.

We have shown that it is possible, important and beneficial to develop formal definitions of a usability framework based on cognitive dimensions. The potential exists to examine alternative or related formalised properties in a similar manner.

Cognitive dimensions promise great potential benefits for the effective assessment and design of complex interactive tools. There is a wide community interested in the dimensions, and the CiDa tool and its analysis represents one approach to strengthening the role of cognitive dimensions. The provision of a more accurate and precise framework for cognitive dimensions would benefit its employment with design and development. However, the study described here illustrates that the development and validation of a framework is not a trivial task. Despite this the results from the study are a positive step towards the validation of formalised cognitive dimensions.

Future work is to develop this approach to validation further, exploring the apparent weakness of our approach for examining premature commitment, and in general broadening the range of dimensions considered.

Acknowledgments. The authors are indebted to Thomas Green and Simeon Yates for their comments on earlier versions of this paper and their assistance in data analysis.

References

1. Green, T. R. G.: Cognitive dimensions of notations. In A. Sutcliffe and L. Macaulay (eds.): People and Computers V. Cambridge University Press (1989)
2. Green, T. R. G., Petre, M.: Usability analysis of visual programming environments: a `cognitive dimensions' framework. In J. Visual Languages and Computing Vol. 7(2) (1996) 131-174

3. Green, T.R.G., Blackwell, A.F.: Design for usability using Cognitive Dimensions. Tutorial session at British Computer Society conference on Human-Computer Interaction HCI'98 (1998)

4. Roast, C.R., Dearden, A., Khazaei, B.: Enhancing contextual analysis to support the design of development tools. In Fincher, S., Markpoulos, P., Moore, D., Ruddle, R. (eds.): People and Computers XVII - Design for Life. Springer Verlag (2004)

5. Roast, C. R.: Modelling unwarranted commitment in information artefacts. In Chatty S. and Dewan P. (eds.): Engineering for Human-Computer Interaction. Kulwer Academic Press (1998) 77-90

6. Roast, C., Khazaei, B., Siddiqi, J.: Formal comparison of program modification. In Stasko J. and Pfeiffer J. J. (eds.): IEEE Symposium on Visual Languages. IEEE Computer Society (2000) 165-171

7. Britton, C., Jones, S.: The untrained eye: how languages for software specification support understanding in untrained users. In Human-Computer Interaction, Vol. 14(1) (1999) 191-244

8. Khazaei, B. and Triffitt, E.: Applying Cognitive Dimensions to Evaluate and Improve the Usability of Z Formalism, Proceedings of the 14th International Conference on Software Engineering and Knowledge Engineering, ACM (2002)

9. Blackwell, A.F., Britton, C., Cox, A. Green, T.R.G., Gurr, C.A., Kadoda, G.F., Kutar, M., Loomes, M., Nehaniv, C.L., Petre, M., Roast, C., Roes, C., Wong, A., Young, R.M.: Cognitive Dimensions of Notations: design tools for cognitive technology. In M. Beynon, C.L. Nehaniv, and K. Dautenhahn (eds.): Cognitive Technology 2001 (LNAI 2117). Springer-Verlag (2001) 325-341

10. Blackwell, A.F., Green, T.R.G.: A Cognitive Dimensions questionnaire optimised for users. In Blackwell A.F. and Bilotta E. (eds.): Proceedings of the Twelfth Annual Meeting of the Psychology of Programming Interest Group. (2000) 137-152

11. Blandford, A., Green, T.R.G.: OSM an ontology-based approach to usability engineering. In Representations in Interactive Software Development. Workshop at Queen Mary and Westfield College, Department of Computer Science (1997)

12. Lavery, D., Cockton, G., Atkinson, M.: Cognitive dimensions: Usability evaluation materials. Technical report, Department of Computing Science, University of Glasgow (1996)

13. Burnett, M., Dagit, J., Lawrance, J., Beckwith, L., Kissinger, C.: Experiences with Cognitive Dimensions presented at Cognitive Dimensions of Notations 10th Anniversary Workshop (Dallas 2005)

14. Blandford, A., Connell, I., Green, T.R.G.: Concept-based Analysis of Surface and Structural Misfits (CASSM) Tutorial Notes. September 2004, available at http://www.uclic.ucl.ac.uk./annb/CASSM.html

15. Connell, I., Blandford, A., Green, T.R.G.: CASSM and cognitive walkthrough: usability issues with ticket vending machines. In Behaviour and Information Technology Vol. 23(5) (2004) 307-320

16. Roast, C. R.: Formally comparing and informing design notations. In Thimbleby, H., O'Conaill, B. and Thomas, P. (eds.): People and Computers XII. Springer Verlag (1997) 315-336

17. Roast, C.R.: Dimension driven re-design - applying systematic dimensional analysis, Proceedings of the 14th Psychology of Programming Interest Group workshop (2002)

18. Green, T. R. G.: The cognitive dimension of viscosity: a sticky problem for HCI. In D. Diaper, D. Gilmore, G. Cockton and B. Shackel (eds.): Human-Computer Interaction — INTERACT '90. Elsevier (1990)

Appendix

Design 1 for the cartoon face tool is represented by the state transition diagram below. The other four designs used in the study shared the same state space, but differed in terms of transitions.

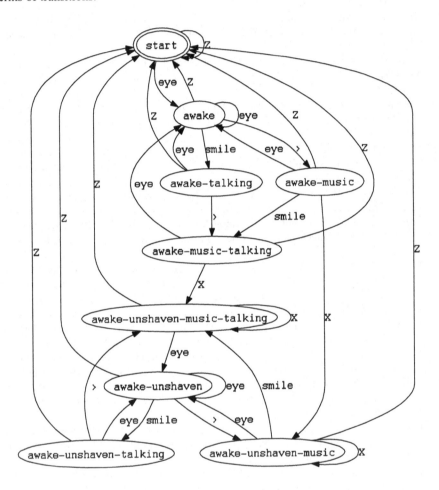

Formal Modelling of Cognitive Interpretation

Rimvydas Rukšėnas[1], Paul Curzon[1], Jonathan Back[2], and Ann Blandford[2]

[1] Department of Computer Science, Queen Mary, University of London, London, UK
{rimvydas,pc}@dcs.qmul.ac.uk
[2] University College London Interaction Centre, London, UK
{j.back,a.blandford}@ucl.ac.uk

Abstract. We formally specify the interpretation stage in a dual state space human-computer interaction cycle. This is done by extending / re-organising our previous cognitive architecture. In particular, we focus on shape related aspects of the interpretation process associated with device input prompts. A cash-point example illustrates our approach. Using the SAL model checking environment, we show how the extended cognitive architecture facilitates detection of prompt-shape induced human error.

Keywords: human error, cognitive architecture, model checking, SAL.

1 Introduction

Interactive systems combine human and computer actors. Their correctness depends on the behaviour of both. It is reasonable, and useful, to say that humans behave rationally: entering interactions with goals and domain knowledge likely to help them achieve their goals. Whole classes of persistent, systematic user errors may occur due to modelable cognitive causes [1]. Often opportunities for making such errors can be reduced with good design [2]. A methodology for detecting designs that allow users, when behaving in a rational way, to make systematic errors will improve such systems.

We previously [3] developed a generic formal cognitive model from abstract cognitive principles, such as entering an interaction with knowledge of the task's subsidiary goals, showing its utility for detecting some systematic user error. Here we describe a development of it. The cognitive architecture previously identified device signals with user perception of them: a gross simplification of the complex process which involves perception, interpretation and evaluation. Similarly, user actions were identified with their corresponding device inputs. Such simplifications can hide design flaws. We address this problem by separating the user and the device state spaces. We also structure the underlying state space of the cognitive architecture to distinguish input signals (originating from user perception), output signals (consequences of user actions) and internal state (user memory). The formal version of our generic user model, module User, is outlined in Sect. 2. Our restructuring introduces intermediate entities, *interpretation* and *effect*, relating the now distinct state spaces (see Fig. 1) and described in detail in Sect. 3. The *effect* is an abstract view of how user actions are translated into device

G. Doherty and A. Blandford (Eds.): DSVIS 2006, LNCS 4323, pp. 123–136, 2007.
© Springer-Verlag Berlin Heidelberg 2007

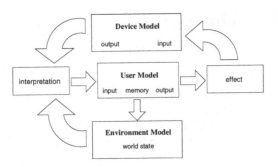

Fig. 1. The cycle of interaction

commands. The importance of such translation is evident in interactive systems involving voice or gesture recognition of user inputs. More detailed modelling of this is left to future work. The *interpretation* is an abstract view of the pathways from device signals and environment objects to the user decision of what they could mean. Blandford and Young [4] also separate user and device descriptions. An important difference (apart from the degree of formality) is our explicit inclusion of the interpretation and effect stages within the cycle of interaction. To illustrate the utility of the changes, we focus here on one use: modelling how the shape (form, size, etc.) of a device prompt affects user (mis)understanding. The shape of a device prompt may restrict or structure the type of information that a user is required to provide.

Dillon [5] argued that the "shape" concept assumes both spatial and semantic characteristics. He found that, as well as using spatial cues, individuals recognise and respond to content and meaning when interpreting requirements. During an interaction there is an inter-coupling of spatial and semantic components of memory. It is therefore likely that the interpretation of a device prompt relies on both spatial and semantic cues. A device prompt may incorporate both of these cue types: e.g. a user may be required to use several different passwords depending on the service required. A fixed digit entry field can act as both a spatial and semantic cue. The location of the password entry field (spatial cue) may correspond to the specific service required, while the size of the entry field (both a spatial and semantic cue) may correspond to the required length of the password and hence inform the user of which password is required (if passwords are of different lengths). Semantic cues are hints based on meaning that help users understand requirements. Dillon and Schaap [6] found that experienced users could better process these semantics, while novices had to rely solely on spatial cues. However, not all semantic cues are based on knowledge of the system. For example, a user with no knowledge of the system can still use the size of the entry field as a semantic cue as it only requires knowledge of passwords.

Information appears to be processed automatically without conscious effort [7]. When cognitive operations are underspecified (e.g., when multiple inputs are possible), humans tend to default to high frequency responses (frequency biasing). The largest single class of action slip errors are due to strong habit intrusions that have structural (spatial) and contextual (semantic) elements in common with planned actions [1]. Detecting cases where device prompt shape can be misunderstood may enable certain types of action slip errors to be avoided.

There are several approaches to formal reasoning about usability. One is to focus on a formal specification of the user interface [8,9]. Most commonly this approach relies on model-checking tools; investigations include whether a given event can occur or whether properties hold of all states. An alternative is formal user modelling, as here. It involves writing formal specifications of both the computer system and the user, then reasoning about their conjoint behaviour. Both device and user are considered as equally central components of the system and modelled as part of the analysis. Duke and Duce [10] formally reason about HCI this way; their approach is well suited to reasoning about interaction that, for example, combines the use of speech and gesture. However, their framework lacks tool support, which would make it difficult to apply in practice. Bowman and Faconti [11] formally specify a cognitive architecture using the process calculus LOTOS, analysing its properties using temporal logic. These approaches are more detailed than ours, which abstracts above cognitive processes. Moher and Dirda [12] use Petri net modelling to reason about users' mental models and their changing expectations over the course of an interaction; this approach supports reasoning about learning to use a new computer system but focuses on changes in user belief states rather than the analysis of desirable properties.

Rushby et al [13] focus specifically on mode errors and the ability of pilots to track mode changes. They formalise plausible mental models of systems and analyse them using the Murϕ state exploration tool. However, the mental models are essentially abstracted system models; they do not rely upon structure provided by cognitive principles. Neither do they model user interpretation.

Campos and Doherty [14] use perception mappings to specify mental models; no formal model of user behaviour is developed. Instead, they reason about the properties of representations of information in the interface. Also, perception in their approach seems to be always deterministic. Bredereke and Lankenau [15] reason about user perception of reality using a refinement based approach. Perception is expressed as a relation from environment events to mental events that could in principle be lossy, corresponding to physical or psychological reasons for an operator not observing all interface events of a system. However, the authors note that in practice they use the relation to rename events and so it is not lossy. This contrasts with our work which explicitly considers imperfect user interpretation. Cerone et al's [16] CSP model of an air traffic control system includes controller behaviour. A model checker was used to look for new behavioural patterns, overlooked by the analysis of experimental data. The classification stage of the interaction cycle of their model is similar to our user interpretation.

2   The Cognitive Architecture in SAL

Our cognitive architecture is a higher-order logic formalisation of abstract principles of cognition and specifies cognitively plausible behaviour [17]. The architecture specifies possible user behaviour (traces of actions) that can be justified in terms of specific results from the cognitive sciences. Real users can act outside

Table 1. A fragment of the SAL language

`x:T`	x has type T
`x' = e`	the new value of x is that of the expression e
`{x:T | p}`	a subset of T such that the predicate p holds
`a[i]`	the i-th element of the array a
`r.x`	the field x of the record r
`r WITH .x := e`	the record r with the field x replaced by the value of e
`g → upd`	if g is true then update according to upd
`c [] d`	non-deterministic choice between c and d
`[](i:T): cᵢ`	non-deterministic choice between the c_i where i is in range T

this behaviour, about which the architecture says nothing. Its predictive power is bounded by the situations where people act according to the principles specified. The architecture allows one to investigate what happens if a person acts in such plausible ways. The behaviour defined is neither "correct" or "incorrect". It could be either depending on the environment and task in question. We do not attempt to model underlying neural architecture nor the higher level cognitive architecture such as information processing. Instead our model is an abstract specification, intended for ease of reasoning.

Our previous formalisation of the cognitive architecture was developed in a theorem prover. The new version is based on the SAL model checking environment [18]. It provides a higher-order specification language and tools for analysing state machines specified as parametrised modules and composed either synchronously or asynchronously. The SAL notation we use is given in Table 1.

We rely upon cognitive principles that give a *knowledge level* description in the terms of Newell [19]. Their focus is on the goals and knowledge of a user. In this section, we discuss the principles and the way they are modelled.

Non-determinism. In any situation, any one of several cognitively plausible behaviours might be taken. It cannot be assumed that any specific plausible behaviour will be the one that a person will follow. The SAL specification is a transition system. Non-determinism is represented by the non-deterministic choice, [], between the named guarded commands (i.e. transitions). Each describes an action that a user *could* plausibly make. For example, in the following, *ReactCommit* is the name of a family of transitions indexed by `i:ReactRange`.

```
TRANSITION
    ([](i:GoalRange): GoalCommit:..) [] ([](i:GoalRange): GoalTrans:..)
[] ([](i:ReactRange): ReactCommit:..) [] ([](i:ReactRange): ReactTrans:..)
[] Exit:..[] Abort:..[] Idle:..
```

Mental versus physical actions. A user commits to taking an action in a way that cannot be revoked after a certain point. Once a signal has been sent from the brain to the motor system to take an action, it cannot be stopped even if the person becomes aware that it is wrong before the action is taken. Therefore, we model both *physical* and *mental* actions. Each physical action modelled is associated with an internal mental action that commits to taking it. In the SAL specification, this is reflected by the pairings of guarded commands: *GoalCommit – GoalTrans* and *ReactCommit – ReactTrans*. The first of the pair models committing to an action, the second actually doing it (see below).

User goals. A user enters an interaction with knowledge of the task and, in particular, task dependent sub-goals that must be discharged. These sub-goals might concern information that must be communicated to the device or items (such as credit cards) that must be inserted into the device. Given the opportunity, people may attempt to discharge any such goal, even when the device is prompting for a different action. We model such knowledge as user goals which represent a pre-determined partial plan that has arisen from knowledge of the task in hand, independent of the environment in which that task will be accomplished. No fixed order is assumed over how user goals will be discharged.

To see how this is modelled in SAL consider the following guarded command *GoalTrans* for doing a user action that has been committed to:

$$\texttt{gcommit}[\texttt{i}] = \texttt{committed} \quad \rightarrow \quad \begin{array}{l} \texttt{gcommit}'[\texttt{i}] = \texttt{done}; \quad \texttt{gcommitted}' = \texttt{FALSE}; \\ GoalTransition(i) \end{array}$$

The left-hand side of $\rightarrow$ is the guard of this command. It says that the rule will only activate if the associated action has already been committed to, as indicated by the i-th element of the local variable array `gcommit` holding value `committed`. If the rule is then non-deterministically chosen to fire, this value will be changed to `done` and the boolean variable `gcommitted` is set to false to indicate there are now no commitments to physical actions outstanding and the user model can select another goal. $GoalTransition(i)$ defines the state update transitions associated with this particular action i.

User goals are modelled as an array `goals` which is a parameter of the `User` module. The user model state space consists of three parts: input variable `in`, output variable `out`, local variable (memory) `mem`; environment is modelled by global variable `env`. All of these are specified using type variables and are instantiated for each concrete interactive system. Each goal is specified by a record with the fields `grd`, `tout`, `tmem` and `tenv`. The `grd` field is discussed below. The remaining fields are relations from old to new states that describe how two components of the user model state, outputs `out` and memory `mem`, and environment `env` are updated by discharging this goal. These relations, provided when the generic user model is instantiated, are used to specify $GoalTransition(i)$ as follows:

```
out' ∈ {x:Out | goals[i].tout(in,out,mem)(x)};
mem' ∈ {x:Memory | goals[i].tmem(in,mem,out')(x)};
env' ∈ {x:Env | goals[i].tenv(in,mem,env)(x) ∧ possessions}
```

The update of `env` must also satisfy a generic relation, *possessions*. It specifies universal physical constraints on possessions, linking the events of taking and giving up a possession with the corresponding increase or decrease in the number of objects possessed. This number is modelled as an environment component.

If the guarded command for *committing* to a user goal (given below) fires, it switches the commit flag for goal i to `committed` thus enabling the *GoalTrans* command. The predicate grd, extracted from the goals parameter, specifies when there are opportunities to discharge this user goal. Because we assign done to the corresponding element of the array gcommit in the *GoalTrans* command, once fired the command below will not execute again. If the user model discharges a goal, without some additional reason such as a prompt, it will not do so again.

$$\begin{array}{ll} \text{gcommit[i]} = \text{ready} \ \wedge \ \text{NOT(gcommitted} \vee \text{rcommited)} & \longrightarrow \quad \text{gcommit}'[\text{i}] = \text{committed;} \\ \wedge \ \text{finished} = \text{notf} \ \wedge \ \text{goals[i].grd(in, mem, env)} & \quad \text{gcommitted}' = \text{TRUE} \end{array}$$

Reactive behaviour. A user may react to an external stimulus, doing the action suggested by the stimulus. For example, if a flashing light comes on a user might, if the light is noticed, react by inserting coins in an adjacent slot. Reactive actions are modelled in the same way as user goals but on different variables, e.g. parameter react of the User module rather than goals. *ReactTransition(i)* is specified in the same way as *GoalTransition(i)*. The array element rcommit[i] is reassigned ready rather than done, once the corresponding action has been executed, as reactive actions, if prompted, *may* be repeated.

Goal based task completion. Users intermittently, but persistently, terminate interactions as soon as their perceived goal has been achieved [2], even if subsidiary tasks generated in achieving the main goal have not been completed. A cash-point example is a person walking away with the cash but leaving the card.

In the SAL specification, a condition that the user perceives as the main goal of the interaction is represented by a parameter PerceivedGoal of the User module. Goal based completion is then modelled as the guarded command *Exit*, which simply states that, once the predicate PerceivedGoal becomes true and there are no commitments to user goals and/or reactive actions, the user may complete the interaction. This action may still not be taken because the choice between enabled guarded commands is non-deterministic. Task completion is modelled by setting the local variable finished to ok:

$$\begin{array}{ll} \text{PerceivedGoal(in, mem)} \ \wedge \ \text{finished} = \text{notf} & \longrightarrow \quad \text{finished}' = \text{ok} \\ \wedge \ \text{NOT(gcommitted} \vee \text{rcommitted)} & \end{array}$$

No-option based task termination. If there is no apparent action that a person can take that will help complete the task then the person may terminate the interaction. For example, if, on a ticket machine, the user wishes to buy a weekly season ticket, but the options presented include nothing about season tickets, then the person might give up, assuming the goal is not achievable.

In the SAL specification, the no-option condition is expressed as the negation of predicates EnabledGoals and EnabledReact. Note that, in such a situation, a possible action that a person could take is to wait. However, they will only do so given some cognitively plausible reason such as a displayed "please wait". The waiting conditions are represented in the User module by predicate parameter Wait. If Wait is false, finished is set to abort in the guarded command *Abort*.

3   Formal Specification of User Interpretation for an ATM

The separation of user and device state spaces means connectors are required to compose the user and device models (recall Fig. 1). If the state spaces of

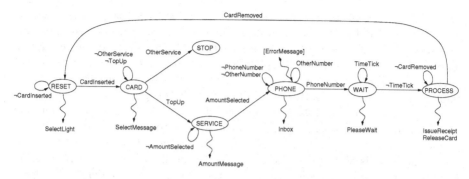

Fig. 2. ATM specification as finite state machine

both models precisely match, these connectors are simply identity mappings. This would yield essentially the same situation as with the shared state space. However, the separated state spaces open up new possibilities for specifying more complex connectors. These allow the formal modelling of the interpretation processes that are occurring in the interaction between the user and the device.

In this section, we consider the user interpretation part of a specific interactive system. Considering such concrete examples will help us to develop in the future an abstract model (as with the user model itself) of user interpretation. We start by specifying the machine and user models of this system.

We use here the task of topping-up a mobile phone based on a real ATM. A finite state machine specification of this device is given in Fig. 2. False machine outputs are omitted. The actual SAL specification, module ATM, is a straightforward translation of this diagram. Since our focus is the top-up task, we omit the specification of other services provided (this corresponds to the diagram's STOP state). Also, as we are illustrating the modelling of user interpretation, in this paper we abstract the authentication process by assuming that PIN entering/verification is a part of the card insertion step.

According to our specification, the ATM initially prompts users to insert a card. Once this is done, the machine provides several touch screen menu options. We assume (and specify in the user model later on) that the user chooses the top-up option. The machine then displays a new menu with several options to select the top-up value; the user can choose any. In response, the machine displays an input box and asks for a phone number. The user interpretation of this request is discussed in detail below. For now it suffices to know that the interpretation can result in two actions: entering a phone number, or entering some other number (we assume the machine can distinguish these two alternatives). In the former case, a receipt is issued and the card is released; in the latter, the machine displays an error message and again prompts for a phone number. The transactions related to the actual top-up process take time. Thus a "please wait" message is displayed during processing. Finally, the machine returns to the initial state once the released card is removed.

The input and output components of the device state space are relevant to the discussion of user interpretation. The input variables of our specification are

CardInserted, TopUp, OtherService, AmountSelected, PhoneNumber, OtherNumber, and CardRemoved (Fig. 2). The output variables are CardMessage, SelectMessage, AmountMessage, Inbox, ErrorMessage, PleaseWait, IssueReceipt, and ReleaseCard. These variables are booleans, except Inbox. It is a record consisting of two fields: option and size. The former specifies whether the request to enter a phone number is displayed, the latter is the size of the input box.

The generic user model User was described in Sect. 2. To analyse our interactive system, we now instantiate that model for the concrete task of topping-up a mobile phone. We start by specifying the state space of our user model.

In general, it is plausible to assume that the specific details of an ATM specification might be unavailable at the time the concrete user model is developed. Even if they are, it could be preferable to specify the user state space in more cognitive terms, not constraining oneself by the existing device specification. First, we consider user perceptions which are represented in the User module by the input variable in. We assume that the user is able to perceive the following signals from the machine: InsertCard, SelectService, SelectAmount, RemoveCard, WaitMessage, and ErrorMessage (their names should be self-explanatory). The user can also perceive the shape of the input box, InboxShape. People usually know their phone numbers, however, they might also have another (different) number on their top-up cards. It is cognitively plausible that the user may be uncertain which number is requested. This confusion is represented in the user model by two distinct components, EnterPhoneNumber and EnterCardNumber. Finally, the user evaluates the state of the machine deciding whether the requested service has been received, modelled by ServiceReceived. These components form a record, In, which is used to instantiate the corresponding type variable in User.

Next, we specify state space components related to the actions users might take. These correspond to the ATM inputs in Fig. 2 and are: CardInserted, TopUp, OtherService, AmountSelected, PhoneNumber, OtherNumber, and CardRemoved. Like the user inputs above, these components form a record, Out. For this paper, the memory component of the User module, Mem, is kept simple. We assume the user remembers only the actions taken in the previous step. Mem is therefore the same record type as Out. Finally, user actions can both affect and be restricted by the environment of our system; we thus have a record type, Env. It includes counters, BankCards and PhoneCards, for the user possessions (cards); values (the balances of the corresponding accounts) of these possessions, BankBalance and PhoneBalance; and the sizes, SizePhone and SizeCard, of the card numbers.

We assume that user knowledge of ATM transactions includes the need to (1) provide a payment card, (2) communicate that the top-up option is required and (3) communicate the top-up value. This knowledge is specified as user goals (elements of array goals) instantiated by giving the action guard and the updates to the output component. For the insert-card goal, the guard is that the person perceives an InsertCard signal and has a bank card. The output action is to set CardInserted to true (Default is a record with all its fields set to false so asserts that nothing else is done). We omit the memory and environment updates:

```
grd  := λ(in,mem,env): in.InsertCard ∧ env.BankCards > 0
tout := λ(in,outO,mem): λ(out): out = Default WITH .CardInserted := TRUE
```

Choosing to top-up and communicating the top-up value are modelled similarly.

We assume that the user can *reactively* respond to device prompts by attending to either spatial or semantic cues (or both) and enter the phone number. This may happen only when the machine state is interpreted as signalling to enter the number by in.EnterPhoneNumber. The number must also not have been entered, as indicated by the memory, in the previous step, unless the person sees an error message requesting that repetition. Formally, the action is specified as follows:

```
grd  := λ(in,mem,env): in.EnterPhoneNumber ∧
                       (NOT(mem.PhoneNumber) ∨ ErrorMessage)
tout := λ(in,outO,mem): λ(out): out = Default WITH .PhoneNumber := TRUE
```

However, as discussed earlier, it is plausible that a prompt for the phone number can be misinterpreted as that for the number on the top-up card instead (a semantic cue). The corresponding reactive action is analogous to the one above. Finally, the user can respond to the prompt for taking back their card:

```
grd  := λ(in,mem,env): in.RemoveCard ∧ NOT(mem.CardRemoved)
tout := λ(in,outO,mem): λ(out): out = Default WITH .CardRemoved := TRUE
```

Goal and wait predicates are the last parameters used to instantiate the User module. We assume that the user considers receiving the requested service as the main goal of the interaction. We also assume that seeing a "please wait" message is the only condition when the user, perceiving no options to act, does not terminate the interaction. The two predicates are specified in SAL as follows:

```
PerceivedGoal = λ(in,mem): in.ServiceReceived
Wait          = λ(in,mem): in.WaitMessage
```

Finally, the ATM user model, ATMuser, is defined by instantiating the generic user model with the parameters (goals, reactive actions, perceived goal and wait condition) just defined.

So far we have specified an ATM and have developed a formal model of its user. The state spaces of the two specifications are distinct. This closely corresponds to reality, since the state of an ATM and the user interpretation of it are not necessarily identical. The changing machine state is first attended to then interpreted by the user. Next we formally specify this interpretation, thus providing a connector for separate state spaces. The specification is written as a new SAL module, interpretation. The module, being a connector, has input variables that are the output variables of ATM, and output variable that is the input (perception) component of the User module, the record in.

We model user interpretation (below) by the SAL definition construct which allows one to describe system invariants. Intuitively, this means that the left-hand side of an equation is updated whenever the value of the right-hand side changes. Here, we assume that the user model directly perceives some of the ATM signals such as prompts for inserting a card, selecting amount, a wait message, etc. Consequently, the first six conjuncts in the definition simply rename the appropriate fields in the record in to the corresponding variables in ATM. Below we discuss in more detail the final three conjuncts.

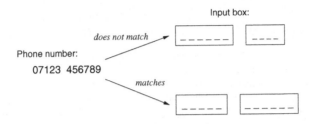

Fig. 3. User interpretation of input boxes

```
DEFINITION in ∈ { x:In |
    x.WaitMessage = PleaseWait ∧ x.ErrorMessage = ErrorMessage ∧
    x.InsertCard = CardMessage ∧ x.SelectService = SelectMessage ∧
    x.SelectAmount = AmountMessage ∧ x.RemoveCard = ReleaseCard ∧
    x.ServiceReceived = IssueReceipt ∧ x.InboxShape = ... ∧
    definition of x.EnterPhoneNumber and x.EnterCardNumber }
```

As explained earlier, the field `ServiceReceived` corresponds to the main goal in our user model. The definition above identifies it with the machine action issuing a receipt. Of course, getting a receipt could not plausibly be the actual user goal, a better candidate for which is to have the mobile phone account increased by the desired amount. The latter, however, is impossible to observe directly, so, with this machine, getting a receipt is the best available approximation.

In this paper, we consider what influence the shape of a machine prompt can have on user interpretation of it. For this, we use input boxes displayed by ATMs (see Fig. 3). There could be many aspects of the shape to investigate; for simplicity, the shape of an input box is modelled as its size in our case studies. In general, however, it could represent any relevant aspect of shape. The definition below identifies shape with size; the condition `Inbox.option` ensures that this identification occurs only when an input box is displayed, otherwise, the user model does not perceive the box at all, as represented by the shape value 0:

```
x.InboxShape = IF Inbox.option THEN Inbox.size ELSE 0 ENDIF
```

The last conjunct in the definition illustrates how shape can affect user interpretation of machine prompts. We present it in four parts below. The first part (conjunct) specifies the situation when there is nothing in the machine state that could be interpreted by the user model as a prompt, or spatial cue, for entering a phone number or the number on a top-up card. This happens when the shape of the input box (possibly not displayed at all) matches neither of the numbers the user could consider as relevant to the prompt:

```
x.InboxShape ≠ env.SizePhone ∧ x.InboxShape ≠ env.SizeCard
⇒ NOT(x.EnterPhoneNumber) ∧ NOT(x.EnterCardNumber)
```

When the shape (size) of the displayed input box matches the phone number and is different from the number on the card, we assume that the user model interprets this as a prompt, or semantic cue, for entering the phone number:

```
x.InboxShape = env.SizePhone ∧ x.InboxShape ≠ env.SizeCard
⇒ x.EnterPhoneNumber ∧ NOT(x.EnterCardNumber)
```

Analogously, the user model can interpret the machine state as a prompt for the number on the top-up card:

```
x.InboxShape ≠ env.SizePhone ∧ x.InboxShape = env.SizeCard
⇒ NOT(x.EnterPhoneNumber) ∧ x.EnterCardNumber
```

Finally, the user can be confused as to which of the two numbers is requested. This may happen when the shape of the displayed box matches both numbers. We assume that the result of user interpretation in this case is random, but it can only yield a prompt for one of the numbers (here XOR is exclusive-or):

```
x.InboxShape = env.SizePhone ∧ x.InboxShape = env.SizeCard
⇒ x.EnterPhoneNumber XOR x.EnterCardNumber
```

Now we have specified all the components of our interactive system. The whole system, denoted system, is modelled in SAL as their parallel composition:

```
(ATMuser [] ATM [] environment) || (interpretation || effect)
```

Here, [] denotes asynchronous (interleaving) composition, whereas || denotes synchronous composition. For brevity, we have not presented the specifications of the effect and environment modules. Informally, the effect module specifies how user actions from ATMuser are translated into the machine commands; in other words, how the output component out is connected to the ATM inputs. In our case study, this translation is simple renaming, analogous to those given in the definition of in above. The environment module contains no transitions; it simply defines constants such as the size of the phone and top-up card numbers.

4   Verification of Interactive Systems

We now present verification examples, focussing on the system aspects influencing user interpretation. We first introduce system properties to verify. Our approach is concerned with two kinds of correctness properties. Firstly, we want to be sure that, in any possible system behaviour, the user's main goal of interaction is eventually achieved. Given our model's state space, this is written in SAL as the assertion (where F means "eventually"): F(PerceivedGoal(in,mem)). Second, in achieving a goal, subsidiary tasks are often generated that the user must complete to complete the task associated with their goal. If the completion of these subsidiary tasks is represented as a predicate, SecondaryGoal, the required condition is specified as: G(PerceivedGoal(in,mem) ⇒ F(SecondaryGoal(in,mem,env))) (where G means "always"). This states that the secondary goal is always eventually achieved once the perceived goal has been achieved. Often secondary goals can be expressed as interaction invariants [3] which state that some property of the model state, that was perturbed to achieve the main goal, is restored.

In the first example, the ATM design's displayed input box has shape (size) larger than strictly needed and it (incorrectly) matches the top-up card number but not the correct but shorter phone number. Our first attempt is to verify that the user model eventually achieves the perceived goal of getting a receipt. Unfortunately, the desired property is not true, and the SAL model checker produces a counterexample which shows both the trace of system states and the actions taken by the user model and the machine. The analysis of the counterexample indicates that the user model loops on entering the top-up card number. Further analysis reveals that this is due to the user (mis)interpreting the ATM prompt for the phone number as that for the card number. This misinterpretation is caused by the input box shape which matches the card number. Of course, this does not mean that every real ATM user is prone to such error or would loop forever. However, the assumptions on which our model of user interpretation is based are cognitively plausible and this error is a consequence of them. Hence, some users are liable to such errors and changes in the ATM design are advisable.

Next, we consider a modified ATM design in which the shape of the displayed box matches the phone number. We assume here that the shape of the card number is different. Now the first correctness property, the user eventually achieving the perceived goal, is satisfied by the interactive system. We thus proceed with the verification of the second property that the user eventually achieves the secondary goal. This is expressed as an interaction invariant, which states that the total value of the user possessions (the balance of the account associated with the payment card plus the top-up card balance) is eventually restored to the initial value. Unfortunately, the verification of this property fails. The counterexample produced indicates that the failure is caused by the user model finishing the transaction as soon as a receipt is issued. Detecting this type of user error, a post-completion error, with its underlying causes and possible remedies, has been discussed in our earlier paper [3]. Here, we just note that such errors could be eliminated by modifying the ATM from Fig. 2 so that a receipt is issued only when the user has removed the card.

Finally, consider the case when the phone and card number both match the shape of the displayed box. The verification of the first correctness property fails. The counterexample produced is as in the first example (when only the card number matched the displayed box). Further analysis reveals that, unlike in that example, the user model can now achieve the perceived goal. Within the SAL environment, this is verified using the assertion EF(PerceivedGoal(in,mem)), where the operator EF states that there is a path such that the corresponding formula is eventually true. This indicates that both user interpretations of the machine prompt are possible, which can lead to the confusion of real ATM users.

5   Summary and Further Work

We have presented a refined version of our cognitive architecture. The state space of the formal user model has been separated from that of the device. This both required and facilitated the abstract modelling of user interpretation of device outputs. We presented a simple case study (available at http://www.dcs.qmul. ac.uk/~rimvydas/usermodel/dsvis06.zip). It illustrates how such abstract models can be used within our verification approach to detect problems in interactive systems related to shape induced confusion over device signal meaning. Our abstract model is a simplification of cognitive interpretation, and clearly not every user of such device will experience the problems our approach reveals.

However, since the abstraction is cognitively plausible, a strong potential for user confusion is there, and a substantial number of users might experience it.

Our cognitive model was not developed directly from a complete psychological theory. Rather an exploratory approach was taken, starting with simple principles of cognition such as non-determinism, goal-based termination and reactive behaviour. However, even the small set of principles is rich enough for plausible erroneous behaviour to emerge that was not directly expected [3].

As SAL provides support for higher-order specifications, the new version of the cognitive architecture remains generic and is instantiated to verify any specific interactive system. Besides the major restructuring described here, the treatment of the underlying state space is simplified in the SAL version where simple variables are used instead of the history functions of the original. Since theorem provers are better for reasoning about abstract properties than concrete ones as here, the ideal is to have an integrated theorem prover + model checker framework. Being developed as a framework for combining various verification tools, including the PVS theorem prover, SAL is a very promising environment for the future development of our verification methodology.

For simple systems as considered here, mechanical verification is unnecessary. The problems detected could be identified by examining the specification of user interpretation. Still, writing a formal specification helps to identify problems, and our framework provides structure to the specification process. Moreover, a combination of several user interpretation pathways would lead to complex specifications, requiring mechanical verification. Finally, the verification of specific systems is only a part of a larger verification framework where the formal specification of user interpretation could be combined with, say, design rules to reason about general properties of interactive systems using a theorem prover.

Other aspects of user interpretation remain to be investigated. An ability to combine information in-the-world with knowledge in-the-head allows individuals to make interpretations. Mandler [20], amongst others, argues that knowledge can be accessed directly or indirectly. When interaction relies on novel associations it is likely to demand more direct attention. However, frequent and familiar interactions use indirect knowledge that involves interpretation. Further work needs to identify when user interpretations are made, what types of spatial and semantic cues are used (see Dillon [5]), and if these can be modelled.

The user interpretation errors detected occur for systematic reasons. A generic model of user interpretation can capture these systematic reasons, thus helping to eliminate errors they cause. While the cognitive architecture is generic, the specification of user interpretation currently is not. It must be written for each specific system from scratch. Considering other aspects of user interpretation will facilitate the development of a generic interpretation model. Finally, we will also investigate the formal modelling of *effect*, the counterpart of user interpretation. It is especially relevant for multimedia based interactive systems. We expect that our changes to and reorganisation of the model will facilitate such modelling, as evidenced by the aspect of user interpretation considered here.

Acknowledgements. This research is funded by EPSRC grants GR/S67494/01 and GR/S67500/01.

References

1. Reason, J.: Human Error. Cambridge University Press (1990)
2. Byrne, M.D., Bovair, S.: A working memory model of a common procedural error. Cognitive Science **21**(1) (1997) 31–61
3. Curzon, P., Blandford, A.E.: Detecting multiple classes of user errors. In: Little, R., Nigay, L. (eds.): Proc. of the 8th IFIP Work. Conf. on Engineering for Human-Computer Interaction. Volume 2254 of LNCS. Springer-Verlag (2001) 57–71
4. Blandford, A.E., Young, R.M.: Separating user and device descriptions for modelling interactive problem solving. In: Nordby, K., Helmersen, P., Gilmore, D., Arnesen, S. (eds.): INTERACT'95. Chapman and Hall (1995) 91–96
5. Dillon, A.: Spatial-semantics: how users derive shape from information space. Journal of the American Society for Information Science **51** (2000) 521–528
6. Dillon, A., Schaap, D.: Expertise and the perception of shape in information. Journal of the American Society for Information Science **47** (1996) 786–788
7. Tulving, E.: Elements of Episodic Memory. Oxford University Press (1983)
8. Campos, J.C., Harrison, M.D.: Formally verifying interactive systems: a review. In: Harrison, M., Torres, J. (eds.): Design, Specification and Verification of Interactive Systems '97. Springer-Verlag (1997) 109–124
9. Markopoulos, P., Johnson, P., Rowson, J.: Formal architectural abstractions for interactive software. Int. Journal of Human Computer Studies **49** (1998) 679–715
10. Duke, D.J., Duce, D.A.: The formalization of a cognitive architecture and its application to reasoning about human computer interaction. Formal Aspects of Computing **11** (1999) 665–689
11. Bowman, H., Faconti, G.: Analysing cognitive behaviour using LOTOS and Mexitl. Formal Aspects of Computing **11** (1999) 132–159
12. Moher, T.G., Dirda, V.: Revising mental models to accommodate expectation failures in human-computer dialogues. In: Design, Specification and Verification of Interactive Systems '95. Springer-Verlag (1995) 76–92
13. Rushby, J.: Analyzing cockpit interfaces using formal methods. Electronic Notes in Theoretical Computer Science **43** (2001)
14. Campos, J.C., Doherty, G.J.: Reasoning about dynamic information displays. In: Jorge, J.A., Nunes, N.J., e Cunha, J.F. (eds.): Interactive Systems. Design, Specification, and Verification. Volume 2844 of LNCS. Springer-Verlag (2003) 288–302
15. Bredereke, J., Lankenau, A.: A rigorous view of mode confusion. In: Proc. of SAFECOMP 2002. Volume 2434 of LNCS. Springer-Verlag (2002) 19–31
16. Cerone, A., Lindsay, P.A., Connelly, S.: Formal analysis of human-computer interaction using model-checking. In: Proc. of the Third IEEE Int. Conference on Software Engineering and Formal Methods (SEFM'05). IEEE Press (2005) 352–362
17. Butterworth, R.J., Blandford, A.E., Duke, D.J.: Demonstrating the cognitive plausibility of interactive systems. Formal Aspects of Computing **12** (2000) 237–259
18. de Moura, L., Owre, S., Ruess, H., Rushby, J., Shankar, N., Sorea, M., Tiwari, A.: SAL 2. In: Alur, R., Peled, D.A. (eds.): Computer Aided Verification: CAV 2004. Volume 3114 of LNCS. Springer-Verlag (2004) 496–500
19. Newell, A.: Unified Theories of Cognition. Harvard University Press (1990)
20. Mandler, G.: Recognizing: the judgement of previous occurrence. Psychological Review **87** (1980) 252–271

Combining Formal Methods and Functional Strategies Regarding the Reverse Engineering of Interactive Applications

J.C. Silva[1,2], José Creissac Campos[1], and João Saraiva[1]

[1] Departamento de Informática/CCTC, Universidade do Minho, Braga, Portugal
{jose.campos,jas}@di.uminho.pt
[2] Grupo de Sistemas e Tecnologias de Informação, IPCA, Barcelos, Portugal
jcsilva@ipca.pt

Abstract. Graphical user interfaces (GUIs) make software easy to use by providing the user with visual controls. Therefore, correctness of GUI's code is essential to the correct execution of the overall software. Models can help in the evaluation of interactive applications by allowing designers to concentrate on its more important aspects. This paper describes our approach to reverse engineer an abstract model of a user interface directly from the GUI's legacy code. We also present results from a case study. These results are encouraging and give evidence that the goal of reverse engineering user interfaces can be met with more work on this technique.

1 Introduction

Enterprise competitiveness in the information age is very much dependent on the quality of the graphical user interfaces (GUIs) being used [10]. However, the quality of large and complex user interfaces is hard to maintain. These very rapidly originate failures, a problem nowadays identified under the *usability* heading. A very large proportion of failures in interactive systems takes place due to erroneous human actions [12]. As pointed out by Leveson [15], human error in computer systems use is often due to errors in their user interface design, and not the sole result of errors performed by the direct users of the systems.

The correctness of the user interface is essential to the correct execution of the overall software. Regarding user interfaces, correctness is expressed as usability: the effectiveness, efficiency, and satisfaction with which users can use the system to achieve their goals [24]. In order for a user interface to have good usability characteristics it must both be adequately designed and adequately implemented, having its target users, their goals, and the operating environment in mind.

Tools are currently available to developers that allow for fast development of user interfaces with graphical components. However, the design of interactive systems does not seem to be much improved by the use of such tools. Interfaces are often difficult to understand and use for end users. In many cases users have problems in identifying all the supported tasks of a system, or in understanding

G. Doherty and A. Blandford (Eds.): DSVIS 2006, LNCS 4323, pp. 137–150, 2007.
© Springer-Verlag Berlin Heidelberg 2007

how to reach them. The problem seems to lie more on the design of the systems, than in their actual implementation.

> *Problems could be largely solved if designers had methods and tools to provide indications about the most effective interaction and presentation techniques to support the possible user activities* [22].

Traditionally design aspects of user interfaces have been the concern of Human-Computer Interaction, while software engineers have been mainly concerned with implementation aspects. Clearly there is a need to enable software engineers to consider aspects of design when developing interactive systems.

Model-based design helps to identify high-level models which allow designers to specify and analyse systems. Different types of models can been used in the design and development of interactive systems, from user and task models to software engineering models of the implementation. The authors are currently engaged in a R&D project (IVY – A model-based usability analysis environment[1]) which aims at developing a model-based tool for the analysis of interactive systems designs. The tool will act as a front end to the SMV model checker, creating an abstraction layer where models of interactive systems can be developed and analysed. The models used are expressed in the MAL interactors language [3], and express both the information present at the user interface and the behaviour of the system in response to user input. In the context of the project we are investigating the applicability of reverse engineering approaches to the derivation of user interface's abstract models amenable for verification of usability related properties.

In this paper we present the initial results of work on investigating the application of strategic programming and slicing to the reverse engineering of user interfaces. Our goal is to produce a fully functional reverse engineering prototype tool. The tool will be capable of deriving abstract models of interactive applications' user interfaces. This will enable reasoning about the design of the system. In particular we are interested in applying automated reasoning techniques to ensure a thorough analysis of all possible behaviours of a given system.

In section 2 we briefly introduce the IVY project. Then in section 3 we describe some related work. Section 4 explains the technique applied in the reverse engineering of graphical user interfaces. Thus, we describe the model-based technique used for reverse engineering interactive systems. In section 5 we shows the application of the actual prototype to a simple system. Finally, in section 6 we present some conclusions and put forward our plans for future work.

2   About the IVY Project

2.1   The Project

IVY follows from the development of I2SMV [3], a compiler enabling the verification of interactive systems' models using the SMV model checker [18]. The

---

[1] http://www.di.uminho.pt/ivy

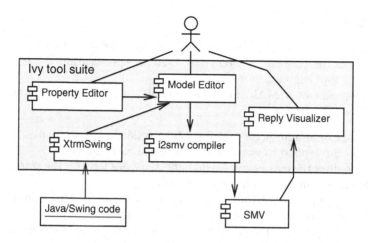

Fig. 1. IVY architecture

objective now is to develop, as a front end to SMV, a model based tool for the analysis of behavioural issues of interactive systems' designs. This tool will not only translate the models into the SMV input language, but fully support the process of modelling and analysis by providing editors, for models and properties, and a reply visualizer for the analysis of the verification process results (see figure 1).

A considerable number of tools for model checking have been proposed. Interactive systems, however, have specificities that make it difficult to use typical model checking tools [3]. Two major types of problem can be identified:

- the richness of the interaction between user and system affects the models;
- the assumptions that must be made about the user's capabilities affects the analysis of the verification results;

Tools are needed that facilitate modelling, and reasoning about the results of the verification, from an interactive systems perspective. In IVY we aim at creating an abstraction layer where models of interactive systems can more easily be developed and analysed.

Being modular, the tool will also act as a test-bed for different styles of modelling/analysis of interactive systems. One approach we are exploring is the use of reverse engineering techniques to enable the generation of models from user interface code. Our goal is to support the verification of existing user interfaces in a semi-automated manner. This will not only be useful to enable the analysis of existing interactive applications, but can also be helpful in a re-engineering process when a existing application must be ported or simply updated. In this case, being able to reason at a higher level of abstraction than that of code, will help in guaranteeing that the new/updated user interface has the same characteristics of the previous one.

2.2   The Language

Interactors act as a mechanism for structuring the use of standard specification techniques in the context of interactive systems specification [7]. In IVY the MAL interactors language from [3] is used.

The definition of a MAL interactor contains a state, actions, axioms and presentation information:

- The state of an interactor is defined by a collection of attributes.
- Actions correspond to events the system can respond to.
- Axioms allow the expression of what effect actions have on the state. In order to describe behaviour, a deontic logic is used:
  - deontic operator $obl(ac)$: ac is obliged to happen some time in the future;
  - deontic operator $per(ac)$: ac is permitted to happen next;
  - model operator $[ac]expr$: $expr$ is true after action ac takes place;
  - $[]expr$: $expr$ is true in the initial state;
  - $per(ac) \rightarrow exp$: ac is permitted only if exp is true;
  - $exp \rightarrow obl(ac)$: if exp is true then action ac becomes obligatory.
- Presentation information allows us to assert that a particular attribute/action is visible. This is done with a *vis* annotation on relevant attributes/actions.

This language allows us to abstract both static and dynamic perspectives of interactive systems. The static perspective is achieved with **attributes** and **actions** abstractions which aggregate the state and all visible components in a particular instant. The **axioms** abstraction formalizes the dynamic perspective from an interactive state to another.

3   Related Work

In the Human-Computer Interaction area, quality is typically addressed by the use of empirical methods that involve testing (a prototype of) the system. These methods work by placing users in front of a system in order to assess its usability. Analytic methods have also been proposed as a means of reducing the effort of analysis. These approaches work by inspection of the system (or a model thereof) and range from less structured approaches such as Heuristic Evaluation [21] to more structured ones such as Cognitive Walkthroughs [16]. In all cases, these approaches are geared towards the analysis of the design of the interactive system, and in particular aspects related to its usability.

The use of mathematically rigorous (formal) models of the interactive systems, as a means of reasoning about usability issues, has also been proposed (see, for example, [3,23]). One advantage of formal approaches is that they enable the thorough verification of the validity of the properties/system under scrutiny. One of their drawbacks is the difficulty in incorporating human considerations in the analysis process. Approaches such as Syndectic Modelling [8] attempt to formalize the user but become too complex to be used in practice. Other approaches have been proposed were specific aspects of human behaviour are included in the models (see for example, [23,4,2]).

In Software Engineering concerns are more geared towards testing the quality of the code produced (absence of bugs) and its correctness vis-a-vis the system's specification. Testing of user interface implementations has also attracted attention.

Testing typically progresses by having the code execute pre-defined test cases and compare the result of the execution with the result of some test oracle. In the case of interactive systems, models of the user interface are needed both to aid the generation of the test cases, and for the test oracle. In this area, the use of reverse engineering approaches has been explored in order to derive such models directly from the existing interactive system.

A typical approach is to run the interactive system and automatically record its state and events. Memon et al. [19] describe a tool which automatically transverses a user interface in order to extract information about its widgets, properties and values. Chen et al. [5] propose a specification-based technique to test user interfaces. Users graphically manipulate test specifications represented by finite state machines which are obtained from running the system. Systa studies and analyses the run-time behaviour of Java software trough a reverse engineering process [25]. Running the target software under a debugger allows for the generation of state diagrams. The state diagrams can be used to examine the overall behaviour of a component such as a class, a object, or a method.

Another alternative is the use of statical analysis. The reengineering process is based on analysis of the application's code, instead of its execution, as in previous approaches. One such approach is the work by d'Ausbourg et al. [6] in reverse engineering UIL code (User Interface Language – a language to describe user interfaces for the X11 Windowing System, see [11]). In this case models are created at the level of the events that can happen in the components of the user interface. For example, pressing or releasing a button.

In the last decade the reengineering of interactive systems has also been investigated by several authors. Moore [20] describes a technique to partially automate reverse engineering character based user interfaces of legacy applications. The result of this process is a model for user interface understanding and migration. The work shows that a language-independent set of rules can be used to detect interactive components from legacy code. Merlo [9] proposes a similar approach. In both cases static analysis is used.

We are using static analysis as in [9,20,6]. When compared to their work our challenges are twofold:

- We are reverse engineering code for graphical user interfaces, as opposed to character based user interfaces in [9,20]. At the moment we are working with Java/Swing (however, our long term goal is to develop a more generic approach).

- We are more interested in models that reflect the design of the user interface and the interaction that it creates, than the actual architecture of the underlying software implementing it. Hence, we need models that are more abstract than those produced in, for example, [19] or [6].

4   A Technique for Reverse Engineering Graphical User Interfaces

The technique explained in this section aids in identifying a graphical user interface abstraction from legacy code. This includes identifying data entities and actions that are involved in the graphical user interface, as well as relationships between user interface components. The goal is to detect components in the user interface through functional strategies and formal methods. These components include user interface objects and actions.

4.1   Graphical User Interface Definition

The most usual class of user interfaces are hierarchical graphical front-ends to software systems. These user interfaces produce deterministic graphical output from user input and system events. A graphical user interface (GUI) contains graphical widgets. Each widget has a fixed set of properties. At any time during the execution of the GUI, these properties have discrete values, the set of which constitutes the state of the GUI.

This paper focuses on techniques to reverse engineer this first class of user interfaces. Another class of user interfaces are web-user interfaces that have synchronization/timing constraints among objects, movie players that show a continuous stream of video rather than a sequence of discrete frames, and non-deterministic GUIs in which it is not possible to model the state of the software in its entirety.

4.2   GUI Slicing Through Strategic Programming

In order to extract the user interface model from a Java/Swing program we need to construct a slicing function [27,17] that isolates the Swing sub-program from the entire Java program. The straightforward approach is to define a explicit recursive function that traverses the Abstract Syntax Tree (AST) of the Java program and returns the Swing sub-tree. A typical Java grammar/AST, however, has 105 non-terminal symbols and 239 productions [1]. As a result, writing such a function forces the programmer to have a full knowledge of the grammar and to write a complex and long mutually recursive function. We use a different approach by using strategic programming. In this style of programming, there is a pre-defined set of (strategic) generic traversal functions that traverse any AST using different traversal strategies (e.g. top-down,left-to-right, etc). Thus, the programmer needs to focus in the nodes of interest only. In fact, the programmer does not need to have a knowledge of the entire grammars/AST, but only of those parts he is interested in (the swing sub-language in our case).

Strategic programming is a form of generic programming that combines the notions of *one-step traversal* and *dynamic nominal type case* into a powerful combinatorial style of traversal construction. Strategic programming allows novel

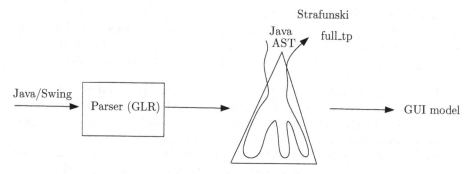

Fig. 2. The reverse engineering process

forms of abstraction and modularization that are useful for program construction in general. In particular when large heterogeneous data structures are involved (e.g. the abstract syntax tree representing a Java program), strategic programming techniques enable a high level of conciseness, composability, and traversal control [29,28]. Strategic programming has been defined in different programming paradigms. In this paper we will use the STRAFUNSKI library [14]: a Haskell [13] library for generic programming and language processing. STRAFUNSKI not only contains the strategic library, but also a powerful GLR parser generator. It contains also a set of grammars for most existing programming languages (for example, a full Java grammar).

In order to explain strategic programming and the STRAFUNSKI library in more detail, let us consider the following JAVA/SWING code fragment:

```
...
addButton = new javax.swing.JButton();
...
```

After parsing this code fragment we obtain the following fragment of the AST:

```
...
Statement(
 StatementWithoutTrailingSubstatement(
  ExpressionStatement(
   semicolon2(
    Assignment(
     AssignmentOp(
      Name2(Identifier-p(["addButton"])),
           equal1,
      StatementExpression(
        ClassInstanceCreationExpression(
        new-comma(ClassOrInterfaceType1(
        Name(Identifier-p(["javax","swing","JButton"]))),
        [])))))))))
...
```

Having the knowledge of this particular fragment of the Java grammar/AST, we are able to define a strategic function that given the complete AST extracts *JButton* object assignments. First, we need to collect the list of assignments in a Java program. We define this function in Haskell/Strafunski as follows:

- We begin by identifying the type of strategy needed to collect the desired information. We make use of the traversal combinator `full_tdTU` in order to define a function that traverses the AST in a top-down fashion (although, in this particular example, we could use a `full_bu` strategy).
- Next, we need to define the *worker* function that will do the work while traversing the AST. This worker function identifies the tree nodes where work has to be done. In the complete Java AST the nodes of interest correspond to the constructor `AssignmentOp` (see AST above). Thus, our worker function simply returns a singleton list with the left-hand side of the assignment and the expression. All the other nodes are simply ignored! The functions *applyTU*, *full_tdTU*, *constTU*, and *adhocTU* are library functions used to construct the results and apply the traversal combinators. Because they are not relevant to understand our techniques, we omit their definitions here.

This function, named `getAssignmentIdentifiers`, looks as follows:

```
getAssignmentIdentifiers :: (Term t) => t -> [([Id],[Id])]
getAssignmentIdentifiers ast =
 runIdentity (applyTU (full_tdTU worker) ast)]
 where
 worker = constTU [] 'adhocTU' getexp
 getexp (AssignmentOp left op exp) = return [(left,exp)]
```

Having collected the list of assignments we can now filter that list in order to produce the list containing all *JButtons* objects in the JAVA/SWING code.

```
getJButtons :: (Term t) => t -> [[Id]]
getJButtons ast = jButton
 where assignments = getAssignmentIdentifiers e
       jButton = [a | (a,b) <- assignments
                  , (b==["javax","swing","JButton"])]
```

Functional strategic combinators allow us to construct programs that only mention those constructors that are strictly relevant to the problem. Furthermore, they work for *any* abstract syntax tree and not only for the Java AST under consideration in this paper. As a result, the strategic function we define not only extracts the Swing fragment from a Java program, but may also be reused to slice another GUI toolkit for other languages/ASTs. Observe that in the Haskell/Strafunski code presented above a small part of it is specific of the Java language/AST. Obviously, we can easily parameterize these functions with that language specific constructors. It also should be noticed that the basic concepts of strategic programming are independent of the programming paradigm.

4.3   User Interface Abstraction

In order to define the slicing functions mentioned above, we defined a small set of abstractions for the interactions between the user and the system. These are the abstractions that we look for in the legacy code:

- User input: Any data inserted by the user;
- User selection: Any choice that the user can make between several different options, such as a command menu;
- User action: An action that is performed as the result of user input or user selection;
- Output to User: Any communication from application to user, such as a user dialogue;

Through the user interface code of an interactive system and this set of abstractions, we can generate its graphical user interface abstraction. To execute this step we combine the STRAFUNSKI library with formal and semi-formal methods, which are mathematically-based languages, techniques, and tools for specifying and verifying systems. The use of formal methods does not guarantee correctness. However, they aid in making specifications more concise and less ambiguous, making it easier to reason about them.

5   An Example

This section shows the application of the prototype to a small example. Basically, the *JClass* system is a simple JAVA/SWING "toy" example allowing for marks management (see figure 3).

Applying the prototype to the application's code, enables us to extract information about all widgets presented at the interface, such as *JButton, JLabel, JComboBox, JTextField, JSlider, JProgressBar, JPanel*, etc. To reverse engineer the graphical user interface of an interactive system it is not necessary to analyse all of the application's functionality. Therefore, irrelevant information from the *JClass* system is discarded by the tool during the slicing phase in order to make the representations much more clear.

Once the AST for the application code is built we can apply different slicing operations as needed. This means we can easily tailor the information (models) we want to extract from the AST (and, thus, from the code).

Currently the prototype enables the extraction of two types of models:

- Interactors models, which capture a more Human Computer Interaction perspective of the system. These models are more oriented towards usability analysis.
- Event-flow graphs which allow the analysis of the code's quality from a software engineering perspective.

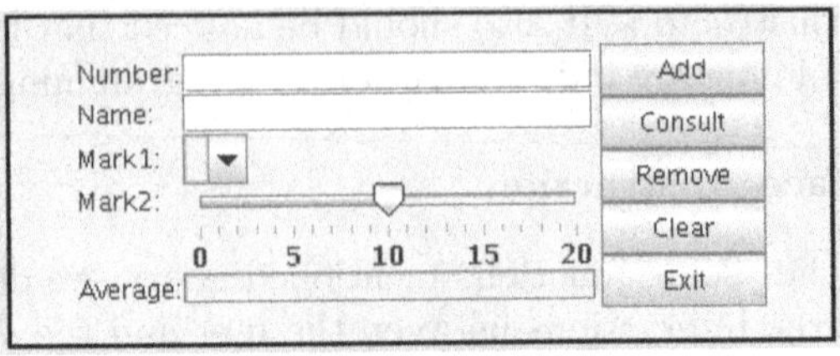

Fig. 3. *JClass* system

In the first case, applied to the code of the *JClass* application, the tool automatically generates an interactor specification including the initial application state and dynamic actions. This interactor contains a set of attributes:

```
interactor JClass
attributes
number, name: String
mark1, mark2, average: Integer
addEnabled, consultEnabled, removeEnabled, clearEnabled,
                                        exitEnabled: Boolean
```

one for each information input widget, and one for each button's enabled status. The names of the attributes are derived from the names of the widget variables in the code. Note that the `String` and `Integer` types must later be defined in the IVY editor.

The interactor also contains a set of actions:

```
actions
   add, open, close, consult, remove, clear, exit,
   setText_name(String), setSelectedItem_mark2(Integer),
   setValue_mark1(Integer), setValue_average(Integer),
   setText_number(Integer)
```

one for each button, and one for each input widget (representing user input). And, finally, a set of axioms:

```
[] number="" & name="" & mark1=10 & mark2=10 & average=0
[] addEnabled=true & clearEnabled=true & exitEnabled=true &
 consultEnabled=false & removeEnabled=false & number="" &
 name="" & mark1=10 & mark2=10 & average=0
[add] number'=number & name'=name & mark1'=mark1 &
 mark2'=mark2 & average'=average & consultEnabled'=true &
 removeEnabled'=true & addEnabled'=addEnabled &
 clearEnabled'=clearEnabled & exitEnabled'=exitEnabled
[consult] number'=number & name'=?ref1? & mark1'=?ref2? &
 mark2'=?ref3? & average'=?ref4? & addEnabled'=addEnabled &
 consultEnabled'=consultEnabled & removeEnabled'=removeEnabled &
 clearEnabled'=clearEnabled & exitEnabled'=exitEnabled
[remove] number'=number name'=name & mark1'=mark1 & mark2'=mark2 &
 average'=average & addEnabled'=addEnabled &
```

```
clearEnabled'=clearEnabled & exitEnabled'=exitEnabled
[clear] number'=?ref5? & name'=?ref6? & mark1'=?ref7? & mark2'=?ref8? &
average'=?ref9? & addEnabled'=addEnabled &
consultEnabled'=consultEnabled & removeEnabled'=removeEnabled &
clearEnabled'=clearEnabled & exitEnabled'=exitEnabled
[setText_name(a)] name'=a & number'=number & mark1'=mark1 & mark2'=mark2 &
average'=average & consultEnabled'=consultEnabled &
removeEnabled'=removeEnabled & addEnabled'=addEnabled &
clearEnabled'=clearEnabled & exitEnabled'=exitEnabled
...
```

The first two axioms define the initial state of the system. The next four define
the effect of the buttons in the interface. The ?refX? expressions represent values
that must be filled in using the IVY editor. To help complete the model, each
expression is a pointer to the Java code which constructs the value to be assign.
Remember that this is a semi-automated process. At least at this stage, we do
not want to go into the semantics of the application's functional layer. The final
axiom defines the effect of user input in the name text field. Similar axioms are
generated for all other set actions, for brevity we include only one here. We have
not included the rendering annotations in the interactor since all attributes and
actions are *visible* (i.e. they are all available to users).

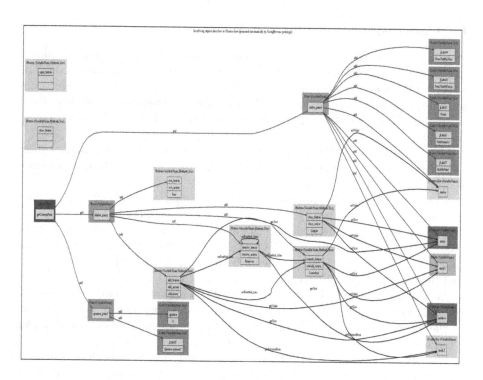

Fig. 4. *JClass* system's partial GUI event-flow graph

Even incomplete, this interactor already includes considerable information regarding the application's interactive behaviour. For example, the fourth axiom expresses the interactive state after executing the *consult* action. We can see that attributes *number, addEnabled, consultEnabled, removeEnabled, clearEnabled* and *exitEnabled* remain unchanged, and that attributes *name, mark1, mark2* and *average* receive new data. Once fully instantiated the model can be used in the IVY tool for verification of its behaviour.

Alternatively the prototype is also capable of generating the *JClass*'s partial event-flow graph (see figure 4). All widgets and their relationship are abstracted to this graph. As an example, blue nodes specify *JButtons* abstractions, arrows specify methods calls from one widget to another.

In this graph, we can see all graphical user interface widgets and their relationships. Through this particular example, we are able to detect all JCLASS's widgets (*JButtons, TextFields, ComboBoxs*, etc) and interactive methods called from these widgets (*setText, getText, getSelectedItem, setEnabled*, etc).

At the same time, the event-flow graph allows us to detect irrelevant widgets in the JCLASS system. In figure 4 these widgets are represented through two disconnected nodes. Basically the JCLASS code used to generate the graph contains two widgets which are not visualized nor manipulated by the system. These are the *open* and *close* nodes in the event-flow graph, which are related to the *open* and *close* actions in the interactor specification actions set.

6   Conclusions and Current Work

In this paper we have shown how strategic programming and slicing techniques can be combined to reverse engineer user interfaces from application code. The results of this work are encouraging and give evidence that the goal of reverse engineering user interfaces can be met. A prototype has been developed that allows us to obtain models of the user interface's structure and (partially) behaviour in an automatic manner.

Currently the tool automatically extracts the software's windows, and a subset of their widgets, properties, and values. The execution model of the user interface is obtained by using a classification of its events.

The approach has also proven very flexible. From the Abstract Syntax Tree representation we are already able to derive both interactor based models, and event flow graphs. In the first case the models capture a user oriented view of the interface. In the second case the models capture the internal structure of the code. This enables us to reason about both usability properties of the design, and the quality of the implementation of that design.

At the moment only a subset of all SWING widgets are being processed by the tool. Our objective has been to investigate the feasibility of the approach. In the future, we will extend our implementation to handle more complex user interfaces.

We will also explore broadening the scope of the approach, both at the input and output of the tool. In the first case we plan to experiment with different programming languages/toolkits, in order to make the approach as generic as possible. In the second case we want to further investigate the possibility of generating different types of models for analysis. For example, we envisage that generating Event Matrixes in the style of [26] will be possible.

Acknowledgments

This work is partially supported by FCT (Portugal) and FEDER (European Union) under contract POSC/EIA/56646/2004.

References

1. Tiago Alves and Joost Visser. Metrication of sdf grammars. Technical Report DI-PURe-05.05.01, Departamento de Informática, Universidade do Minho, 2005.
2. Ann Blandford, Richard Butterworth, and Paul Curzon. Models of interactive systems: a case study on programmable user modelling. *International Journal of Human-Computer Studies International Journal of Human-Computer Studies*, 60:149–200, 2004.
3. José C. Campos and Michael D. Harrison. Model checking interactor specifications. *Automated Software Engineering*, 8(3-4):275–310, August 2001.
4. José Creissac Campos. Using task knowledge to guide interactor specifications analysis. In J. A. Jorge, N. J. Nunes, and J. F. Cunha, editors, *Interactive Systems: Design, Specification and Verification — 10th International Workshop, DSV-IS 2003*, volume 2844 of *Lecture Notes in Computer Science*, pages 171–186. Springer, 2003.
5. J. Chen and S. Subramaniam. A gui environment for testing gui-based applications in java. *Proceedings of the 34th Hawaii International Conferences on System Sciences*, january 2001.
6. Bruno d'Ausbourg, Guy Durrieu, and Pierre Roché. Deriving a formal model of an interactive system from its UIL description in order to verify and to test its behaviour. In F. Bodart and J. Vanderdonckt, editors, *Design, Specification and Verification of Interactive Systems '96*, Springer Computer Science, pages 105–122. Springer-Verlag/Wien, June 1996.
7. D. J. Duke and M. D. Harrison. Abstract interaction objects. *Computer Graphics Forum 12(3), 25-36*, 1993.
8. D.J. Duke, P.J. Barnard, D.A. Duce, and J. May. Syndetic modelling. *Human-Computer Interaction*, 13(4):337–393, 1998.
9. Merlo E., Gagne P. Y., Girard J.F., Kontogiannis K., Hendren L.J., Panangaden P., and De Mori R. Reverse engineering and reengineering of user interfaces. *IEEE Software, 12(1), 64-73*, 1995.
10. B. Lientz e E. Swanson. *Software Maintenance Management*. Addison-wesley edition, 1980.
11. Dan Heller and Paula M. Ferguson. *Motif Programming Manual*, volume 6A of *X Window System Seris*. O'Reilly & Associates, Inc., second edition, 1994.
12. E. Hollnagel. *Human Reliability Analysis: Context and Control*. Academic press edition, 1993.
13. Simon Peyton Jones, John Hughes, Lennart Augustsson, et al. Report on the Programming Language Haskell 98. Technical report, February 1999.
14. R. Lammel and J. Visser. A STRAFUNSKI application letter. Technical report, CWI, Vrije Universiteit, Software Improvement Group, Kruislaan, Amsterdam, 2003.

15. Nancy Leveson. *Safeware: System Safety and Computers*. Addison-Wesley Publishing Company, Inc., 1995.
16. Clayton Lewis, Peter Polson, Cathleen Wharton, and John Rieman. Testing a walkthrough methodology for theory-based design of walk-up-and-use interfaces. In *CHI '90 Proceedings*, pages 235–242, New York, April 1990. ACM Press.
17. Andrea De Lucia. Program slicing: Methods and applications. *IEEE workshop on Source Code Analysis and Manipulation (SCAM 2001)*, 2001.
18. Kenneth L. McMillan. *Symbolic Model Checking*. Kluwer Academic Publishers, 1993.
19. Atif Memon, Ishan Banerjee, and Adithya Nagarajan. GUI ripping: Reverse engineering of graphical user interfaces for testing. Technical report, Department of Computer Science and Fraunhofer Center for Experimental Software Engineering, Department of Computer Science University of Maryland,USA, 2003.
20. M. M. Moore. Rule-based detection for reverse engineering user interfces. *Proceedings of the Third Working Conference on Reverse Engineering, pages 42-8, Monterey, CA*, november 1996.
21. Jakob Nielsen and Rolf Molich. Heuristic evaluation of user interfaces. In *CHI '90 Proceedings*, pages 249–256, New York, April 1990. ACM Press.
22. Fabio Paternò. *Model-Based Design and Evaluation of Interactive Applications*. Springer-Verlag, London, 2000.
23. John Rushby. Using model checking to help discover mode confusions and other automation surprises. *Reliability Engineering and System Safety*, 75(2):167–177, February 2002.
24. ISO/TC159 Sub-Commitee SC4. Draft International ISO DIS 9241-11 Standard. International Organization for Standardization, September 1994.
25. T. Systa. Dynamic reverse engineering of java software. Technical report, University of Tampere, Finland, 2001.
26. Harold Thimbleby. User interface design with matrix algebra. *ACM Transactions on HUman-Computer Interaction*, 11(2):181–236, June 2004.
27. Frank Tip. A survey of program slicing techniques. *Journal of Programming Languages*, september 1995.
28. Eelco Visser. Program transformation with Stratego/XT: Rules, strategies, tools, and systems in StrategoXT-0.9. In Lengauer et al., editors, *Domain-Specific Program Generation*, Lecture Notes in Computer Science. Spinger-Verlag, November 2003. (Draft; Accepted for publication).
29. Joost Visser. *Generic Traversal over Typed Source Code Representations*. PhD thesis, University of Amsterdam, February 2003.

An Ontological Approach to Visualization Resource Management

Richard Potter and Helen Wright

Department of Computer Science, The University of Hull, Hull, UK
R.Potter@dcs.hull.ac.uk,
H.Wright@hull.ac.uk

Abstract. The desire for increasingly intuitive and immersive visualization systems has created a need for diverse resources that support the human-computer interface. Visualization laboratories have growing sets of these specialised resources and managing them has become a complicated and lengthy task. Choosing and utilising resources in a given visualization requires extensive information about each to be available. This paper presents an ontological approach to the description of resources, their capabilities, and their software interfaces. Using this ontology, a software design for the support of resource detection, choice and utilisation is presented. By breaking the dependency of visualizations on specific resources, adaptability and portability is improved.

Keywords: Visualization, Ontology, Hardware Abstraction, HCI.

1 Introduction

As available visualization hardware diversifies, support of the human-computer interface becomes increasingly important. Indeed, resources and the users' interactions with them have been identified by Brodlie et al [1] as two of five key responsibilities of an ideal visual supercomputing infrastructure. Using a taxonomic approach to manage input devices was suggested when visualization was still in its infancy (see for example [2]). Since that time the number and variety of devices has continued to grow, whilst many that were considered by [2] and at the time were rare have become ubiquitous. Visualization, too, has matured. Recent work has highlighted the benefits of an ontological approach to visualization description [3, 4]; in particular [4] notes the superior ability of an ontology to convey a pre-agreed meaning (compared with taxonomy and terminology), which in turn renders it processable by machine. Formal (machine-readable) specification of ontologies is now available via a number of standards, the most recent of which is the web ontology language (OWL) provided by the World Wide Web Consortium (W3C) [5]; these standards enable semantic reasoning over the ontology. This paper proposes a novel approach to managing diverse visualization hardware by linking these two threads, that is, device description and ontology.

G. Doherty and A. Blandford (Eds.): DSVIS 2006, LNCS 4323, pp. 151–156, 2007.
© Springer-Verlag Berlin Heidelberg 2007

2   A Resource Description Ontology

Our aim is to be able to choose resources dynamically and integrate them into a visualization as they become available. We thus describe the ontology as comprising a number of inter-referenced taxonomies dealing with visualization hardware and their software interfaces.

Individual resources are identified in the hardware taxonomy and grouped under headings such as data-glove, mouse, monitor, joystick, etc. A resource's capabilities are described using two further taxonomies. One describes the user actions which can be detected by the resource, such as vocal action or movement action. The other taxonomy describes the sensory experience that the resource stimulates in the user, grouped according to the sense which is stimulated. For example, joysticks are moved by the user, which is classed as a movement action; some also have a force feedback component which is classed as a tactile sensory experience. These capabilities can be thought of as the resource's inputs and outputs. A computer monitor, by contrast, supports no user action but its output stimulates their visual sense.

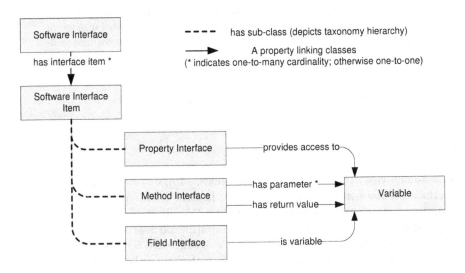

Fig. 1. A depiction of the links between the software interface, software interface item, and variable taxonomies, used to describe software interfaces

Available software interfaces, such as APIs and device drivers, are listed in the software interface taxonomy; the operations and values they make available are described in the taxonomy of software interface items and are grouped as properties, method calls, and fields (fig. 1). Each software interface item has an associated variable of a known type, for example, the '5DT data-glove driver version 1.02' provides a method call called 'fdGetSensorRaw' which returns a floating point value. Variables are described as enumerations, conditional variables or value fields. Enumerations are numeric values which represent members of a finite set of related objects, e.g. a set of hand gestures. A conditional variable is used when the result of an operation is dependent on another variable, usually included as a parameter to a method. The description of a conditional variable will include references to the possible values that may be returned and a reference to the value on which it is dependent. A value represents any other operation result where there is an associated data type. Finally, the ontology refers back to the interaction and sensory experience taxonomies to describe the meaning and purpose of the variables; this can be seen in fig. 2.

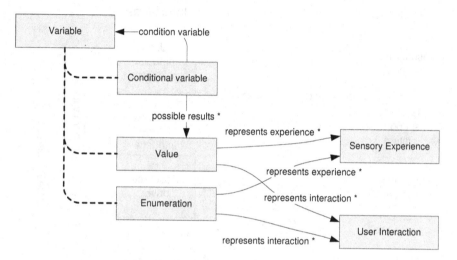

Fig. 2. A depiction of the links within the variable taxonomy, and between this and the interaction and sensory experience taxonomies

3   Software Support for the Management of Visualization Resources

Having developed a machine readable framework for the description of resources, software support for the management and utilisation of resources can be provided. This can be considered in three parts: the detection and description of available resources, choosing appropriate resources for a given visualization, and integrating the visualization and chosen resources.

The detection of resources and population of the description ontology can, to some extent, be automated through queries to the operating system. Standards such as the Human Interface Description (HID) framework [6] provide some information regarding a device's interaction with users. Additional information must be entered manually; community maintenance of the ontology would reduce this effort.

Wright et al [7] describe the factors associated with choosing the right resource for a given visualization. The ontological approach taken by this project allows semantic reasoning to be employed to match requests for information (made by the visualization system) to appropriate resources. This support mechanism for choosing resources has the advantage of decoupling the visualization system from the hardware. Interactions between these are facilitated by a proposed architecture which uses the factory design pattern [8] to create a dynamic interface component, as shown in fig. 3.

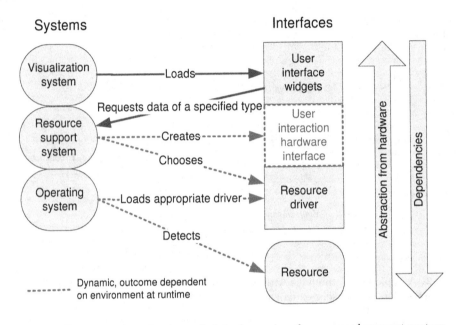

Fig. 3. The generation of a dynamic interface using the proposed support system

A further abstraction of the visualization from the hardware can be achieved through an adaptation of the work on direct image interaction for computational steering by Chatzinikos and Wright [9]. This work involved embedding graphical user interaction components, or 'widgets', into the rendered output of a visualization to enable contextual user interaction. These components can be adapted to make the necessary calls to the proposed system, completely separating it from the visualization. Again, this can be seen in fig. 3.

4   Conclusions and Future Work

This paper has presented an ontology for the formal description of human-computer interface resources and proposed a system to abstract visualizations from these resources using the ontology. Prior work to abstract user interfaces from core application functionality exists in the software engineering field (for example [10, 11]) but the application of semantic technologies to visualization is unique. Also unique is the equal weight given by the ontology to both aspects of human-computer interfaces, that is, users' actions and the experiences that are delivered to them. This contrasts with current work in the field such as [12] which focuses on the management of output hardware and [13] which focuses on input. Completion of this work will provide a framework for direct image interaction for computational steering, which adapts to and utilises the diverse set of available resources.

The current focus of this project is to automate population of the ontology using software-based data gathering and inference tools. The importance of this requirement was highlighted whilst manually entering a description for the '5DT Data-glove 16'. This was a lengthly process exacerbated, firstly, by a lack of relevant documentation (though it was the most comprehensively documented device trialled) and, secondly, by difficulties extracting information from software manually. Automation does however lead to a trade-off regarding the completeness of resource description. Limiting descriptions to the information which is machine-extractable reduces the input burden on users but restricts the information available for choosing appropriate devices. For example, the footprint of a device [2] (i.e. space on the user's desk) may be an important factor to the user but this detail is unlikely to be available for automatic extraction.

Implementation of the proposed support system will be tested using two case studies. One is a software simulation of parasite infrapopulation dynamics on live hosts. This study will test the system on a bespoke visualization based on a complex scientific model. The other is an extension of the Resource Aware Visualization Environment (RAVE) project [12] to support input devices as well as output.

There are two foreseeable factors which will influence the effectiveness of the support system. Firstly, visualizations are often required to respond to data and events in real-time; the computations of the support system may affect this. Secondly, the proposed abstractions will influence the design of visualization widgets [9] and, whilst it is hoped that the system will simplify widget design, the possible ramifications must be explored.

Acknowledgements. This work was partially funded by the Department of Computer Science at the University of Hull. The authors would like to thank James Ward, Dr James Osborne and Prof Roger Phillips of the Department of Computer Science at the University of Hull for their role in supporting this project and for numerous useful discussions. We are grateful to Dr Cock van Oosterhout of the Department of Biological Sciences at the University of Hull and Dr Joanne Cable of the University of Cardiff for proposing the host-parasite dynamics case study. This has been used to generate the requirements for this project and its conversion to a steered application was supported by the Hull Environmental Research Institute. Thanks also to Dr Ian Grimstead, University of Cardiff, for his support regarding the RAVE project.

References

1. Brodlie, K., Brooke, J., Chen, M., Chisnall, D., Fewings, A., Hughes, C., John, N., Jones, M., Riding, M., Roard, N.: Visual Supercomputing: Technologies, Applications and Challenges. In: Computer Graphics Forum, Vol. 24(2). Eurographics (2005) 217–245
2. Card, S., Mackinlay, J., Robertson, G.: The design space of input devices. In: CHI'90, Proceedings of the SIGCHI conference on human factors in computing systems. ACM Press, New York, NY, USA (1990) 117–124
3. Duke, D., Brodlie, K., Duce, D.: Building an Ontology of Visualization. In: VIS'04, Proceedings of the conference on Visualization. IEEE Computer Society, Washington, DC, USA (2004) 598–607
4. Duke, D., Brodlie, K., Duce, D., Herman, I.: Do You See What I Mean? In: IEEE Computer Graphics and Applications, Vol. 25(3). IEEE Computer Society Press, Los Alamitos, CA, USA (2005) 6–9
5. Bechhofer, S., van Harmelen, F., Hendler, J., Horrocks, I., McGuinness, D., Patel-Schneider, P., Stein, L.: OWL Web Ontology Language Reference. W3C, http://www.w3.org/TR/owl-ref (2004)
6. USB Implementers' Forum: Universal Serial Bus (USB) Device Class Definition for Human Interface Devices (HID). Usb.org, http://www.usb.org/developers/devclass_docs/HID1_11.pdf (2005)
7. Wright, H., Chatzinikos, F., Osborne, J.: Visualization: Choosing the Right Tool for the Right Job. In: Cox, S. (ed.): AHM03, Proceedings of 2nd UK e-Science All Hands Meeting. Nottingham, UK (2003) 318-321
8. Gamma, E., Helm, R., Johnson, R., Vlissides, J.: Design Patterns: Elements of Reusable Object-Oriented Software. Professional Computing Series, Addison Wesley (1995)
9. Chatzinikos, F., Wright, H.: Enabling Multi-Purpose Image Interaction in Modular Visualization Environments. In: Erbacher, R., Chen, P., Roberts, J., Groehn, M, Borner, K. (eds.): VDA'03, Proceedings of SPIE Visualization and Data Analysis. (2003)
10. Bodart, F., Hennebert, A., Leheureux, J., Provot I., Sacr, B., Vanderdonckt, J.: Towards a Systematic Building of Software Architecture: the TRIDENT Methodological Guide. In: Bastide, R., Palanque, Ph. (eds.): DSV-IS'95, Eurographics Workshop on Design, Specification, Verification of Interactive Systems. Eurographics (1995) 237–253
11. Singh, G., Green, M.: Automating the Lexical and Syntactic Design of Graphical User Interfaces: The UofA* UIMS. In: ACM Transactions on Graphics, Vol. 10(3). (1991) 213–254
12. Grimstead, I., Avis, N., Walker, D.: RAVE: Resource-Aware Visualization Environment. In: Cox, S. (ed.): UK e-Science All Hands Meeting 2004. Nottingham, UK (2004)
13. Buxton, W.: A three-state model of graphical input. In: INTERACT '90, Proceedings of the IFIP TC13 Third International Conference on Human-Computer Interaction. North-Holland (1990) 449–456

Visual Design of User Interfaces by (De)composition

Sophie Lepreux[1,2], Jean Vanderdonckt[1], and Benjamin Michotte[1]

[1] IAG/ISYS, Université catholique de Louvain, Place des Doyens 1,
B–1348 Louvain-la-Neuve (Belgium)
[2] LAMIH – UMR CNRS 8530, Université de Valenciennes et du Hainaut-Cambrésis,
Le Mont-Houy, F-59313 Valenciennes Cedex 9 (France)
{lepreux, vanderdonckt, michotte}@isys.ucl.ac.be,
sophie.lepreux@univ-valenciennes.fr

Abstract. Most existing graphical user interfaces are usually designed for a fixed context of use, thus making them rather difficult to modify for other contexts of use, such as for other users, other platforms, and other environments. This paper addresses this problem by introducing a new visual design method for graphical users interfaces referred to as "visual design by (de)composition". In this method, any individual or composite component of a graphical user interface is submitted to a series of operations for composing a new interface from existing components and for decomposing an existing one into smaller pieces that can be used in turn for another interface. For this purpose, any component of a user interface is described by specifications that are consistently written in a user interface description language that remains hidden to the designers' eyes. We first define the composition and decomposition operations and individually exemplify them on some small examples. We then demonstrate how they can be used to visually design new interfaces for a real-world case study where variations of the context of use induce frequent recomposition of user interfaces. Finally, we describe how the operations are implemented in a dedicated interface builder supporting the aforementioned method.

1 Introduction

In most commercial interface builders (e.g., Macromedia DreamWeaver, Microsoft Visual Studio) and research interface editors (e.g., Glade, TrollTech), the predominant method for visually building a Graphical User Interface (GUI) consists of dragging widgets from a palette, dropping them on a working area, and editing their properties until the results are satisfactory. This method makes sense since the GUI is visual by nature and direct manipulation of constituting widgets remains natural, flexible, and modifiable [1,2]. However, when it comes to reusing parts or whole of an existing GUI to design another one, most interface builders force the designer to produce an incessant sequence of "copy/paste" operations, if supported, with little or no support for recomposing a new GUI from these elements. In particular, the designer should copy widgets one by one and perform relayouting operations (e.g., resizing, realignment, rearrangement) individually. This situation frequently occurs when an

G. Doherty and A. Blandford (Eds.): DSVIS 2006, LNCS 4323, pp. 157–170, 2007.

existing GUI needs to be adapted for a new context of use, which the GUI was not designed or thought for. If the context of use is considered as the combination of a user (or a user stereotype) working on a given computing platform in a specific environment [3], any variation of one or many of these aspects may lead to a GUI redesign. In the case of multi-platform GUIs [4,5,6], it is impossible to copy/paste GUI elements from one interface builder to another one, unless the interface builder is itself multi-platform. Even in that case, little or no support is provided for reforming a new GUI from fragments coming from existing GUIs. In the case of multi-language GUIs, existing tools prevent designers from just translating the resources in one language and obtain a new GUI for another language.

On the method side, reusability of existing GUIs is often promoted as a desirable method for ensuring consistency, reducing development effort, fitting a particular GUI to the purpose of a given task. In particular, users frequently report that they need to constantly switch from one application to another to fulfill a given task when it was not possible to re-assemble existing components of existing GUIs to form a new one. Again, little or no methodological guidance exists in current development methods to help designers reusing parts or whole of their design to initiate a new development process.

This paper addresses the lack of support for reusing existing developments of GUIs by introducing a visual design method based on three concepts: *decomposition* disassembles an existing GUIs into individual or composite elements that can be further reused for other designs; *composition* assembles individual and composite elements to form a new GUI that fits the purpose of a given task; *recomposition* performs a suite of decompositions and compositions to support re-design of existing GUIs for new contexts of use.

Various simplified forms of decomposition and composition already exist as reported in Section 2 devoted to the state of the art, but we are not aware of any integrated method that is intended to support reusability at a high level of design that does not force people to constantly apply physical and lexical operations. Section 3 presents a reference framework that will be extensively used in the rest of the paper: any GUI will be described in the terms defined by this framework to maintain editable specifications of the GUI of interest. Section 4 defines a series of operators for decomposition and composition: each operator is logically defined, explained, motivated and exemplified with a simple example. Section 5 validates the method by applying these operators on a real-world case study in an interface builder implemented for this purpose. Section 6 concludes the paper by reporting on the main advantages and shortcomings of the work and suggesting some avenues for future work.

2   Related Work

Due to the nature of our problem, the following state of the art is decomposed into two categories: decomposition and composition.

Decomposition. The Covigo library (http://www.covigo.com) supports a simple form of decomposition called *pagination*, where a web page is decomposed into smaller pieces to be used on a smaller screen: special tags are inserted in a HTML web page at run-time to decompose it into smaller pieces. Simple heuristics such as breaking every fifth <tr> or breaking by size are used. Here, the pagination is fully automated, with the attendant risk that it does not break the UI logically. On the other hand, RIML [7] supports manual pagination, thus leaving the decomposition quality under the designer's control and responsibility: it defines additional mark-up for specifying the layout and pagination capabilities of web pages that are then rendered through a dedicated Web adaptation engine. Watters and Zhang [8] segment HTML forms into a sequence of smaller forms, using partition indicators such as horizontal lines, nested lists and tables. Complex layout relationships (e.g., use of tables for layout purpose) probably constitute a bottleneck for such approaches.

To overcome the language restriction, another group of approaches relies on a generic GUI description in a User Interface Description Language (UIDL) that is at a higher level than the markup and programming languages. Major UIDLs such as UIML [4], SunML [9], XIML [10] support decomposition as their UI description can be split into logically related chunks. Again, the designer is responsible for this operation without any support. Göbel et al. [6] describe web-based dialogs in a device-independent way through "DLL dialog", which is a composition of containers and elements. Containers whose elements must appear together are called atomic. Elements are assigned weights indicating their resource requirements in terms of memory and screen size. Fragments with similar weights are generated, while respecting the integrity of atomic containers. Navigation elements are added to permit navigation between dialog fragments. No indication is given on how weights should be assigned to leaf elements, which is a difficult task, especially for multiplatform rendering. Ye & Herbert [11] apply similar heuristics for decomposing a XUL UI description by relying on the hierarchy of widgets and containers, while respecting the value of a 'breakable' attribute attached to each component, which has to be explicitly provided by the designer. PIMA [12] also relies on a UIDL, which is converted into multiple device-specific representations, including a decomposition process. Like other approaches, PIMA's algorithm uses grouping constraints as well as information on size constraints. MORALE [13] is a suite of tools for assembling GUIs with their associated definitions, but all (de)composition operations are restricted to cut/-copy/paste primitives.

While the aforementioned decomposition methods mostly work on a hierarchy of GUI widgets, ROAM [5] consider a tree structure combining a task hierarchy and a layout structure. The tree nodes are annotated as splittable or unsplittable depending on the decomposition possibilities. ROAM's does not really decomposes an existing GUI as it merely moves the extra widgets that do not fit onto a new GUI. Graceful degradation [14] addresses the decomposition problem, but only for the purpose of obtaining GUIs for more constrained platforms, one dimension of the context of use, but not the only one. AUIT [15] automatically generate code generation for JSP and servlet implementations depending on parameters from any platform/user/task combination. A set of XSLT transformation scripts convert the XML-encoded logical screen design into several GUIs.

Composition. Several environments attempt to compose a new GUI by assembling fragments coming from the same or different GUIs. They only differ by the level where the composition is performed. Scalable Fabric [16] is a smart environment where documents associated with interactive applications are grouped depending on their semantic relationships in the user's task. Haystack [17] is a platform for personalizing information spaces and applications for a particular user depending on her tasks. WinCuts [18] recompose GUIs by duplicating parts or whole of a GUI into a new one that corresponds to the users' task. Similarly, Composable UIs [19] define viewports on GUIs to form a new UI by putting the viewports side by side. A detachable UI [20] is a GUI portion that can migrate from one computing platform to another one with re-assembling on the target.

In summary, we observed that major approaches for (de)composition are often language- or platform-dependent to some extend, do not identify independent high-level design primitives for recomposition, are usually supported at the physical level (e.g., as in [18,19,20]) or the application level without any flexibility, are typically considering decomposition merely for screen constraints or multi-platform support. Little or no methodological guidance is provided for this purpose, although it is identified as a major design activity [1,2]. We are not aware of any research that provides a systematic set of (de)composition primitives applicable to any GUI.

3   Reference Framework

To allow high-level design operations on any GUI, we should rely on a high level description of the initial user interface. This description will be expressed in the UsiXML (User Interface eXtensible Markup Language – http://www.usixml.org [21]) UIDL. The principles set out below are, however, generally applicable to any UIDL such as UIML [4], SunML [9] or XIML [10]. UsiXML is structured according to the four abstraction levels of the 'CAMELEON reference framework' [3] for multi-target UIs (Fig. 1).

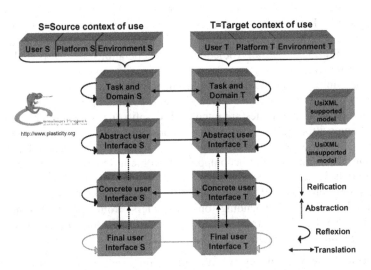

Fig. 1. The four abstraction levels used in the framework

A *Final User Interface* (FUI) refers to an actual UI rendered either by interpretation (e.g., HTML) or by code compilation (e.g., Java). A *Concrete User Interface* (CUI) abstracts a FUI into a description independent of any programming or markup language in terms of Concrete Interaction Objects, layout, navigation, and behavior. An *Abstract User Interface* (AUI) abstracts a CUI into a definition that is independent of any interaction modality (such as graphical, vocal or tactile). An AUI is populated by *abstract components* and *abstract containers*. Abstract components are composed of facets describing the type of interactive tasks they are able to support (i.e., input, output, control, navigation). The *Tasks & Concepts* level describes the interactive system specifications in terms of the user tasks to be carried out and the domain objects of these tasks. As (de)composition operations will be defined independently of any context of use (including the computing platform), the CUI level is the best candidate for a formal definition. Therefore, this level is more detailed in the subsequent paragraphs.

A CUI may be obtained by forward engineering from the T&C level, the AUI level or directly. A CUI is assumed to be described without any reference to any particular computing platform or toolkit of that platform [21]. For this purpose, a CUI model consists of a hierarchical decomposition of CIOs. A *Concrete Interaction Object* (CIO) is defined as any UI entity that users can perceive such as text, image, animation and/or manipulate such as a push button, a list box, or a check box. A CIO is characterized by attributes such as, but not limited to [21]: *id, name, icon, content, defaultContent, defaultValue.*

4   (De)composition Operations

In this section, (de)composition operations are first defined based on the UsiXML concepts of a Concrete User Interface. Since the UI is represented in UsiXML terms and since it is a XML-compliant language, operations could be defined thanks to tree algebra, with which operations could be logically defined on the XML tree and directly performed. El-bekaï et al. defined a set of operators to comparison (similarity, equivalence and subsumption) and others operators adapted to database [22]. We adapt their notation presented in the next part to decomposition and composition goal in the second part. Then, an implementation is described of a tool that supports a method based on these operations.

4.1   Relation Between UsiXML, XML and Tree Algebra

Since each GUI is described in UsiXML terms as a Concrete User Interface as indicated in the previous section, each GUI is internally represented as a tree of XML elements.

Thus, the correspondence proposed by [22] gives that the basic elements of a UsiXML UI, i.e. a XML tree, could be defined logically:

- XML document → Tree (T)
- Element → Root node (R), parent (P), child (C) node
- Leaf → child (C) node, atomic (A) values

Fig. 2 shows the relationships between a GUI (top left), its UsiXML specifications (top right) and its internal structure as a XML tree in order to perform the operations.

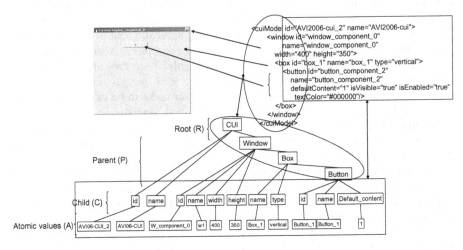

Fig. 2. An UI, its UsiXML and its tree representation

4.2 Presentation of the Operators

A first part presents a few operators associated to the decomposition, whereas a second part presents a few operators linked with the composition.

4.2.1 Operators Supporting Decomposition
This part defines two basic operators working on the internal structure of the UsiXML specifications. Other operators such as *Cut, Projection, and Complementary* are defined with the same principle but are not presented here.

Selection

$$\sigma(T)(E) \rightarrow T$$

Pre : let T a tree and *E* an Expression

$$T_2(R) = T_1(R)|E(R) = true \tag{1}$$

Post : $\sigma(T_1)(E) = T_2$ $T_2(P) = T_1(P)|E(P) = true$

$$T_2(C) = T_1(C)|E(C) = true$$

The *Selection* operator which works upon tree and an expression is defined in (1). This operator aims at keeping the node which corresponds to the expression. For example, Fig. 3 apply the expression E={output} to an UI and its result. The resulting UI is the same as in the input UI with only the "output" elements.

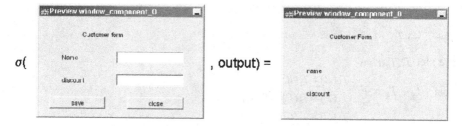

Fig. 3. Example of the selection operator

Intersection

$$T \cap T \to T$$

Pre : let $T_1, T_2 trees$

$$T_3(R) = T_1(R) \tag{2}$$
$$\text{Post}: T_1 \cap T_2 = T_3 \quad T_3(P) = T_1(P) + T_2(P) - 2(T_1T_2(P))$$
$$T_3(C) = T_1(C) + T_2(C) - 2(T_1T_2(C))$$

The intersection operator is defined in (2). It is a binary operator; it takes two trees as input. The output is new XML data containing elements, root node, parent nodes and child nodes which are in one of two trees data model. The intersection operator applied on two similar interfaces will give the interface shown in Fig. 4.

In this algorithm, the different elements are compared. We have stated that two elements are identical or similar if they have the same type (i.e. button), the same name in one language (i.e. save) and all the required attributes. As the size and the color are optional arguments, we consider that they can be different. In this case the resulting button keeps only the options which are identical in the two tested button.

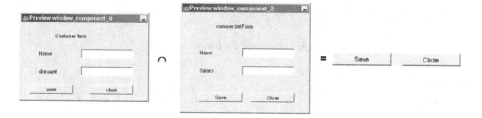

Fig. 4. Example of the intersection operator

4.2.2 Operators Supporting Composition

This part defines two basic operators on the internal structure of the UsiXML specifications. Other operators, such as "Difference" operator are defined with the same principle but are not presented here. This difference operator takes two trees as input and gives a tree as output. The output tree is the very first input tree without the elements which are included in the two input trees.

Fusion

$$T + T \rightarrow T$$

Pre : let T_1, T_2 *trees*   (3)

$$\text{Post :} \quad T_1 + T_2 = T_3 \quad \begin{array}{l} T_3(R) = T_1(R) \\ T_3(P) = T_1(P) + T_2(P) \\ T_3(C) = T_1(C) + T_2(C) \end{array}$$

The fusion operator is defined in (3). It is a binary operator; it takes two trees as input. The output is new XML data containing elements, root node, parent nodes and child nodes which are in the two trees data model. The fusion operator applied on two interfaces, following the algorithm 1, will give the interface shown in Fig. 5.

```
%algorithm1: The two trees T1 and T2 are merge at the %level
R+1 to form the T3 window.

IF (direction = vertical)
Then        Add box (vertical B')
            %Modify the window size:
               T3.height = T1.height + T2.height
               T3.width = T1.width

IF (direction = horizontal)
Then        Add box (horizontal B').
            %Modify the window size:
               T3.height = T1.height
               T3.width = T1.width + T2.width

Add T1(R+1) in box B', Add T2(R+1) in box B'.
```

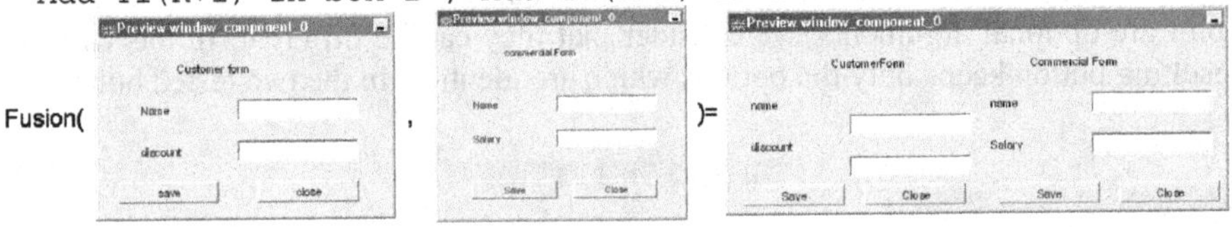

Fig. 5. Example of the fusion operator

Union

$$T \cup T \rightarrow T$$

Pre : let T_1, T_2 *trees*   (4)

$$\text{Post :} \quad T_1 \cup T_2 = T_3 \quad \begin{array}{l} T_3(R) = T_1(R) \\ T_3(P) = T_1(P) + T_2(P) - (T_1 T_2(P)) \\ T_3(C) = T_1(C) + T_2(C) - (T_1 T_2(C)) \end{array}$$

The output of the union operator consists of new XML data containing elements, root node, parent nodes and child nodes in the two input trees data model without the duplication of any elements such root nodes, parent nodes and child nodes. The union is disjoint: duplicates are purged. This operator is defined in (4). To illustrate this operator, one example of result is shown in Fig. 6. However, if the two "name" elements are considered as identical then the result could be different. Since the duplicates are purged, the Area text associated to the name which is present in the same structure and content in the two input interfaces will be purged in the output user interface. The result is presented Fig. 7(a). The Union operator does not take into account the place of the element in the interfaces so the result can be as shown in Fig. 7(b). In this case, we could consider some of the operators as 'presentation-independent', that is they are not sensible to physical aspects of the GUI such as position, size, arrangement, colors, fonts, style. However, if such a need arises, it is still possible to incorporate these constraints as conditions.

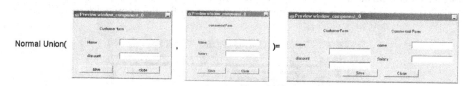

Fig. 6. An example of expected user interfaces from union of the two user interfaces

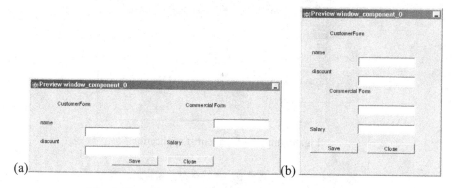

Fig. 7. The other results expected from the Union operator

4.3 Implementation

Some of the above operations have been directly implemented in GrafiXML, a graphical interface builder that automatically generates UsiXML specifications as opposed to final code for other builders. GrafiXML has been implemented in Java 5.0 and today consists of more than 90,000 lines of Java code. It can be freely downloaded from http://www.usixml.org as it is an open source project regulated by Apache 2.0 open licence and available on SourceForge. GrafiXML is able to automatically generate code of a UI specified in UsiXML into (X)HTML or Java. For the purpose of the examples below, we will rely on the Java automated code generation.

5 Case Studies

The operators defined here above can be used in two cases. At the *design time,* they can be used by the designers to create the user interfaces. For example, the user interfaces which are built to one application or to a set of applications of the firm have to respect a graphic charter. With the operator, the designer can reuse some of the elements of the user interfaces. This is already illustrated by the examples associated to the operators. This case is not presented here but is presented in [23]. The second case of use is at *run time*. It is integrated in the reuse issue which has introduced the component idea. The first issue in this domain is the composition of the components. If we consider the business component as a component with user interfaces, one issue in the domain of HCI is to compose the user interfaces of the business components. The using of business components and of their user interfaces brings to the user interfaces composition issue. If we consider that the user interfaces are specified with UsiXML, the union operator is particularly interesting for the composition.

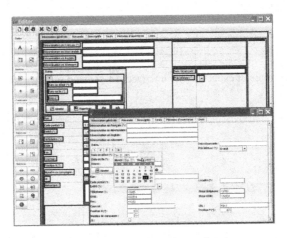

Fig. 8. Initial UI for a tourist application

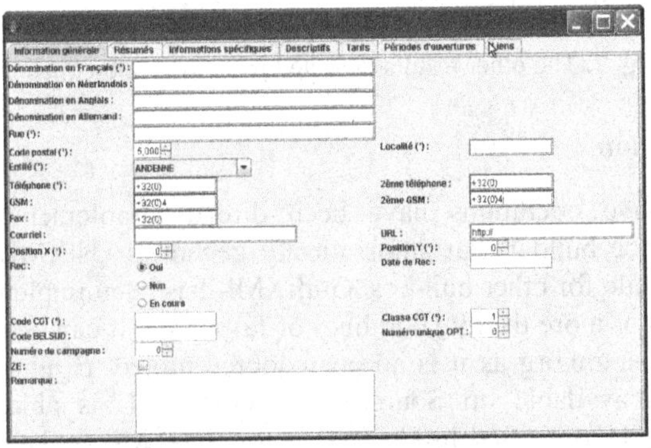

Fig. 9. Initial UI for an event management application

Let us now consider another case study taken in the domain of tourism. In this domain, it happens frequently that some parts of the same information should be reproduced in different UI for different events (e.g., hotel information, tourist trip including hotel booking, booking a hotel, etc.). Fig. 8 reproduces a screenshot of a Concrete User Interface edited in the editor and its preview in Java (obtained by Java automated code generation). This view is particularly appreciated by designers and developers (and even end users) as it combines the design view and the final view, which is pretty close to the UI as the end user will see. In order to define a precise layout, a matrix of lines and guides could be defined to align objects in lines and columns.

Fig. 9 reproduces another UI for an event management application, also taken in the same domain. The two UIs only differ from a few fields, here the dates of the events in Fig. 8 and the comment in Fig. 9. Therefore, if we want to identify the common part of these two UIs, the intersection operator performs the operation, as defined previously, to identify common parts of both trees and then rebuilds a new tree with the identified elements. This operator re-generates new UsiXML specifications. This intersection is reproduced in Fig. 10. Note in Fig. 10 that the designer did not need to do anything: all common elements were identified, a new layout was produced so as to mimic the initial one and all objects have been laid out and aligned to preserve the initial constraints. Therefore, there was no need to re-position, re-align, or re-arrange the widgets.

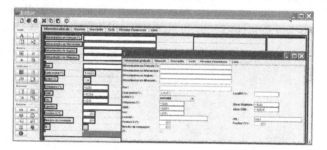

Fig. 10. Intersection of UIs found in Fig. 10 and 11

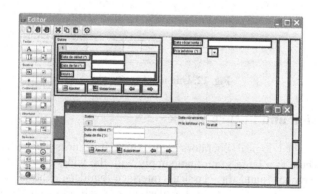

Fig. 11. Difference between Fig. 10 and 11

Similarly, Fig. 11 illustrates the application of the difference operator, in this case Fig. 8 – Fig. 9. Therefore, Fig. 11 only contains those widgets of Fig. 8 that are not present in Fig. 9. Again, these widgets are identified and re-laid out so as to form an entirely new UI that is ready to test with the end user. Note that it is even possible to define new operators or composition of individual operators. As soon as this intersection is identified, it is possible to submit again this intersection to any other operation (here, a sequence of global copy/paste) so as to define a new operator by composition. The composition of UI operators is inspired from the macro-commands from the domain of command languages where several individual commands applied to some objects could be grouped together into a macro-command. In this way, the designer is able to define her/his own combination of operators and repetitions on demand. At any time, each operator works on the underlying UI model expressed in UsiXML. Without this characteristic, it would have been almost impossible to program these operators in a classical interface builder where all widgets are physically defined. Instead, they are here logically defined, thus allowing logical operations. At any time, the code of the final UI can be produced.

The last example showed Fig. 12 concerns the (vertical) union operator. This operator allows composing two interfaces without repetition. In this case, two parts of information are repeated, the designation and the piece of information. These common parts are viewed in the Fig. 10 which presents the intersection. So these elements are not duplicated by the union operator. All the elements are placed with the respect of the initials UIs. In this case, if the fusion operator is used, then all the elements of each interface are laid-out. The common elements will be presented twice.

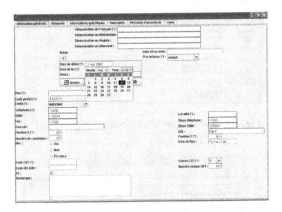

Fig. 12. Union of Fig. 8 and 9

6   Conclusion and Future Work

We have described logical operators with which it is possible to manipulate UI portions or whole at a large grain than simply with the widget level that is the most common technique found in classical interface builders. Therefore, instead of manipulating one widget at time for designing a UI (an activity that is time consuming and tedious), it is possible to manipulate UI fragments as such. Then, and only then, cut/copy/paste operations could be applied. The main difference is that these operations are logically applied as opposed to a physical application where all individual widgets need to be re-positioned, re-sized, and re-arranged. Re-positioning, re-sizing, and re-arrangement are the most frequently executed operations in interface builders, consequently to redesigning a UI or reusing a previously designed UI. This situation also often occurs when UI templates are used.

The operators which have been introduced are logically defined based on the tree algebra and adapted to the domain of user interfaces. These operators were described with an example and more developed in the case study. Using of the operators from the tree algebra is appropriate because the user interfaces are specified in UsiXML and because the XML documents can be processed like trees.

Acknowledgments

We gratefully thank the support from the SIMILAR network of excellence (The European research taskforce creating human-machine interfaces SIMILAR to human-human communication), supported by the 6th Framework Program of the European Commission, under contract FP6-IST1-2003-507609 (http://www.similar.cc). The authors thank also the Nord-Pas de Calais regional authority (Projects MIAOU and EUCUE) and the FEDER (Fonds Européen de Développement Régional, European Fund for Regional Development) for supporting a part of this work.

References

1. Brown, J.: Exploring Human-Computer Interaction and Software Engineering Methodologies for Creation of Interactive Software. SIGCHI Bulletin 29, 1 (1997) 32–35
2. Morch, A.: Tailoring tools for system development. Journal of End User Computing 10, 2 (1998) 22–29
3. Calvary, G., Coutaz, J., Thevenin, D., Limbourg, Q., Bouillon, L., Vanderdonckt, J.: A Unifying Reference Framework for Multi-Target User Interfaces. Interacting with Computer 15, 3 (2003) 289–308
4. Ali M.F., Pérez-Quiñones M.A., Abrams M.: Building Multi-Platform User Interfaces with UIML. In: Seffah, A., Javahery, H. (eds.): Multiple User Interfaces: Engineering and Application Framework. John Wiley, Chichester (2004) 95–118
5. Chu, H., Song, H., Wong, C., Kurakake, S., Katagiri, M.: Roam, a Seamless Application Framework. Journal of System and Software 69, 3 (2004) 209–226
6. Göbel, S., Buchholz, S., Ziegert, T., Schill, A.: Device Independent Representation of Web-based Dialogs and Contents. In Proc. of IEEE Youth Forum in Computer Science and Engineering YUFORIC'01 (Valencia, November 2001). IEEE Computer Society Press, Los Alamitos (2001)
7. Spriestersbach, A., Ziegert, T., Grassel, G., Wasmund, M., Dermler, G.: Flexible Pagination and Layouting for Device Independent Authoring. In Proc. of WWW'2003 Workshop on Emerging Applications for Wireless and Mobile Access (2003)
8. Watters, C., Zhang, R.: PDA Access to Internet Content: Focus on Forms. In Proc. of the 36th Annual Hawaii Int. Conf. on System Sciences HICSS'03 (Big Island, January 2003). IEEE Computer Society Press, Los Alamitos (2003) 105–113
9. Dery-Pinna, A.-M., Fierstone, J., Picard, E.: Component Model and Programming: a First Step to Manage Human-Computer Interaction Adaptation. In Proc. of 5th Int. Symposium on Human-Computer Interaction with Mobile Devices and Services MobileHCI'2003 (Udine, September 8-11, 2003). Lecture Notes in Computer Science, Vol. 2795. Springer-Verlag, Berlin (2003) 456–460

10. Eisenstein, J., Vanderdonckt, J., Puerta, A.: Model-Based User-Interface Development Techniques for Mobile Computing. In Lester J. (ed.): Proc. of 5th ACM Int. Conf. on Intelligent User Interfaces IUI'2001 (Santa Fe, January 14-17, 2001). ACM Press, New York (2001) 69–76

11. Ye, J., Herbert, J.: User Interface Tailoring for Mobile Computing Devices. In Proc. of 8th ERCIM Workshop « User Interfaces for All » UI4All'04 (Vienna, June 28-29, 2004). Lecture Notes in Computer Science, Vol. 3196, Springer-Verlag, Berlin (2004) 175–184

12. Banavar, G., Bergman, L.D., Gaeremynck, Y., Soroker, D., Sussman, J.: Tooling and System Support for Authoring Multi-device applications. Journal of Systems and Software **69**, 3 (2004) 227–242

13. Rugaber, S.: A Tool Suite for Evolving Legacy Software. In Proc. of IEEE Int. Conf. on Software Maintenance ICSM'99 (Oxford, 30 August-3 Sep. 1999). IEEE Comp. Society Press, Los Alamitos (1999) 33–39

14. Florins, M., Vanderdonckt, J.: Graceful Degradation of User Interfaces as a Design Method for Multiplatform Systems. In Proc. of Int. Conf. on Intelligent User Interfaces IUI'04 (Funchal, January 13-16, 2004). ACM Press, New York (2004) 140–147

15. Grundy, J.C., Hosking, J.G.: Developing Adaptable User Interfaces for Component-based Systems. Interacting with Computers **14**, 3 (2001) 175–194

16. Robertson, G., Horvitz, E., Czerwinski, M., Baudisch, P., Hutchings, D., Meyers, B., Robbins, D., Smith, G.: Scalable Fabric: Flexible Task Management. In Proc. of ACM Conf. on Advanced Visual Interfaces AVI'2004 (Gallipoli, May 25-28, 2004). ACM Press, New York, (2004) 85–89

17. Quan, D., Huynh, D., Karger, D.R.: Haystack: A Platform for Authoring End User Semantic Web Applications. In Proc. of International Semantic Web Conference (2003)

18. Tan, D.S., Meyers, B., Czerwinski, M.: WinCuts: Manipulating Arbitrary Window Regions for more Effective Use of Screen Space. In Proc. of ACM Conf. on Human Aspects in Computing Systems CHI'2004 (Vienna, April 2004). ACM Press, New York (2004) 1525-1528

19. Leventhal, E., Grubis, A.: Composable User Interfaces. The MITRE Corporation, Bedford USA (2004)

20. Grolaux, D., Vanderdonckt, J., Van Roy, P.: Attach me, Detach me, Assemble me like You Work. In Costabile, M.-F., Paternò, F. (eds.): Proc. of 10th IFIP TC 13 Int. Conf. on Human-Computer Interaction INTERACT'2005 (Rome, September 12-16, 2005), Lecture Notes in Computer Science, Vol. 3585, Springer-Verlag, Berlin (2005) 198–212

21. Limbourg, Q., Vanderdonckt, J., Michotte, B., Bouillon, L., Lopez, V.: USIXML: a Language Supporting Multi-Path Development of User Interfaces. In Proc. of 9th IFIP Working Conf. on Engineering for Human-Computer Interaction jointly with 11th Int. Workshop on Design, Specification, and Verification of Interactive Systems EHCI-DSV-IS'2004 (Hamburg, July 11-13, 2004). Lecture Notes in Computer Science, Vol. 3425. Springer-Verlag, Berlin (2005) 200–220

22. El Bekai, A., Nick Rossiter, B.: A Tree Based Algebra Framework for XML Data Systems. In Proc. of the 7th Int. Conf. on Enterprise Information Systems ICEIS'2005 (Miami, May 25-28, 2005) (2005) 305–312

23. Lepreux, S., Vanderdonckt, J.: Toward a support of the user interfaces design using composition rules. In Calvary, G., Pribeanu, C., Santucci, G., Vanderdonckt, J. (eds): Proc. of the 6th International Conference on Computer-Aided Design of User Interfaces (CADUI'2006). (Bucharest, Romania, June 5-8, 2006) Chapter 19, Springer-Verlag, Berlin, (2006)

Exploring the Specification of Haptic Interaction

Shamus P. Smith

Department of Computer Science,
Durham University, Durham DH1 3LE,
United Kingdom
shamus.smith@durham.ac.uk

Abstract. Visual technologies have directly influenced the specification and implementation of virtual environments and the user interactions that can be supported. However, recent advances in haptic devices have facilitated new levels of virtual environment interaction by the development of environments where it is possible to touch and *feel* virtual objects. Such environments support a richer set of possible user interactions.

This paper explores haptic specification for virtual environment interaction. The aim is to provide a *sketch* of interaction to enable analysis of usability requirements in an example haptic technology.

Keywords: Virtual environments, interaction specification, haptic interaction, design tools, usability.

1 Introduction

Traditionally virtual environments have been visually oriented. A contributing factor has been the technological constraints on providing a richer sense-based environment [9]. In the last decade visual technologies have matured and it is common to find virtual environments using a range of visual-oriented technology, for example monitors, head-mounted displays, surround-screen displays, workbenches and hemispherical displays [3].

Interaction in virtual environments, and the potential for complex and realistic interactions, has been driven by the dominance of these visual technologies. This has limited the veracity of the resulting interaction. Stanney et al. [22] note that "multimodal interaction may be a primary factor that leads to enhanced human performance for certain tasks presented in virtual worlds." To be able to touch or *feel* virtual objects has been constrained to bulky and expensive equipment. However, recent advances in technology has meant that haptic devices are now being used in all manner of applications [23] including medical device simulation, computer aided design, visualisation and the graphic arts [1]. Virtual environments using sight and touch are quite feasible, but the effects of sensory interaction are complex and vary from person to person.

The use of haptic technology has added to the challenge of developing virtual environments that meet the needs of users. In particular the addition of

G. Doherty and A. Blandford (Eds.): DSVIS 2006, LNCS 4323, pp. 171–184, 2007.
© Springer-Verlag Berlin Heidelberg 2007

tactile and kinesthetic cues[1] have implications for the developers of virtual environments and the tools they use during the specification, design and implementation phases of such systems. A fundamental difference between visual and haptic-based interaction is the necessity to explicitly consider physical feedback to and from the system in haptic interaction, in addition to any visual feedback. It is important that the additional realism afforded by the haptic feedback is not at the cost of (i) the user, for example by compromising usability, or (ii) the designer, for example by biasing the development to particular technologies.

This paper explores how the specification of haptic interaction can clarify the physical and virtual interactions enabled by haptic technology. Analysis of such specifications is a fundamental step in supporting the requirements of both virtual environment users and designers. An existing specification notation for virtual environments, called Flownets [19], is utilised to investigate haptic interaction. Willans and Harrison [26] note that such specifications abstract from implementation issues and support a requirement-centered rather than implementation-centred approach. Designs can be driven by what the user requires rather than specific technologies. This is clearly advantageous in terms of usability [13,26].

The remainder of the paper is organised as follows. Section 2 overviews the specification of virtual environment interaction and describes an example graphical notation, called Flownets, in the context of a navigation-based interaction technique. Next a haptic-oriented case study will be presented and a haptic specification model produced. In Section 4 usability issues as highlighted by the Flownet specification will be analysed. This will be followed by a discussion of Flownet use for haptic specification. Some conclusions are drawn in Section 6.

2   Specifying Virtual Environment Interaction

The very nature of virtual environments makes them difficult to describe and model. Virtual environments are dynamic environments and due to their continuous nature, defining salient and useful aspects of them is extremely difficult. At an initial stage of design it would be desirable if there was a useful way of *sketching* the flow of an interaction at a high level of abstraction, for requirements gathering and design specification. This would provide a basis for pre-implementation evaluation of the environment and could then be developed into a more detailed model for mapping onto an implementation [19,26].

Previous work has examined virtual environment interaction specification in order to compare interaction techniques [19] and provide a basis to identify and discuss issues such as usability [10]. In addition, formal and semi-formal specifications (see for example [5, chapt. 17 & 18]) can reduce undesirable interaction behaviour in the final system by limiting features of the design that may be ambiguously implemented [6,12,19].

---

[1] *Tactile cues* are perceived as information about surface texture, temperature, pressure and pain. *Kinesthetic cues* are perceived as information about joint angles and muscular length and tension [3].

Navarre et al. [12] describe the use of a formalism called Interactive Cooperative Objects (ICO) in order to model virtual environment behaviour. They aim to (i) determine the impact of changing input devices and/or interaction techniques, (ii) detect similarities and dissimilarities in interaction behaviour and (iii) measure any interaction effects that allow the prediction of user behaviour. However, Navarre et al. [12] do not consider the issue of continuity, as they observe that when it comes to low level modelling the events produced and processed are always dealt with in a discrete manner. Although this may be the case for virtual environment technology, the participating user will perceive continuous feedback [2] in both the visual and haptic, i.e. contact, pressure and temperature, representations.

Jacob et al. [8] consider the essence of a non-WIMP dialogue, such as in a virtual environment, as a set of continuous relationships most of which are temporary. Interaction can be explicitly described by a data-flow component for describing continuous relationships and an event-based component for describing discrete interactions. More recently, Shaer and Jacob [17] consider the need to model physical interaction, concurrent dialogues and combined intentional and passive interaction in the next-generation of user interfaces.

Wüthrich [27] examines the use of systems theory to construct a model of a virtual reality system. The model focuses on 3D input and considers discrete and continuous input and system state changes. Wüthrich aims to build a deterministic view of the system categorising the input by device and action types in order to provide a mathematical binding between input devices and a virtual reality development toolkit. Abstracting the discrete and continuous input into a general model can simplify the software code needed to support interfacing particular hardware devices to a virtual reality system.

In order to capture the continuous and discrete nature of virtual environment interaction Smith, Duke and Massink [19] use a graphical notation, called Flownets, based on hybrid systems research[2]. A Flownet is a graphical description of the dialogue between a user and an interactive system. Such descriptions are often used to reason about the usability of an interface [26]. One general principle is that interactive systems should accurately render their state to the user so that they do not suffer mode confusion [4]. Mode confusion results from misidentification of an interface's behaviour, i.e. a difference between the actual interface behaviour and what was expect by the user [4]. The following sections will present an overview of the Flownet notation and describe how such mode issues can be considered in the context of a virtual environment navigation technique.

2.1   Flownet Example: Navigation Using Two-Handed Flying

Two-handed flying (THF) [11] is a specialised type of flying which exploits proprioception, the person's sense of the position and orientation of their body and

---

[2] Hybrid systems are systems consisting of a mixture of discrete and continuous components.

limbs. Direction of flight is defined by the vector between the user's two hands and the flight speed is specified by the distance between the user's hands (see Figure 1 - from [11]). Flight is stopped by moving the hands into a *dead zone*, a minimum hand separation.

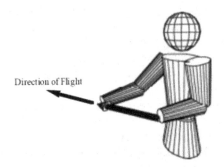

Direction of Flight

Fig. 1. Two-handed flying

Figure 2 shows a representation of the THF technique in the Flownet notation. A more detailed description of this notation has been discussed elsewhere [19,25] but will be illustrated here within an example. Figure 3 shows the components of the Flownet notation.

In this model there are three unique *external plugs*[3]. These are the continuous flow from the "hand positions" and the Boolean *control arcs* from the techniques "enable" and "disable". A control arc signals a control dependency in the model. Initially, the user triggers the interaction by some, unspecified, enable mechanism (1) which is part of the application or the environment in which THF is used. This enables the "start" *transition*. This transition also has an *inhibitor arc* so that the interaction cannot get restarted while the user is currently flying. The start transition passes a token to the "not flying" *state*. The user will remain in this state until their hands are moved outside the THF dead zone. This condition is detected by a *sensor* on the "hand positions" flow (2). The sensor spans the flow and acts as a function from the continuous flow content to a discrete boolean.

Once the user's hands are moved outside the THF dead zone, the active token is passed to the "flying" state (3). In this state a *flow control* is activated. The flow control acts as a valve on the continuous loop for transforming the user's current position and speed. The continuous loop in this example is comprised of three components; the flow control (3), a *transformer* (4) and a *store*. A transformer applies a transformation to a flow to yield a modified content. In Figure 2 the "update position, speed" transformer takes the current values from the continuous flow and updates them using the current value on the "hand positions" flow (4). This is then passed to the store. A store is a source and repository for information that is consumed or produced by a continuous flow. If

---

[3] The "hand positions" plug is repeated on the diagram for clarity.

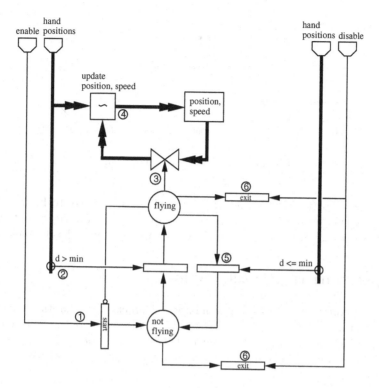

Fig. 2. Two-handed flying Flownet

the user's hands are moved back into the THF dead zone, a sensor on the user's hand positions would trigger a transition (5) back to the stationary position. Finally, while in either state, if the user wishes to exit the technique, a disable control arc can be triggered (6) which de-activates all states.

2.2   THF Flownet Analysis

Figure 2 highlights the modes/states of the interaction and the events that cause the transitions between modes. Also, there is a clear separation of the discrete processes, the control processes in the bottom of the diagram, and the continuous processes, the continuous loop in the top of the diagram. When the technique is active, and the user is flying, the user is receiving continuous visual-feedback based on their changing position and speed of travel. However, there is no such feedback when the user's hands are in the dead zone and the user is stationary. In this state, it is not clear whether the interaction technique is active or not [26]. If the user was to attempt to use a hand-based gesture, e.g. to point to an object or to try and select an object, then they could easily become disorientated as they fly off in the resulting indicated direction, at possibly great speed. If input

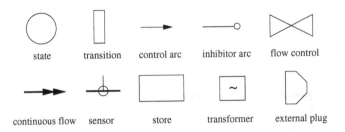

Fig. 3. Flownet notation components

devices based on the user's hand position and/or gesture are to be overloaded with interaction techniques for selection, manipulation and navigation, then discovering such usability issues are critical early in a system's development.

3   Specifying Haptic Interaction

Providing a comprehensive overview of haptic interaction and haptic technologies is outside the scope of this paper (see [1,3,23]). Instead the relevant haptic properties will be highlighted through the specification of haptic interaction in the context of a particular example based on a neurosurgery training simulator [7].

3.1   Neurosurgery Training Domain

Hansen et al. [7] describe a virtual environment for neurosurgery training where a user interacts with a virtual brain model using a haptic device to teach the correlation between brain deformation and applied pressure. The aim of the system is to provide an environment where doctors can practice using a brain spatula without endangering human or animal subjects (See Figure 4 - from [15, pg243]).

The system enables a user to apply a rigid virtual spatula onto a deformable virtual brain while providing suitable haptic and visual feedback. Haptic interaction is provided by a ground-referenced force feedback arm (see Figure 5 - from [7]) and in addition to haptic feedback, the system maps forces on the virtual brain into a colour so that the force distribution in the tissue can be monitored. The tissue is marked red when forces exceed a certain threshold.

The aim of the system is to allow the user to study the correlation between tissue deformation and force in order to quickly find the appropriate force needed in any given situation. In addition, Hansen et al. [7] hope that the user will learn not to apply too much force which can lead to irreversible and severe brain damage.

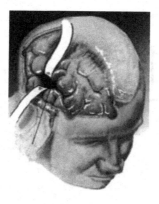

Fig. 4. Brain retraction using two spatulas

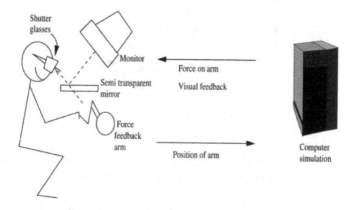

Fig. 5. Setup for the virtual brain spatula simulator

3.2   Flownet Specification

The interaction supported by this setup has been modelled in two Flownets (see Figures 6 and 7[4]). The addition of the haptic dimension to the interaction requires the modelling of both device-based and virtual interaction. In Figure 6, the states of the haptic device are modelled. The transition from stationary to moving states is triggered by appropriate force pressure from the user's hand on the device. When in the *device moving* state, the device's position and orientation are transformed by a combination of the force from the user's hand and any haptic feedback returned from the virtual component of the system, in this case *contact feedback* and *deformation feedback*. The generation of the virtual feedback is modelled in Figure 7.

---

[4] These figures include an extension to the original Flownet notation [19] by the addition of a double circle state to indicate the start state of the Flownet.

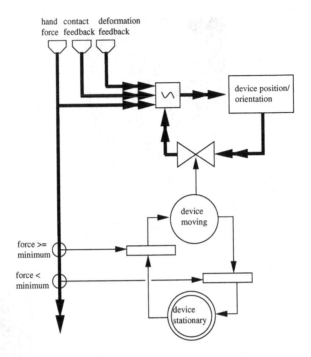

Fig. 6. Haptic device Flownet

Biggs and Srinivasan [1] identify a primary classification of haptic interactions with real and virtual environments based on three elements: "(i) free motion, where no physical contact is made with objects in the environment; (ii) contact involving unbalanced resultant forces, such as pressing an object with a fingerpad; (iii) contact involving self-equilibrating forces, such as squeezing an object in a pinch grasp." The states in Figure 7[5] are based on this classification with states for *free* motion, object *contact* and object *deformation*. An additional state representing excessive force being applied, with the brain tissue suffering *damage*, is provided. The transition from free and contact states is determined by the presence of collision detection events, determined by a sensor on the haptic device's position and orientation[6]. When in contact with the virtual object, the *contact feedback* is updated by it's current value modified by a function of the virtual brain model and the device's current position and orientation. This transformer is an encapsulation of the *haptic rendering* provided by the system.

Once in contact with the virtual brain tissue, deformation occurs when spatula movement is present. As with the contact feedback, the deformation feedback is determined by it's current value and the relative positions of the haptic device

---

[5] The external plug *device position / orientation* and the store *virtual brain model* are unique entities and are duplicated on the diagram for layout clarity.

[6] The generation of collision detection events has been simplified as it is outside the scope of the interaction specification and therefore not modelled further.

and the virtual brain model. Also the brain model itself is transformed while in this state, represented to the user as visual feedback.

If excessive force as determined by some damage threshold function, in this case a sensor attached to the *device position / orientation* external plug, the interaction moves to the *damaged* state. Haptic feedback is still provided via the continuous flow from the *deformation feedback* store and an alternative transformation of the brain model is applied to provide red visual indicators on the tissue being damaged. The Flownet provides a rich description of the haptic interaction. In addition, the construction of such a specification highlights the complex nature of the interaction.

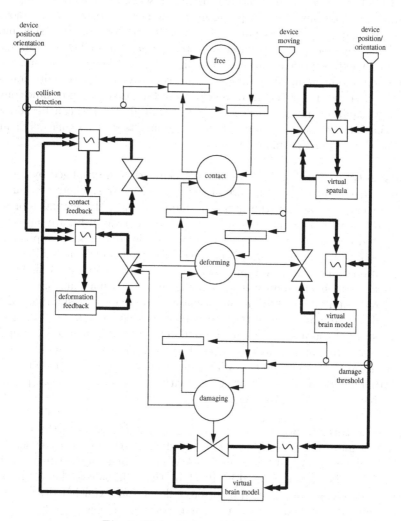

Fig. 7. Virtual interaction Flownet

4   Specification Analysis

Many "what if" questions can be answered in an unambiguous way based on such a specification [10]. For example what would happen if, while deforming the brain tissue, the user suddenly released the haptic device? Answering such a question from the textual descriptions of the interaction in [7] would be difficult, if not impossible. Based on the specification in Figure 7 such an action would result in a transition to the *contact* state and then depending on the nature of the physical device, a possible transition to the *free* state. If the device is self-centering, for example like many joysticks, such a transition to the *free* state would occur. Such questions are important when developers are required to make design decisions when mapping interaction requirements to the most appropriate technology [20]. Newman and Lamming [13] observe that such models of activity are especially invaluable in making *usability* predictions. Six usability requirements supported by such specifications are the active actors, type of interaction, mode changes, undo operations, cognitive load and indication of errors [10]. This list is not meant to be complete but serves to show how common usability requirements of interfaces, see for example [14,18], can be addressed using the Flownet specification. These requirements will be considered in the context of the brain spatula example.

Active actors - How the objects in the specification are changed by the interaction is determined by the nature of the connecting arcs. There are four main actors in this interaction; the user, the haptic device, the virtual representation of the spatula and the virtual brain model. As seen in Figure 6 the user is represented by the *hand force* external plug that is continuously applied to the haptic device during the interaction. The device itself is determined by it's original position and orientation that is transformed, when moving, by the user and any virtual forces. The representation of the virtual spatula is unchanged during the interaction and it's position and orientation are continuously updated when triggered by the movement of the haptic device. This happens regardless of the current state of the interaction in Figure 6. The virtual brain model is updated during *deforming* and *damaging* states. In this interaction the main actors are all transformed by continuous flows triggered by explicit user behaviour. Thus the virtual environment does not change without user participation, promoting a desirable user-centered interaction.

Type of interaction - The continuous and discrete parts of the interaction are clearly indicated in the Flownets. In addition, there is a clear separation between the generation of haptic feedback via the stores on the left-hand side of Figure 7 and the visual oriented feedback on the right side of the diagram. The continuous feedback is triggered by discrete flows from explicitly described state changes and sensor reading from particular continuous flows.

Mode changes - One problem that can occur in user interfaces are mode changes that escape the attention of the user and that may lead to confusion.

As seen in Figure 7 there are four main states to this interaction. However, only two of the later states have explicit visual feedback on the mode change, via the visual deformation and damage indication. Therefore the user must rely on the accuracy of the haptic rendering of collision events and the user's ability to notice them. This has implications for the required veracity of the haptic rendering, specified in the *contact feedback* transformer, and any physical user requirements based on human variability in their sensitivity to haptic events. It may be appropriate, based on the user population, to add explicit mode change indicators to every state change, for example by visual or audio cues.

Undo operations - An *undo* feature is not explicitly mentioned in [7]. The continuous nature of the virtual brain deformation, and the potential damage from too much force, does not lend itself to undo actions as there are no clear start and finish points to the interaction. Although, at a low level, computer systems are clearly discrete with step-by-step programs and users' actions being converted into streams of events [5, pg 618], in the brain spatula example an undo feature may be counter to the pedagogical aims of the simulator. Hence this will not be considered further here.

Cognitive load - Triggers for mode changes are an important part of a successful interaction. In this example the user has to remember the various modes of operation that are related to the different phases of brain tissue manipulation. The majority of triggers are based on the haptic response from the system and the users' interpretation of this feedback. It may be appropriate to provide on-screen information, attached to the activation of the discrete states, to indicate particular states of the simulation to allow the user to focus on the force/pressure training and not interface specific issues.

Indication of errors - Hansen et al. [7] note that the simulator can map all levels of force into colour so that the force distribution in the tissue can be monitored. However, they observe that "assigning all kinds of colours to the brain tissue will reduce realism." Therefore tissue is just marked red when forces exceed a certain threshold. The indication of red tissue, via inappropriate amounts of force, is the error indicator in this interaction. In the Flownet this is represented explicitly in the transformation of the virtual brain model while in the *damaged* state.

5   Discussion

It is common for the developers of virtual environments to be concerned with the use of system resources. Typically there are minimum requirements for response times for both visual and haptic feedback. Low temporal resolution of a haptic display can adversely affect quality, causing unintended vibrations and making virtual objects feel softer than intended [3, pg 71] while slow visual frame rates can lead to visual lag, which has been linked with cybersickness symptoms [22].

The resources needed to produce continuous feedback in a virtual environment can be identified in the Flownet by examining the active transformer nodes as associated to each state. In Figure 7, both the *deforming* and *damaging* states have three active transformer nodes; (i) generating deformation feedback for the haptic device, (ii) updating the visual feedback via the virtual brain model and (iii) updating the visual representation of the virtual spatula. In these most active states, system resources must be distributed between these transformations while still providing a quality of service. For a designer, this becomes particularly important if new feedback mechanisms are to be added. For example, if an audio cue during brain deformation was to be added to the simulation, the designer must consider how this could be achieved without degradation to the current system. Such a view of interaction provides a basis for the designer to consider alternative trade-offs in the feedback configuration of the system.

The complex nature of haptic interaction manifests itself in the complexity of the Flownet models. In this paper the first use of concurrent Flownet models has been presented. Concurrency is required to model the physical and virtual requirements of the haptic interaction. Modelling of concurrency will be required in systems that have multiple interaction techniques or additional multi-modal features.

Flownets are a high level representation and, as such, are a simplification of the final implemented interaction. The aim has been to improve accessibility of the models to a wider audience. As a result, some information is not explicitly represented. For example, the exact details of the continuous flow transformations as represented by the transformer nodes are not specified. In the haptic example this is the exact details of the haptic rendering, and associated algorithms for the *contact feedback* and *deformation feedback* transformers. Similarly, the internal makeup of the store nodes are not explicitly defined, for example the graphical transformations of the virtual brain model. The focus has been on highlighting the modal nature of the interaction and how this may effect usability. If more haptic-oriented issues are to be analysed, then the contents of the transformer and store nodes could be made explicit in order to model the continuous tactile cues, such as temperature and pressure, and/or kinesthetic cues, such as tension. This will not be discussed further here.

Flownets provide the basis for an inspectable design model that can be used to identify requirements that an implementation must support. The diagrams provide a mechanism to communicate the specifics of the interaction to developers. Early in the design process, the exact details of the transformations and the composition of the stores will be secondary to identifying the interaction requirements. There are obvious benefits to eliciting as much operational knowledge about a design as early as possible before costly decisions have been made and need undoing [16,21]. This is a first step in mapping design requirements - or from retrospective analysis, redesign requirements - onto technology capabilities [20]. If a more formal model is required, Flownets provide a basis for further refinement, for example to a HyNet [24] model, a hybrid modelling specification supported by formal semantics (see [10]).

6   Conclusions

This paper has described the use of Flownets for the specification of haptic interaction to provide a *sketch* of interaction in a haptic-oriented virtual environment. The resulting specification is useful in documenting features of the interaction, the consideration of haptic/visual issues and in identifying questions about the usability of the haptic technology.

Previous Flownet specifications focused on visually-orientated interaction techniques, specifically navigation in virtual environments. A haptic interaction environment has been successfully modelled, including the concurrent physical and virtual components of the interaction. The resulting specification turned out to be useful in answering specific questions about the usability of the haptic interface.

Future work includes producing specifications to analyse additional characteristics of haptic interaction and provide a platform to begin both further, more detailed, interaction decomposition and general abstractions of the models. The aim is to provide specification tools for the application of virtual environment technologies to support the required user-based multi-modal interactions.

References

1. S. James Biggs and Mandayam A. Srinivasan. Haptic interfaces. In K. M. Stanney, editor, *Handbook of Virtual Environments*, pages 93–115. Lawrence Erlbaum Associates, New Jersey, 2002.

2. Monica Bordegoni, Umberto Cugini, Piero Mussio, and Maristella Matera. The role of continuity in haptic interaction systems. In *CHI 2000 Workshop: Continuity in Human Computer Interaction*, L'Aia, Netherlands, April 2000.

3. Doug A. Bowman, Ernst Kruijff, Joseph J. LaViola Jr., and Ivan Poupyrev. *3D User interfaces: Theory and Practise*. Addison Wesley, USA, 2005.

4. Asaf Degani, Michael Shafto, and Alex Kirlik. Modes in automated cockpits: Problems, data analysis and a modelling framework. In *36th Israel Annual Conference on Aerospace Sciences Conference*. Haifa, 1996.

5. Alan Dix, Janet Finlay, Gregory D. Abowd, and Russell Beale. *Human-Computer Interaction*. Pearson/Prentice Hall, Harlow, England, third edition, 2004.

6. Emmanuel Dubois, Luciana P. Nedel, Carla M. Dal Sasso. Freitas, and Liliane Jacon. Beyond user experimentation: notational-based systematic evaluation of interaction techniques in virtual reality environments. *Virtual Reality*, 8:118–128, 2005.

7. Kim V. Hansen, Lars Brix, Christian F. Pedersen, Jens P. Haase, and Ole V. Larsen. Modelling of interaction between a spatula and a human brain. *Medical Image Analysis*, 8:23–33, 2004.

8. Robert J. K. Jacob, Leonidas Deligiannidis, and Stephen Morrison. A software model and specification language for non-WIMP user interfaces. *ACM Transactions on Computer-Human Interaction*, 6(1):1–46, March 1999.

9. Roy S. Kalawsky. *The Science of Virtual Reality and Virtual Environments*. Addison-Wesley, 1993.

10. Mieke Massink, David Duke, and Shamus Smith. Towards hybrid interface specification for virtual environments. In D. J. Duke and A. Puerta, editors, *Design, Specification and Verification of Interactive System '99*, Springer Computer Science, pages 30–51, New York, 1999. Springer-Verlag/Wien.

11. Mark R. Mine, Frederick P. Brooks Jr., and Caro H. Sequin. Moving objects in space: Exploiting proprioception in virtual-environment interaction. In Turner Whitted, editor, *SIGGRAPH 97*, pages 19–26. ACM SIGGRAPH, 1997.

12. David Navarre, Philippe Palanque, Rèmi Bastide, Amèlie Schyn, Marco Winckler, Lucianna P. Nedel, and Carla M. D. S. Freitas. A formal description of multimodal interaction techniques for immersive virtual reality applications. In M. F. Costabile and F. Paternò, editors, *Human-Computer Interaction (INTERACT 2005)*, volume LNCS 3585, pages 170–183. Springer, 2005.

13. William M. Newman and Michael G. Lamming. *Interactive System Design*. Addison-Wesley, Harlow, UK, 1995.

14. Jakob Nielsen. *Usability Engineering*. AP Professional, Boston, 1993.

15. J. L. Poppen. *An Atlas of Neurosurgical Techniques*. W. B. Saunders Company, Philadelphia, 1960.

16. Mike Scaife and Yvonne Rogers. Informing the design of a virtual environment to support learning in children. *International Journal of Human-Computer Studies*, 55(2):115–143, 2001.

17. Orit Shaer and Robert J. K. Jacob. Toward a software model and a specification language for next-generation user interfaces. In *ACM CHI 2005 Workshop: The Future of User Interface Design Tools*, April 2005.

18. Ben Shneiderman. *Designing the User Interface: Strategies for Effective Human-Computer Interaction*. Addison-Wesley, third edition, 1998.

19. Shamus Smith, David Duke, and Mieke Massink. The hybrid world of virtual environments. *Computer Graphics Forum*, 18(3):C297–C307, 1999.

20. Shamus P. Smith and David J. Duke. Binding virtual environments to toolkit capabilities. *Computer Graphics Forum*, 19(3):C–81–C–89, 2000.

21. Shamus P. Smith and Michael D. Harrison. Editorial: User centred design and implementation of virtual environments. *International Journal of Human-Computer Studies*, 55(2):109–114, 2001.

22. Kay M. Stanney, Ronald R. Mourant, and Robert S. Kennedy. Human factors issues in virtual environments: A review of the literature. *Presence*, 7(4):327–352, August 1998.

23. Steven Wall and Stephen Brewster. Editorial: design of haptic user-interfaces and applications. *Virtual Reality*, 9(2-3):95–96, 2006.

24. Ralf Wieting. Hybrid high-level nets. In J. M. Charnes, D. J. Morrice, D. T. Brunner, and J. J. Swain, editors, *1996 Winter Simulation Conference*, pages 848–855, Coronado, California, USA, 1996.

25. James S. Willans. *Integrating behavioural design into the virtual environment development process*. PhD thesis, University of York, 2001. Technical Report YCST 2002/02.

26. James S. Willans and Michael D. Harrison. A toolset supported approach for designing and testing virtual environment interaction techniques. *International Journal of Human-Computer Studies*, 55(2):145–165, 2001.

27. Charles A. Wüthrich. An analysis and a model of 3d interaction methods and devices for virtual reality. In D. J. Duke and A. Puerta, editors, *Design, Specification and Verification of Interactive System '99*, Springer Computer Science, pages 18–29, New York, 1999. Springer-Verlag/Wien.

Analysis of Pointing Tasks on a White Board*

G. Faconti and Mieke Massink

Consiglio Nazionale delle Ricerche, Istituto ISTI, Pisa, Italy
{G.Faconti,M.Massink}@isti.cnr.it

Abstract. We study the variations in two dimensional (2D) pointing tasks on a traditional white board of a group of subjects by means of capturing their movement traces in an automatic way with the Mimio device. Such traces provide detailed insight in the variability of 2D pointing relevant for example for the design of computer vision based gestural interaction. This study provides experimental evidence that for medium large distances Fitts' model, and Welfords and Shannons variants, continue to show a linear relationship between movement time (MT) and the index of difficulty (ID) with a high correlation for the ranges considered. The expected increased sensitivity to changes in ID for these larger distances are confirmed. Nearly all movements show three phases: a planning phase, a ballistic phase and an adjustment phase. Finally, we show that the arrival time at the target resembles a log-normal distribution.

1 Introduction

One of the challenges in Human-Computer Interaction is to let computers support activities that humans already perform in their daily life with the tools and environment they are used to work with. The computer support to such activities should ideally interfere as little as possible with the human activities but nevertheless provide a real augmented reality.

However, in order to provide real-time and adequate support to the user, the computing system needs to operate in a tightly coupled, continuous way with the activities of the user and its environment. The increase of computing power, the miniaturisation and the enormous developments in devices for data-acquisition such as video cameras and related image analysis software have stimulated much research and experimentation with computer vision based gestural interaction techniques for human-computer interaction [3,4].

Although computer vision based techniques potentially enable a direct and continuous interaction between user and computer, the tight coupling requires that the software is able to keep up with user's movements. This is a challenging enterprise in particular due to the variability of human behaviour even in simple and repetitive tasks. Systems that do not manage to keep up sufficiently close or behave unpredictably may constrain the user's activities and disturb or even

---

* Research partially funded by EU Integrated Project Sensoria, contract n. 016004.

G. Doherty and A. Blandford (Eds.): DSVIS 2006, LNCS 4323, pp. 185–198, 2007.

interrupt higher-level cognitive activities that are performed in parallel with the pointing behaviour [2].

One kind of application that has received considerable attention in the literature is that of finger tracking. Finger tracking is a computer vision technique that allows a computer in combination with a video camera to follow finger movements of users when they are working, for example, with a white board. Used in combination with a projector, finger tracking can be used as part of an augmented reality application for the white board. In such a setting the user uses a mix of common physical and virtual devices such as pens and erasers for the white board and projected virtual buttons for operations such as copy and paste. A nice experimental example of such a device is the Magic Board [3,11].

Experimental design of the Magic Board required an investigation of the velocity of the natural pointing movements that people perform when using a white board. At the time of its design experiments were performed to estimate such velocity using a video camera that captured the position of the user's finger with a frequency of 25 images per second. These data have been analysed image per image in a non-automatised way [3].

There exist also well-known and useful models, such as Fitts' law and its many variants that provides us with an estimate of movement times based on an index of difficulty and an index of performance. However, such models typically provide only *mean* movement times and for distances of at most 40 cm. which involve usually smaller limb groups, such as fingers, wrist and forearm, than those involved in 2D pointing on a white board. These models have been mainly developed to predict the time to position a cursor or to select a target employing devices such as the mouse, a touch pad and numerous other devices that can be found in traditional desk-top computers [10,13,1,15]. Some studies suggest that movements that involve large limbs are more sensitive to changes in the index of difficulty [10,12].

Pointing in the context of a white board involves much larger distances over which we expected the velocity to vary considerably during single movements. In this paper we therefore revisit the finger pointing experiment for the white board, but instead of a video camera we use the Mimio [8], a high-resolution ultrasonic position capturing device that can be attached to a normal white board and which can be used to register automatically and in real-time the exact trajectory of a pen that is moved over the white board by the user. This allows for a much more detailed analysis than was possible with a video camera. We study the trajectories of adult subjects for simple pointing tasks on a white board. We investigate to what extend Fitts' model is appropriate for these larger movements. We also investigate the maximal velocity of the pen in relation to the distance from the target and the distribution of the time to reach the target for various distances. Such distributions provide information about the variability of the pointing behaviour, which is usually not completely random, but rather well-approximated by stochastic distributions. Such distributions in their turn are useful in stochastic models of combined user and system behaviour such as discussed in some of our earlier work [5].

Sect. 2 describes the design of the experiment and in Sect. 3 we analyse the obtained data. Sect. 4 presents a discussion. An extended version of this article is available as technical report [6].

2   The White Board Pointing Experiment

For the experiments we have asked 18 participants to perform a number of pointing tasks on a white board with the Mimio device. In this section we provide more details on the participants and the experimental set-up.

2.1   Participants

18 participants took part in the experiment (12 male and 6 female), aged between 17 and 54 years, with an average age of 40 years. They were students, Researchers and Professors at University, and teachers at High School. All of them were native Italian speakers with normal or adjusted to normal vision and right-handed.

2.2   Apparatus

For the experiments a Mimio capture bar device [8] was used for the measurement of positional data. The capture bar was positioned over a vertically mounted white board of 1050 mm. high and 1400 mm. wide, positioned at 1200 mm. from the floor, as illustrated in Fig. 1. It was connected through a Universal Serial Bus (USB) port to a portable computer equipped with a Pentium III 850MHz processor and 128 Mbytes of memory. x and y co-ordinates of the position of the tip of a Mimio provided pen, held by the participant while sliding over the board, were recorded in mm. and time-stamped at the computer. The pen resembles conventional markers used for writing on white boards. The difference is that in the Mimio pen the conventional marker is enclosed in a hard plastic wrapper which is slightly larger than that of the marker pen it contains carrying infrared and ultrasound transmitters. The device is ergonomically designed to be held and used by a person as if it was a traditional marker with slightly increased diameter. When the device is pushed against the board, as normally happens when writing, a micro-switch is operated and two signals (infrared and ultrasound) are generated that are sensed by the capture bar. When the device is released from the board, the micro-switch stops the generation of the signals. We have used the version of the pen that does not leave an ink-trace on the board in order not to distract the participants with already drawn lines while performing the experiment. The Mimio is able to determine the current position of the device relative to the board by triangulation with a resolution of 0.35 mm. and a frequency of 87 Hz.

2.3   Stimuli

Two sets of stimuli were presented marked on the board by means of circles of black ink. Both sets were formed by five circles with diameters measuring

20 mm. and 10 mm. respectively. We have opted for circles rather than squares, such as in other 2D pointing experiments [15], because of their invariance of the width to the angle of approach of the target. The targets were placed at the following positions (measurements are from the bottom-left corner of the white board): position 1 (150 mm. horizontal, 700 mm. vertical); position 2 (950 mm., 700 mm.); Centre (600 mm., 450 mm.); position 3 (150 mm., 200 mm.); and position 4 (950 mm., 200 mm.) - see Fig. 1 for illustration. The positions reflect a reasonably representative set of pointing movements that are likely to occur when using a normal white board.

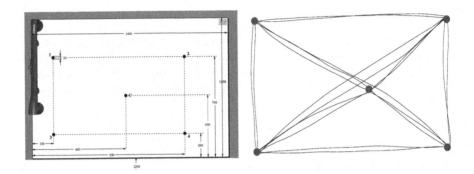

Fig. 1. Board with capture bar and position of stimuli (left) and trajectories of a single subject (right)

2.4   Procedure

The design of the experiment was that of a fully-crossed, within subjects factorial design with repeated measures. The participants were each provided with a Mimio pen for a practise trial before the beginning of the experiment. The trial was the same for all subjects and consisted of writing their name on the board.

The basic task of participants in the experiment was to connect two circles by pointing to the first with the pen, pushing it slightly on the board and sliding it to the second circle at a velocity that feels natural to the participant, according to verbal instructions. The sliding of the pen over the board is needed for the Mimio device to capture the trajectory. The five circles on the board gave 20 types of movement that a participant could be asked to perform. One response for each type of movement was obtained during the experiment. The movement types included both directions between the central circle and each of the four corner circles and also those between the four corner circles in the horizontal, vertical, and diagonal planes as shown in Fig. 1 on the right where the trajectories corresponding the 20 movements of a single subject are drawn. Tasks were presented in a random order for each participant.

Participants were instructed as follows in Italian:

"On the board in front of you five circles are marked. The outer circles are numbered 1, 2, 3 and 4 (Experimenter demonstrates by pointing to each position). The central circle is simply denoted by the letter 'C'. Your task is to connect to circles with the pen you are holding according to my instructions. First I will tell you which circle to start at - I will say, for example, "From 1 ...". I will then tell you which circle you should move to - I will do this by giving you the label of the circle, for example "... to C". You should move your hand at a speed that feels natural to you sliding the pen across the board. Try to get the tip of the pen close to the centre of each target."

3   Data Analysis

The experimental data collected following the process described in the previous section were classified based on the distance of the two circles to be connected and the width of the target circle. Consequently, we identified (i) long diagonal movements (LD) from 1 to 4, from 2 to 3, and vice versa, (ii) middle diagonal movements (MD) from 1 and 3 to C, and vice versa, (iii) short diagonal movements (SD) from 2 and 4 to C, and vice versa, (iv) horizontal movements (HO) from 1 to 2, from 3 to 4, and vice versa, (v) vertical movements (VE) from 1 to 3, from 2 to 4, and vice versa (see Fig. 1). The five classes were replicated for the large and the small target respectively. This led to the identification of ten classes consisting of 18×4 measurements each. It might have been reasonable to split each class into two; one for each different direction of movement (i.e. left to right and right to left or downward and upward). However, given the rather small number of trials for each movement in this explorative study we decided to keep the above mentioned classes and examine the results for indications for the need for further refinement in future experiments.

3.1   Fitts' Law Analysis of Overall Data

Our analysis started from a consideration of Fitts' law [7] as one of the rare quantitative tools available in user interface research and development.

The length of movements studied in this experimental setting exceeds that usually considered in evaluating devices such as for example mice and tablets. As a consequence, the participants in our experiments need to use different limbs and muscles to perform the pointing tasks than in the usual Fitts' law experiments. The above observation justifies the potential for validating Fitts' formal relationship in the case of a white board equipped with a Mimio device although the main objective of our work aims at finding performance distributions and variations in pointing behaviour rather than the mean values of human perceptual-motor performance.

The usual form of Fitts' law predicts that the movement time MT needed to point at a target of width W at distance D is logarithmically related to the inverse of the spatial relative error $\frac{2D}{W}$, that is:

$$MT = a + b \log_2 \left(\frac{2D}{W} \right) \tag{1}$$

where a and b are empirically determined constants [12].

There exist a number of well-known variations of Fitts' law such as Welford's variation [18,19]:

$$MT = a + b \log_2 \left(\frac{D}{W} + 0.5 \right) \tag{2}$$

and Shannon's original theorem [16]:

$$MT = a + b \log_2 \left(\frac{D}{W} + 1 \right) \tag{3}$$

The logarithmic factor in the formulas, called the index of difficulty ID, describes the difficulty to achieve the pointing task [12]. The index of performance IP, defined as $IP = \frac{ID}{(MT-a)}$, gives a measure of the information capacity of the human motor system, analogous to channel capacity C in Shannon's theorem [16].

In our analysis we compared all above variants of Fitts' law. Also, we used the method described in [15] to compute the effective target size W_e in a two dimensional space to replace W in the above equations. The effective target size reflects the actual size of the target based on what the participants really did. Equation (3) with W replaced by W_e is also used in the new standard for pointing devices ISO9241-9 [14]. The use of W_e instead of W is believed to increase the accuracy of the model in general.

The overall results obtained from our experiments for all pointing tasks of all participants is given in Table 1. The table reports the results for the width of the targets considered (20 mm. and 10 mm.), the effective width W_e and the distance D. The index of difficulty ID, the mean movement time MT and the index of performance (or throughput) IP have been calculated using W_e for the three variants of Fitts' law: Fitts (ID_F, IP_F), Welford (ID_W, IP_W) and Shannon (ID_S, IP_S). The last column in Table 1 gives the mean velocity for each combination of target and distance.

The results for Welfords variant are presented graphically in Fig. 2 together with a first order fit of the data to the logarithmic component of Welfords variant, the correlation coefficient of 0.98, the regression coefficient of 0.675 s/bit and its regression constant of -1.658 s. The results for Fitts' law and Shannon's variant are very similar with correlation coefficient 0.98 and 0.99 resp., regression coefficient 0.667 s/bit and 0.682 s/bit resp. and regression constant -2.274 s. and -1.711 s. resp. All results show a linear relationship between movement time and the index of difficulty with a high correlation as has also been observed in many other Fitts' law studies involving finger, wrist and forearm muscles in computer input control [12,13]. A difference with the results reported in [12] on Fitts' results for the tapping experiment involving distances of between 2 and 16 inches is the regression coefficient (slope). In Fitts' experiments the slope

Table 1. Data from experiment with Mimio capture bar and pen

W (mm)	W_e (mm)	D (mm)	Mov. Type	ID_{eF} (Bits)	ID_{eW} (Bits)	ID_{eS} (Bits)	MT (sec)	IP_{eF}^* (Bits/s)	IP_{eW}^* (Bits/s)	IP_{eS}^* (Bits/s)	Velocity (cm/s)
20	17.98	430.1	SD	5.58	4.61	4.64	1.518	1.47	1.45	1.44	28.33
20	18.21	500.0	VE	5.77	4.81	4.83	1.615	1.48	1.47	1.45	30.96
20	18.27	514.9	MD	5.82	4.84	4.87	1.637	1.49	1.47	1.45	31.45
20	18.35	800.0	HO	6.45	5.46	5.48	1.954	1.53	1.51	1.50	40.94
20	19.12	943.4	LD	6.62	5.63	5.65	2.138	1.50	1.48	1.47	44.13
10	7.83	430.1	SD	6.78	5.79	5.81	2.160	1.53	1.52	1.50	19.91
10	8.25	500.0	VE	6.92	5.93	5.95	2.295	1.51	1.50	1.49	21.79
10	8.07	514.9	MD	6.99	6.01	6.02	2.384	1.50	1.49	1.47	21.60
10	8.28	800.0	HO	7.59	6.60	6.82	2.744	1.51	1.50	1.53	29.15
10	8.42	943.4	LD	7.81	6.81	6.82	3.097	1.45	1.43	1.42	30.46
						Mean	2.152	1.50	1.49	1.47	
						StDev	0.501	0.02	0.03	0.03	

(*) Calculated using $IP = ID/(MT - a)$ where a is the regression constant.

for the experiment in which a stylus of 1 oz was used is 0.1089 s/bit and for the 1-lb stylus 0.1240 s/bit, which are both much lower than the regression coefficient found for the white board experiment. So, the index of difficulty has more influence on the movement time in the case of the white board than in the case of traditional desktop computer interfaces such as mouse and joy-stick. This result is in line with an hypothesis made in earlier research by Langolf et al. [10] in which it was found that IP decreased as the limb changed from the finger to the wrist to the forearm, i.e. involving increasingly larger limbs.

The mean velocity presented in Table 1 is much lower than the maximum velocity reported in [3]. In their experiments a maximum velocity of 200 cm/s has been observed in pointing tasks where participants were asked to start from one extreme of the white board, i.e. covering approximately 120 cm., and put a mark with a pen on the other extreme in a fast way. This shows, as expected, that the mean movement time and distance is not a satisfactory predictor of the maximal velocity that may occur in pointing movements over medium large distances.

In order to get better insight in the variation of the velocity during pointing tasks on the white board we analyse the obtained trajectories in the following sections.

3.2   Convergence Patterns

According to Jagacinski et al. [9] researchers have postulated in the past two classes of models that attempt to explain the movement processes underlying the relationship between target width and distance. One class postulates that the movement is composed of a sequence of discrete sub-movements of uniform duration and uniform relative accuracy as found by Crossman et al. [9]. The

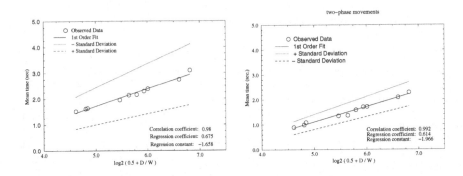

Fig. 2. Welford's variant of Fitts' law in the case of aggregate data (left) and considering only the ballistic and planning phases (right)

other class argues for the existence of two basic structural components; an initial impulse or ballistic component and a sequence of finer adjustments when approaching the target such as proposed by Welford [19]. Welford suggested based on these ideas that Fitts' index of difficulty should be reformulated into two terms in which the first term corresponds to an open-loop initial approach to the target, and the second term to a visually feedback controlled final alignment with the target. However, in experiments performed by Jagacinski et al. [9] with movements performed with a joystick between targets projected on a display of 38 cm by 28 cm the data collected were insufficient to establish conclusively whether the first sub-movement was regulated by an open- or closed-loop control. MacKenzie reports however that experiments have shown that movements that take less than 200 ms are ballistic and those with a duration over 200 ms are controlled by visual feedback [12] at page 118. This result has been obtained in the context of traditional Fitts' law experiments, so for amplitudes of at most 40 cm.

Fig. 3 shows some examples of the velocity (top) and of the distance (bottom) profiles computed from trajectory and time-stamp data for different subjects and trials. From the graphs on the left, three phases are clearly identifiable during a movement:

– an *initial planning* phase characterised by a low velocity profile followed by
– a *ballistic* phase characterised by a high increase and subsequent decrease of the velocity profile followed by
– an *adjustment* phase characterised by a low velocity.

The graphs on the right show different examples of the velocity and distance profiles which have only two phases: a ballistic phase and an adjustment phase. In other words, in many trajectories the planning phase is not visible. The most likely explanation for this difference is the set-up of the experiment. In fact, participants have a view of the starting and target candidate circles for a trajectory on the board before they start operating the marker. That way, they might build a mental image of the board in advance and work on that image directly during the performance; that is, the planning phase is implicitly performed and the pointing task starts with the ballistic movement. Control over the position and size of the target is put in place at the end of the ballistic phase when adjustment is necessary. This requires a refresh of the mental image and the focusing on the image of the target. Consequently, the behaviour of participants doesn't show significant qualitative variations once the performance is started. It is interesting to note that each participant always adopts the same behaviour across multiple tasks (i.e. the presence/absence of the planning phase is invariant with respect to tasks for a subject). Apparently, a learning effect from previous knowledge of the position of the targets in the board is not appreciated. This may be due to the small number of tasks each subject is asked to perform together with the focusing on the current task only. However, two different strategies of operation are clearly revealed at this stage of our analysis. Further experiments are needed to study this phenomenon in a more controlled way. However, all subjects showed a trajectory with a ballistic phase followed by an adjustment phase when approaching the target.

If we correct the obtained data for the planning phase, i.e. we leave out the part of the trajectory that clearly concerns the planning phase, we obtain an even better fit of Welford's variant presented in Fig. 2 (right).

A further observation shown in Fig. 3 is that the velocity of the movement varies considerably as a function of the distance to the target. Moreover, velocities of more than 2 to 3 times as high as that of the average velocities based on Fitts' model can be observed. We discuss issues related to velocity in more detail in Section 3.4. In the next section we first look in more detail to the different phases of the pointing movements.

3.3   Distance Covered and Time Spent in the Movement Phases

The bar charts on the left of Fig. 4 show the mean percentage of the distance covered within the three distinguished phases of a movement, and the bar charts on the right show the mean percentage of time spent in those phases, for each of the indicated trials. It is evident that almost all of the distance was covered within the ballistic phase, while in the planning and the adjustment phases the distance covered is negligible. This occurred uniformly across all trials with minimal variations.

Considering the time spent to perform a complete movement, the variation across phases changes significantly. While the ballistic phase keeps taking most of the time, both planning and adjustment phases cannot be neglected.

The figure shows that the variation across target sizes of the percentage covered both in distance and in time during the planning phase is minimal. On the contrary, the adjustment phase duration depends on the size of the target both for distance and time: the bigger the target the shorter is the duration of the adjustment.

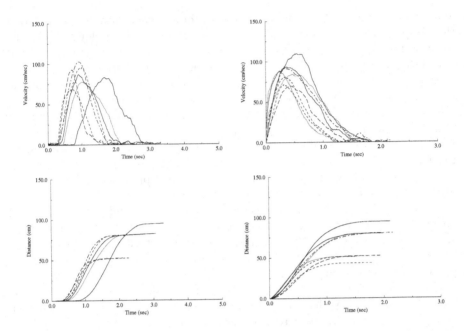

Fig. 3. Velocity (top) and distance (bottom) sample profiles with planning (left) and without planning (right) phases

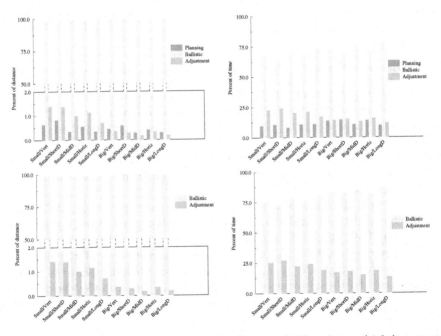

Fig. 4. Percent distribution of movements in distance (left) and time (right) per test

3.4   Observed Maximal Velocity

Table 2 shows the maximal velocities that have been observed for each distance and each target width. It also shows the mean of the maximal velocities reached by the participants and the standard deviation. The highest velocity of 196.69 cm/s has been reached for the target of 20 mm. and the horizontal movement of 80 cm in a movement from point (1) to point (2) on the board. This is slightly less than the maximal velocity reported in [3] which was 200 cm/s. The latter however was obtained for a larger distance (120 cm.) and no clear target size. It can also be observed from this table that the highest *mean maximal* velocity is reached for the long diagonal and that this mean velocity decreases with the distance, with a minor exception for the short diagonal and the vertical movements for the small target.

Interestingly, from the same table we can also observe that the maximum velocity reached is not only depending on the distance that needs to be covered but also on the target size. Apparently, the ballistic movement is performed more cautiously and slower if a smaller target needs to be reached.

Table 2. Maximal observed velocity for each type of movement

Target (mm.)	Movement Type	Max Velocity (cm/s)	Mean Velocity (cm/s)	St. Dev.
20	Long diagonal	178.47	95.29	33.12
20	Horizontal	196.69	91.41	30.80
20	Mid diagonal	162.69	79.18	31.01
20	Vertical	149.58	76.18	30.84
20	Short diagonal	171.07	69.56	26.99
10	Long diagonal	109.66	67.35	18.81
10	Horizontal	102.66	67.16	19.27
10	Mid diagonal	99.94	54.25	17.66
10	Vertical	95.68	48.95	15.11
10	Short diagonal	92.79	49.22	14.85

3.5   Variability of Arrival Times

Fitts' law studies typically do not address the distribution or variability of movement times but are aiming at the development of a valid model for the prediction of average movement times for different indices of difficulty and performance. Although Fitts' law has many important applications, there are situations in which the *variability* of the movement times is an important factor, such as in the case of direct interaction via computer vision techniques. It is well-known that human behaviour is quite variable, even in case of simple tasks, however, it is not completely random. Swain and Goodman [17], among others, observed for example that reaction times are rather well described by log-normal probability distributions. These are similar to normal distributions but skewed somewhat to the faster end of the distribution.

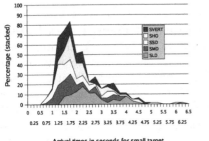 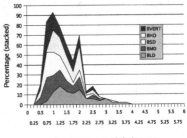

Arrival times in seconds for small target   Arrival time in seconds for big target

Fig. 5. Distribution of arrival time for small (left) and big (right) target for the different types of movement

In Fig. 5 the distribution of the arrival times for the two sizes of the target and the various types of movements are shown. On the horizontal axes the arrival time (in seconds) is shown. The vertical axes shows the percentage of trajectories that reached the target by that time in a *stacked* way. The numbers have been obtained by grouping the trajectories in slots of 0.25 seconds each. All trajectories have been renormalised by removing potential planning phases from the trajectories. Fig. 6 shows *non-stacked* distributions for the long diagonal trajectories for the small and the big target as an example.

It can be observed that the distributions are indeed skewed to the faster part of the distribution and resembles somewhat a log-normal distribution. However, in a number of cases a second, lower, peak can be observed toward the slower part of the distribution. This could be explained by the fact that movements of the same length, but in different directions have been grouped together. For example, moving from left to right might be much easier (and thus faster) for most people than moving from right to left. A further factor is that the number of movements considered in this study has been relatively limited. Further experimentation is needed to find out whether these distributions will be reproduced and would fit more closely to a log-normal distribution as these first data are suggesting.

4   Discussion

We have studied the pointing behaviour of adults performing simple pointing tasks on a white board. Such tasks involve movements over larger distances, and thus involving different limbs and body muscles than are usually considered in Fitts' law studies.

Although the study was limited in its set-up for what concerns the number of participants, and the number of trials that they were asked to perform, the use of an ultrasonic high-resolution movement capturing device provided interesting and detailed data on the structure of the movements and the variation of the velocity over each trajectory. Our results show a linear relationship between

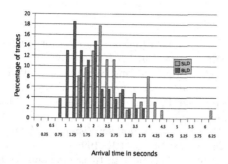

Fig. 6. Distribution of arrival time for small target, long diagonal (SLD) and big target, long diagonal (BLD)

movement time and the index of difficulty with a high correlation as in most Fitts' law studies for traditional pointing and tapping tasks. The main difference is that the regression coefficient was found to be much higher for pointing movements on the white board than in traditional Fitts' law experiments. This is in line with earlier findings that movements involving larger limbs are more sensitive to the index of difficulty. Furthermore, the obtained trajectories showed a clear number of phases in the structure of the movements. An initial planning phase, followed by a ballistic phase and an adjustment phase could be distinguished, although in some trajectories the planning phase was missing. This last aspect is most likely due to the way the experiments have been set-up. We plan to conduct further experiments in order to control this aspect as well as other aspects that seem relevant for the results, such as arm-length (reach), person's length and direction of movement.

The ballistic phase of the movements showed that velocities were reached that were significantly higher than the average velocity derived from the measured distance and movement times. Moreover, the velocity is clearly influenced by the size of the target. Furthermore, the data seems to suggest that the arrival times for each combination of distance and target follow a log-normal distribution. Further experimentation is needed to investigate this hypothesis in more detail.

For what concerns the design of vision based tracking techniques, the results of the experiments show that the velocity of the pointing movement varies considerably. Such knowledge could be used for improvement of the adaptive tracking techniques. For example, it could be investigated whether the initial part of the ballistic movement could be used to predict with a good accuracy in which direction and where the movement is heading.

Although limited in scope and number of participants, the current experiment shows nevertheless a number of interesting phenomena that would be worth to investigate further within the context of a larger experiment which we are currently carrying out.

References

1. J. Accot and S. Zhai. Beyond Fitts' law: models for trajectory-based HCI tasks. In S. Pemberton, (Ed.), *CHI-Conf. on Human Fact. in Comp. Sys.*. ACM, 1997.
2. P. Barnard and J. May. Representing cognitive activity in complex tasks. *Int. Journ. on Human-Computer Interaction*, 14:92–158, 1999.
3. F. Bérard. Vision par ordinateur pour l'interaction homme-macine fortement couplée, 1999. Ph.D. thesis.
4. R. Cipolla and A. E. Pentland. *Computer Vision for Human-Machine Interaction.* Cambridge Univ. Press, Cambridge, UK, 1998.
5. G. Doherty, M. Massink, and G. Faconti. Reasoning about interactive systems with stochastic models. In C. Johnson, (Ed.), *DSVIS* . Springer, 2001. LNCS 2220.
6. G. Faconti, and M. Massink. Analysis of pointing tasks on a white board – Extended version. CNR-ISTI Technical report 2006-TR-24, CNR, 2006.
7. P. M. Fitts. The information capacity of the human motor system in controlling the amplitude of movement. *Journ. of Exp. Psychology*, 47:381–391, 1954.
8. Mimio interactive whiteboard, 2005. http://www.mimio.com.
9. R. J. Jagacinski, D. W. Repperger, M. S. Moran, S. L. Ward, and B. Glass. Fitts' law and the microstructure of rapid discrete movements. *Journ. of Exp. Psychology: Human Perception and Performance*, 6(2):309–320, 1980.
10. G. D. Langolf, D. B. Chaffin, and J. A. Foulke. An investigation of Fitts' law using a wide range of movement amplitudes. *Journ. of Motor Behav.*, 8:113–128, 1976.
11. F. Letessier, J. Bérard. Visual tracking of bare fingers for interactive surfaces. In *ACM Symposium UIST, Santa Fe, NM, USA*, 2004.
12. I. S. MacKenzie. Fitt's law as a research and design tool in human-computer interaction. *Int. Journ. of HCI*, 7:91–139, 1992.
13. I. S. MacKenzie and R. Balakrishnan. Performance differences in the fingers, wrist, and forearm in computer input control. In S. Pemberton, (Ed.), *ACM-CHI Conf. on Human Factors in Comp. Sys.*. ACM Press, 1997.
14. I. S. MacKenzie and W. Soukoreff. Card, english, and burr (1978) – 25 years later. In *Extended Abstracts of the ACM-CHI Conf. on Human Factors in Computing Systems*, pages 760–761. ACM, 2003.
15. A. Murata. Extending effective target width in Fitts' law to a two-dimensional pointing task. *Int. Journ. of Human-Computer Interaction*, 11(2):137–152, 1999.
16. C. E. Shannon and W. Weaver. The mathematical theory of communication, 1949.
17. A. D. Swain and H. E. Guttmann. Handbook of human reliability analysis with emphasis on nuclear power plant applications - final report, 1983. Technical Report NRC FIN A 1188 NUREG/CR-1278 SAND80-0200. Prepared for Division of Facility Operations; Office of Nuclear Regulatory Research; Nuclear Regulatory Commission; Washington D.C. 20555.
18. A. T. Welford. The measurement of sensory-motor performance: survery and reappriasal of twelve years' progress. *Ergonomics*, 3:189–230, 1960.
19. A. T. Welford. Fundamentals of skill, 1968.

Mixed-Fidelity Prototyping of User Interfaces

Jennifer N. Petrie and Kevin A. Schneider

Department of Computer Science, University of Saskatchewan,
Saskatoon, SK S7N 5C9, Canada

Abstract. We present a new technique for user interface prototyping, called mixed-fidelity prototyping. Mixed-fidelity prototyping combines and supports independent refinement of low-, medium-, and high-fidelity interface elements within a single prototype. Designers are able to investigate alternate, more innovative designs, and are able to elicit feedback from stakeholders without having to commit too early in the process. The approach encourages collaboration among a diverse group of stakeholders throughout the design process. For example, individuals who specialize in specific fidelities, such as high-fidelity components, are able to become involved earlier on in the process.

We developed a conceptual model called the Region Model and implemented a proof-of-concept system called ProtoMixer. We then demonstrated the mixed-fidelity approach by using ProtoMixer to design an example application.

1 Introduction

User interface prototyping is a process for creating mock-ups representing the user interface of the final software system. Prototypes serve as a common language between stakeholders, offering a way for designers to explore design ideas and elicit feedback from stakeholders prior to committing to designs. Prototypes aid in refining requirements and may be used as a specification for developers. Prototyping is important in arriving at a well-designed user interface.

Different fidelities of prototypes can be explored during the prototyping process: low-, medium-, and high-fidelity. Fidelity refers to how closely the prototypes resemble the final product in terms of visual appearance, interaction style, and level of detail [17]. Each fidelity of prototype uses different techniques and mediums and each is important at specific stages in the design process [14]. The commonly accepted best practice of prototyping encourages starting with low-fidelity prototypes then moving to medium- and finally to high-fidelity, refining whole prototypes at each fidelity prior to advancing to a higher-fidelity.

We have identified some shortcomings with this current best practice. Designers typically only work on one fidelity at a time and, while prototyping is often termed 'iterative', designers often only iterate within a specific fidelity. These shortcomings force designers to make decisions on some design issues earlier than desired as well as undesirably delay investigating other more pressing issues. Also, because different fidelities are performed on different mediums and tools, there is a lack of traceability in the

G. Doherty and A. Blandford (Eds.): DSVIS 2006, LNCS 4323, pp. 199–212, 2007.
© Springer-Verlag Berlin Heidelberg 2007

process and transitioning back or forth between fidelities requires significant effort. Furthermore, this practice does not encourage novel designs to be explored. Also, current practice lacks collaboration between various stakeholder groups, such as end users and software developers. These shortcomings are evident in and reinforced by the existing support tools.

To address these shortcomings we have developed the mixed-fidelity prototyping approach. Mixed-fidelity prototyping involves combining multiple fidelities within a single prototype. This allows designers to independently explore and refine individual elements within a prototype, while maintaining the element within the context of the overall design. By mixing fidelities, we aim to enhance the collaboration throughout the prototyping process by bringing together various stakeholder groups earlier on and allowing for more active participation. We utilize a large interactive display workspace in this research to further encourage collaboration.

In the remainder of this paper, we discuss related work on prototyping techniques and tools as well as collaborative large display projects. Next, we describe the mixed-fidelity prototyping approach further and include a conceptual model we developed, called the Region Model, for supporting the approach. We also provide an overview of a proof-of-concept system called ProtoMixer. Finally, an example design session is presented where ProtoMixer is used to design an example application to illustrate the approach.

2   Background

Low-fidelity prototypes are best used early in the design process when trying to understand user requirements and expectations [14]. Low-fidelity prototypes are created on physical mediums such as paper, whiteboards, or chalkboards. Freehand sketching is one of the most common techniques for low-fidelity prototyping as it allows for ideas to be left intentionally vague and informal [11] and it encourages thinking [16].

Medium-fidelity prototypes are refined versions of the low-fidelity prototypes and are created on the computer. Medium-fidelity prototypes are commonly created using multimedia design tools, interface builders, or scripting languages such as tcl/tk [12].

High-fidelity prototypes are refined versions of the medium-fidelity that typically have some level of functionality implemented and may link to some sample data. High-fidelity prototypes are computer-based prototypes that are often developed using interface builders or certain scripting languages to speed up the process. High-fidelity prototypes are particularly useful for performing user evaluations as well as for serving as a specification for developers and as a tool for marketing and stakeholder buy-in [14].

The majority of prototypes are developed using some type of support tool. One of the most widely used class of tools is Interface Builders, such as Microsoft® Visual Basic®, Borland® Delphi™, and Metrowerks™ CodeWarrior™. Interface Builders aid designers in creating and laying out interfaces by allowing for interface components to be dragged into position on the desired screen. Interface Builders may be used for high-fidelity and, to a lesser extend, medium-fidelity prototyping. Interface builders are restrictive in terms of what designs designers can build as well as the order in which designers have to build it and they require significant time and effort to create a prototype.

Another widely used class of tools is Multimedia Design tools, which includes commercial tools such as Macromedia® Director® and Flash® as well as Apple® Hyper-Card® and tools from the research community such as DEMAIS [1] and Anecdote [5]. Multimedia design tools are useful in creating and demonstrating storyboards in medium-fidelity prototyping as they allow for creation of images that can represent user interface screens and components as well as for playing out navigational transitions from one screen to the next. On the negative side, the interactivity supported by multimedia design tools is very limited, usually to only basic mouse clicks, and so is support for creating functionality and tying in data.

A number of tools support freehand sketching. SILK [9], one of the first tools to support informal sketching of user interfaces, also provided support for transitioning to a higher-fidelity through automatic interface component transformation to working components. DENIM [10] is a tool aimed at supporting the early stages of web design through informal sketching and provides for creating and running designs of different levels of granularity (from sitemap to storyboards to individual pages) [10].

In recent years, researchers have shown considerable interest in attempting to bridge the gap between interface and software design through a series of workshops [6,7,8]. Gurantene et al. [4] argue for using high-fidelity prototypes as a bridging artifact. However, prototyping tools lack support for the diverse roles of user interface designers, graphic artists, software engineers, and end users.

Design workspaces and, more specifically, work surfaces influence collaboration [2,15]. For instance, work surfaces help focus designers attention and aid in expressing creativity. Furthermore, workspaces provide a medium for designers to communicate through with actions such as drawing, writing notes, and gesturing to emphasize or reference previously made points. For these reasons, design teams must have suitable workspaces. We use large displays in our research as large display workspaces are conducive to collaboration, allowing for multiple people to simultaneously work directly at the surface while allowing for everyone in the room to be aware of the workspace content.

3   Mixed-Fidelity Prototyping

Mixed-fidelity prototyping involves combining multiple fidelities within a single prototype. As an example, consider having a sketched screen design that contains various sketched elements. The sketch may also contain images in place of sketched elements and also could have one or more interface elements presented as high-fidelity working components. The sketched elements or images may also be given some form of behavior similar to what they would possess at traditional higher-fidelities.

Mixed-fidelity prototyping allows designers the opportunity to focus on a specific interface issue, by exploring it at higher-fidelities and making refinements as needed. In the mean time, other aspects of the prototype may be left at a lower-fidelity, delaying decisions while allowing designers to redirect their time and efforts to the more pressing design issue(s). Also, by leaving other elements at lower-fidelities, designers are able to explore the higher-fidelity elements while keeping them within the context of more complete screen designs.

Mixed-fidelity prototyping varies from the traditional process, which limits iteration to occur within the current fidelity. Also, traditional practice does not encourage advancing to the next higher-fidelity until ideas have been refined at the current fidelity and does not encourage skipping fidelities. Finally, traditional practice discourages iterating to a higher-fidelity at the element level, rather only once the whole prototype is ready for advancement. Figure 1 depicts the limited iterative nature of the traditional prototyping process.

Fig. 1. Traditional prototyping process with limited iteration opportunities

Mixed-fidelity prototyping is a fully iterative process. Designers may advance to any higher-fidelity at any point in time as well as revert back to any earlier fidelity as desired. Also, mixed-fidelity prototyping allows iterative refinement at the element level rather than only for the overall design. Figure 2 show the iterations possible with our mixed-fidelity approach.

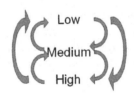

Fig. 2. Mixed-fidelity prototyping as a fully iterative process

Prior to developing our model and prototype we designed several collaborative prototyping scenarios. We used these scenarios to discover unique issues that could be addressed with mixed-fidelity prototyping. We identified the following novel or key concepts: (1) mixing elements of multiple fidelities in a single prototype, (2) transitioning between the fidelities as ideas are refined, (3) integrating domain-specific data and functionality, (4) exploring novel interactive elements, (5) comparing alternative designs, and (6) recording the design process. These issues are not easily possible or supported under current practice and with existing tools.

4   The Region Model for Mixed-Fidelity Prototyping

We developed a conceptual model, called the Region Model, to support mixed-fidelity prototyping. Prototypes are composed of multiple elements on the design space. Prototypes are composed using the region metaphor by overlaying regions on other regions to arrive at a desired design. Overlaid regions are related in a parent-subregion hierarchy. The root region is also referred to as the *design space*. Figure 3 illustrates how regions can be used to compose prototypes.

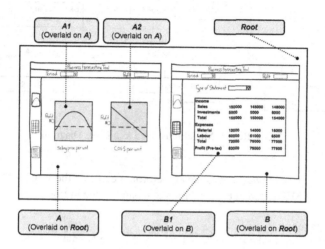

Fig. 3. Using the concept of regions to compose prototypes

Regions have both visual properties as well as associated behaviors. The visual presentation or form that a region takes is represented as *assets*, where assets may be sketches, images, or high-fidelity widgets, for example. A region have spatial and visual attributes, such as x, y, and z coordinates, width and height, as well as color and transparency. A region may be associated with a layout algorithm to automatically position its subregions. Finally, regions have a history list, which are clones of themselves over a period of time.

Behavior is represented as *scripts* that are bound to regions, where the scripts perform manipulations on regions. Scripts are made up of *commands*, which are used to perform basic manipulations on regions such as modifying their size or position.

Regions may be connected through *relationships*. Relationships specify that a change in one region's properties affect other regions. Relationships may exist for two main purposes: to bind behaviors and to indicate navigational flow.

The Region Model can be used to describe the current and historical state of the prototypes being designed as well as the design space itself and how alternative prototypes are arranged within the design space. Figure 4 is a UML Class Diagram illustrating the major concepts in the Region Model.

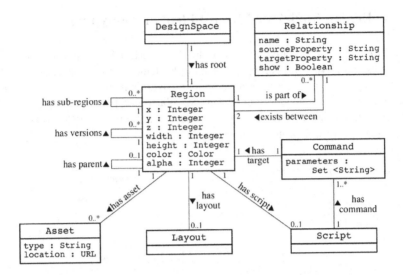

Fig. 4. Region Model illustrated as a UML Diagram

An XML[3] based notation was developed for specifying the Region Model. Below is an example XML document describing the design space in Figure 3.

```
<DesignSpace>
    <Region name="Root" x="..." y="..." ... parentRegion="null">
        <Region name="A" x="..." y="..." ...  parentRegion="Root">
            <Asset type="Image" location="..."/>
            <Region name="A1" x="..." y="..." ... parentRegion="A">
                <Asset type="Image" location="..."/> </Region>
            <Region name="A2" x="..." y="..." ... parentRegion="A">
                <Asset type="Image" location="..."/>  </Region>
        </Region>
        <Region name="B" x="..." y="..." ... parentRegion="Root">
            <Asset type="Image" location="..."/>
            <Region name="B1" x="..."   y="..." ... parentRegion="B">
                <Asset type="Image" location="..."/>  </Region>
        </Region>
    </Region>
</DesignSpace>
```

5   ProtoMixer: Software Support for Mixed Fidelity Prototyping

ProtoMixer, shown in Figure 5, is a proof-of-concept system developed to support the mixed-fidelity prototyping approach. ProtoMixer is implemented in Java and the graphics rendering is with Java2D. ProtoMixer is intended to be an easy to use, lightweight system, much in the same manner as a basic drawing editor. All objects may be positioned anywhere on the workspace, which is the same as the canvas in a drawing

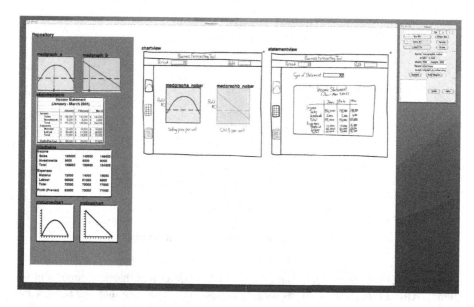

Fig. 5. Screenshot of ProtoMixer

editor; placement of objects is not restricted by frames and borders as with other tools like Interface Builders. Also, there are no menu bars; all system operations are either performed directly on the object or through a simple command panel (cf. Figure 6).

ProtoMixer supports the integration of elements of any fidelity through the use of assets. In the current version of ProtoMixer, assets may be of these types: sketch, image, and widget, where each of these types clearly corresponds to a fidelity. These assets can then be created outside of ProtoMixer using tools and mediums that designers are accustomed to. For example, sketches can be created on paper and then be scanned as images and imported into ProtoMixer. As well, images can be created in the designers' favorite multimedia application. High-fidelity components can be coded in an Interface Builder or from scratch and be imported into our system. These components may be any of Java's pre-built widgets, such as high-level control components (like JTables and JTextFields) as well as lower-level general purpose container objects such as JPanel and JscrollPane. ProtoMixer also allows for custom-built components, as long as they extend from JComponent class. ProtoMixer also provides limited support for sketching directly within the tool.

Prototypes are composed in ProtoMixer by overlaying regions on top of other regions. Visual properties can then be adjusted for regions by specifying new values in the command panel. Then prototypes and/or their elements can be given behavior through a few different approaches: constraints, animation, and bindings. ProtoMixer supports generic binding between high-fidelity elements using the observer design pattern.

ProtoMixer offers a variety of features, too many to discuss in this paper (see [13] for further details). For example, it supports automatic layout of prototypes and/or their elements. It also supports prototype storyboarding through animating the navigational flow between the prototype screens by either highlighting the screens in order of

Fig. 6. Screenshot of ProtoMixer's command panel

navigation or by laying screens out on top of one another and flashing through in sequence. Also, ProtoMixer supports logging of design activities for undoing actions and supports importing and exporting of the design space contents.

A set of commands is built in to ProtoMixer to manipulate properties of regions. For example, there are commands to scale, move, select, clone and animate regions. Manipulating properties is important in constructing prototypes as well as in managing the design space. Commands can be grouped into scripts, stored and later recalled.

ProtoMixer utilizes a large display workspace, currently running on four 30" Apple Cinema Displays® each at a resolution of 2560x1600 pixels for a total of 16 megapixels. The high-resolution workspace allows for multiple designs to be worked on and for multiple designers to participate in the design session.

6   Example Mixed Fidelity Design Session

In this section, to illustrate the mixed fidelity prototyping approach, we look at an example design session for prototyping a business forecasting tool, used by businesses for estimating their revenue and expenses and ultimately profit for some future period. Forecasting involves estimating a number of factors and with so many factors and possible values for each factor, it is most effective to take a visual approach where users can play through different situations and have the effects visualized in charts on the fly. In this example application, adjusting the factor value (x axis value) on charts causes a shift in the corresponding chart's profit curve as well as causes the underlying financial statements to be updated. Note that this application is for illustrative purposes and the mixed-fidelity approach is intended to generalize beyond this domain.

We start by sketching designs using an external drawing application. Note that we also could have drawn the designs on paper and then scanned them in as images. We then import these sketches into ProtoMixer as images and specify them as regions' assets (done through an XML input file). All of the sketches are then displayed in ProtoMixer in the Repository Region. Refer to Figure 7 for the initial state of ProtoMixer.

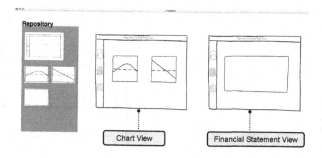

Fig. 7. Initial sketches of two views of forecasting data

(1) Mixing multiple fidelities in a single prototype. We proceed with prototyping by adding further details to the sketches such as labels for the chart axes and pull-down menus for selecting cost and revenue drivers as well as the desired time period.

Next we want to give the sketched charts a more refined look, so we create medium-fidelity images of the charts using an external tool. We import these assets and overlay them on top of the sketched versions on the Chart View.

Now we turn to working on refining the table element in the Financial Statement View. We sketch out example data to put into the table and then import that new sketch. As we are confident the table will be used in the final design, we move it to high-fidelity. Specifically we create a new region and set its asset to be a JTable widget. This region is then overlaid on top of the sketched table. The prototypes created thus far are shown in Figure 8.

(2) Transitioning between the fidelities as ideas are refined. After reviewing the prototypes at that point, we come up with a new design for more interactive charts which involves changing the appearance of the charts. Rather than starting from scratch, ProtoMixer allows us to turn off a layer to hide the images of the charts, thus reverting to the original sketched charts. Using ProtoMixer's built-in sketching feature, we update the sketches to include a vertical guide bar, to emphasize which x value the user has specified. Then we create and import medium-fidelity images matching these refined charts and overlay them onto the sketches. The resulting designs are shown in Figure 9.

(3) Integrating domain-specific data and functionality. We now make some high-fidelity updates to give the users a better appreciation for what the final software will be. First off, we add real data to the high-fidelity data component by setting the JTable's data and updating the region's asset to point to the new table. Then we insert a high-fidelity text field on top of the low-fidelity version. Next we connect the table's data to the profit field, as the profit's value is calculated based on the table data. This connection is done using the high-fidelity binding feature. From now on, modifying the table automatically updates the profit text field. The resulting design is shown in Figure 10.

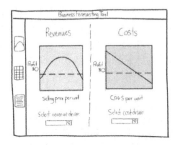 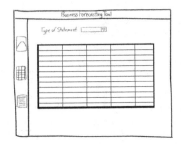

Fig. 8. Medium-fidelity charts and a high-fidelity table have been mixed on refined sketches

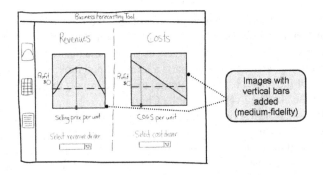

Fig. 9. 'Chart View' after adding updated images of charts

(4) Exploring novel interactive elements. Next we further explore the charts' behavior and interactivity. We want the x-axis of the chart to behave like a slider bar so the user can then slide through the different x-values and have the effects on the other chart visualized immediately by shifting the curve. Such a design is rather unique and is not implemented in any standard toolkit.

We start off by creating a series of medium-fidelity images that illustrate their appearance at some instance in time. Next we set these new charts as the assets of the most recent charts. We are careful to add the charts in sequential order to allow for animation of the chart's behavior. We now animate the charts by using the flash animation feature to see the resulting effects of moving sliders.

Now we need to move to a higher-fidelity design with these chart components, giving them some actual behavior. We work on the main chart area first. As Java's standard toolkit does not offer a chart widget, we implement a simple one on our own to look like the sketched charts. Then we need to use a slider widget for specifying an active x-axis value, so we make use of the JSlider from Java's standard toolkit. We overlay the chart on the sketched chart and then position the slider along the chart's x-axis.

Now that we have the key elements to create our novel chart component, we need to connect them together so a slider's value modifies the other chart's curve. We do this by

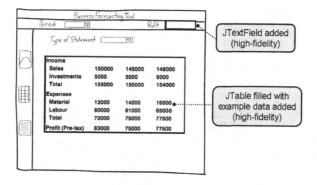

Fig. 10. 'Financial Statement View' after adding the high-fidelity text field and table with data

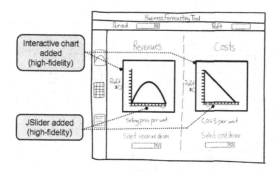

Fig. 11. 'Chart View' after composing a lightweight novel chart element

binding the high-fidelity chart and slider components, again using the binding feature. Now we can see that dragging one chart's slider modifies the other chart and this can be demonstrated to other stakeholders. The resulting design is shown in Figure 11.

(5) Comparing alternative designs. Now we want to explore an alternative layout for the prototype. We sketch out an alternate layout idea, which tries to incorporate the charts and financial statements in the same view so no details are hidden from the user. We import this sketch as well as a sketched version of our current layout and use the automatic layout feature to position the two designs side-by-side. We then want to annotate the two designs with pros and cons of each. We annotate them by creating two high-fidelity JTextArea widgets and type the annotations into the text areas. These annotations can then be associated with a particular design and hidden and unhidden as desired. The resulting state of ProtoMixer is shown in Figure 12.

6) Recording the design process. Later on assume that a software developer is working on the full implementation of the chart components. As no standard component exists, the developer needs to get a thorough understanding of what this chart does and how evolved into the current chosen design. The developer uses ProtoMixer to look back

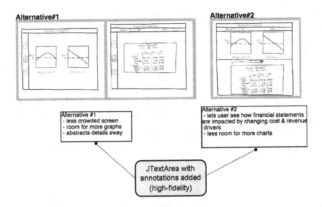

Fig. 12. Annotating the two alternate layouts with pros and cons

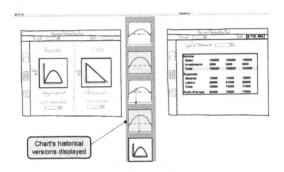

Fig. 13. Center region displays historical versions of the Revenue Chart

at previous versions, or more specifically, the evolution of the chart using the view versions feature. ProtoMixer then pops up a new region next to the specified chart with all of the versions. This state is shown in Figure 13.

7 Conclusion

This research presented a new approach to user interface prototyping called mixed-fidelity prototyping. Mixing fidelities allows designers the flexibility to focus on one specific aspect of a prototype at a time, by exploring that aspect in the various fidelities. In turn, our approach allows for designers to defer the exploration of less urgent issues, unlike current techniques and tools that heavily restrict designers in their workflow. For example, with Interface Builders designers are immediately forced to choose a layout and specific component types when composing a prototype. Our approach also allows individuals with expertise in a specific fidelity to be involved in that fidelity earlier on. For example, a software developer can begin implementing a high-fidelity component for the prototype at an early stage.

Our approach also addresses some of the issues or shortcomings with the current prototyping practice: multiple fidelities may be explored at any given time, iteration may occur between any of the fidelities, user interface designers may better collaborate with each other and with other stakeholders, and potentially more innovative user interface designs may follow. Also, our approach adds continuity and traceability to the process by offering a single unified tool for prototyping in while allowing for designers to still take advantage of paper and whiteboard-based designs that they are familiar with.

ProtoMixer has several benefits over other existing prototyping tools. With ProtoMixer, prototypes can be composed of multiple fidelities, and elements are easily refined and transitioned between different fidelities. Individual elements can be tied into data and functionality, and can be executed inside prototypes. As well, traditional informal practices such as sketching and storyboarding are supported on the mediums that designers are accustomed to. Furthermore, ProtoMixer aids the designers by recording the history of the design process. Finally, ProtoMixer is designed for collaborative use on a high-resolution, large display workspace.

A secondary aspect of this research was to enhance the collaborative nature of prototyping by utilizing a large display workspace. Previous work has shown the benefits of using large displays in collaborative settings and in design settings in particular. Large displays seem ideal for this domain of prototyping, a visually rich, team-based domain. While we did not formally evaluate the benefits of using a large display workspace, it is evident that exploring multiple designs at once, whether it be exploring alternatives or exploring more than one screen design at once, requires more resolution than available on traditional-sized displays. Using tiled high-resolution displays to create a large-display workspace is conducive to our Regions Model and supports our approach well.

Preliminary use of the prototype has been positive, however, a next step in this research is to perform a field study to further evaluate mixed-fidelity prototyping using ProtoMixer. It may be interesting to compare the results of expert versus novice designers, and to evaluate the usefulness of ProtoMixer as a single-user versus a collaborative tool.

References

1. BAILEY, B. P., KONSTAN, J. A., AND CARLIS, J. V. Demais: designing multimedia applications with interactive storyboards. In *Proceedings of the ninth ACM international conference on Multimedia* (2001), ACM Press, pp. 241–250.

2. BLY, S. A. A use of drawing surfaces in different collaborative settings. In *Proceedings of the ACM conference on Computer-supported cooperative work* (1988), ACM Press, pp. 250–256.

3. BRAY, T., PAOLI, J., SPERBERG-MCQUEEN, C. M., MALER, E., AND YERGEAU, F. Extensible markup language (XML) 1.0 (third edition). W3 Recomendation available at: http://www.w3.org/TR/2004/REC-xml-20040204 - Accessed on November 3, 2005.

4. GUNARATNE, J., HWONG, B., NELSON, C., AND RUDORFER, A. Using evolutionary prototypes to formalize product requirements. In *Bridging the Gap II Workshop at ICSE* (2004).

5. HARADA, K., TANAKA, E., OGAWA, R., AND HARA, Y. Anecdote: a multimedia story-boarding system with seamless authoring support. In *Proceedings of the fourth ACM international conference on Multimedia* (1996), ACM Press, pp. 341–351.

6. JOHN, B. E., BASS, L., KAZMAN, R., AND CHEN, E. Identifying gaps between hci, software engineering and design, and boundary objects to bridge them. In *Workshop at CHI'04* (2004).

7. KAZMAN, R., BASS, L., AND BOSCH, J. Bridging the gaps between software engineering and human-computer interaction. In *Workshop at ICSE'03* (2003).

8. KAZMAN, R., BASS, L., AND JOHN, B. E. Bridging the gaps ii: Bridging the gaps between software engineering and human-computer interaction. In *Workshop at ICSE'04* (2004).

9. LANDAY, J. A., AND MYERS, B. A. Interactive sketching for the early stages of user interface design. In *Proceedings of the SIGCHI conference on Human factors in computing systems* (1995), ACM Press/Addison-Wesley Publishing Co., pp. 43–50.

10. LIN, J., NEWMAN, M. W., HONG, J. I., AND LANDAY, J. A. Denim: finding a tighter fit between tools and practice for web site design. In *Proceedings of the SIGCHI conference on Human factors in computing systems* (2000), ACM Press, pp. 510–517.

11. LIN, J., THOMSEN, M., AND LANDAY, J. A. A visual language for sketching large and complex interactive designs. In *Proceedings of the SIGCHI conference on Human factors in computing systems* (2002), ACM Press, pp. 307–314.

12. OUSTERHOUT, J. K. *Tcl and the Tk toolkit*. Addison-Wesley Longman Publishing Co., Inc., 1994.

13. PETRIE, J. Mixed fidelity prototyping of user interfaces. Master's thesis, University of Saskatchewan, 2006.

14. RUDD, J., STERN, K., AND ISENSEE, S. Low vs. high-fidelity prototyping debate. *interactions 3*, 1 (1996), 76–85.

15. TANG, J. C., AND LEIFER, L. J. A framework for understanding the workspace activity of design teams. In *Proceedings of Conference on Computer-supported cooperative work* (1988), ACM Press, pp. 244–249.

16. TVERSKY, B. What does drawing reveal about thinking? In *Proceedings of Visual and spatial reasoning in design* (1999), pp. 93–101.

17. WALKER, M., TAKAYAMA, L., AND LANDAY, J. A. High-fidelity or low-fidelity, paper or computer medium? In *Proceedings of the Human Factors and Ergonomics Society 46th Annual Meeting* (2002), pp. 661–665.

A Hybrid Approach for Modelling Early Prototype Evaluation Under User-Centred Design Through Association Rules

María Paula González, Toni Granollers, and Jesús Lorés

Departament of Computer Science – Universitat de Lleida
C/Jaume II, 69 – 25001 Lleida, Spain
{mpg,toni,jesus}@diei.UdL.es

Abstract. One of the main activities in User Centred Design (UCD) is prototype evaluation, which is traditionally performed by means of an Evaluation Stage that looks for the redefinition of the prototype requirements, involving quantitative and qualitative usability testing techniques. This paper describes a new approach in which the traditional methodology for performing the Evaluation Stage under UCD is embedded in a framework with capabilities for mining association rules. This allows to minimise the impact of the interpretation bias of the evaluation team when analysing ambiguous user statements in natural language.

Keywords: UCD – Evaluation Stage – Data mining – Association Rules.

1   Introduction and Motivations

During the last decade, User-Centred Design (UCD) principles have proven to be successful cutting costs in software development and increasing user satisfaction and productivity [1]. When a software system is iteratively produced under UCD a number of intermediate prototypes $\mathcal{P}_1, \ldots, \mathcal{P}_n$ are developed. Between a prototype $\mathcal{P}_i$ and its successor $\mathcal{P}_{i+1}$ several intermediate stages are involved, such as the *Evaluation Stage*(ES)[1] whose main goal consists in contrasting the usability[2] features of the prototype $\mathcal{P}_i$ against its requirements in order to refine them. The main components for performing the ES for a prototype P_i are shown in full lines in Fig. 1. Given the design of P_i and its requirement specification R_i, different usability evaluation techniques are applied by the software development team (DT) with an active user role. The aim of such techniques is to refine the current set of requirements R_i transforming it into a new requirement definition R_{i+1} for a new (still undeveloped) prototype P_{i+1}. This redefinition

---

[1] In what follows we assume that the Evaluation Stage is always performed early during the software development process (i.e. we focus on early prototypes) and under a UCD perspective.

[2] Usability is defined by the ISO 9241-11 norm as "the extent to which a product can be used by specified users to achieve specified goals with effectiveness, efficiency and satisfaction in a specified context of use".

G. Doherty and A. Blandford (Eds.): DSVIS 2006, LNCS 4323, pp. 213–219, 2007.
© Springer-Verlag Berlin Heidelberg 2007

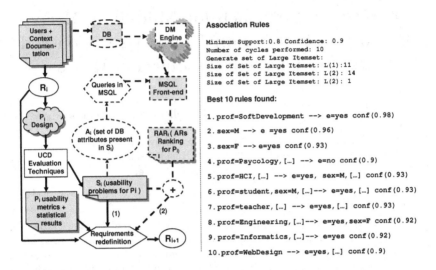

Fig. 1. Left: Schema of the Evaluation Stage for a prototype P_i (full lines represent the traditional approach whereas dotted lines stand for the new components introduced for integrating association rule mining). **Right:** Ranked list RAR_1 of association rules (best 10 out of 50 found) for the experiment in Section 4 ([...] means that more attributes were present in the rules, but without direct relation with this experiment).

is carried out by performing both a *quantitative* and a *qualitative usability estimation* of P_i to make explicit its usability features and problems, which will be then contrasted against R_i [1].

Qualitative usability estimation of a prototype P_i is commonly carried out by techniques based on the interpretation of the DT when analysing user statements expressed in natural language [7]. The output of such techniques is a a set $S_i = \{s_1, \ldots, s_k\}$ of usability problems (statements in natural language) that are used to contrast the current requirements of P_i against its design (as the usability problems in S_i express the problematic features in the design of P_i) in order to redefine those current requirements [1] (arrow (1) in Fig. 1). As a result, a new requirement definition R_{i+1} is generated to be considered in the next cycle of the iterative software production, where a new prototype P_{i+1} will be designed on the basis of R_{i+1}. The interpretation bias of the DT when analysing ambiguous user assertions leads to some lack of objectiveness. For this reason, one of the most significant challenges in the ES is to define a usability testing process that combines high expressiveness, minimum risk and a maximal objectiveness level.

This paper describes the main features of a new, hybrid approach in which the traditional methodology of the ES for prototypes is embedded in a framework with capabilities for mining *association rules*. These rules will allow to automatically find unbiased cause-effect relationships in data coming from the definition of the requirements of $\mathcal{P}_i$. As a result, the DT will be able to use these relationships to reinforce their understanding of qualitative usability problems detected during the ES of $\mathcal{P}_i$ in order to improve the requirement definition for the next prototype $\mathcal{P}_{i+1}$.

2   Mining Association Rules: Fundamentals

Datamining involves a collection of techniques for the analysis of large data sets in order to discover patterns of interest and extract potentially useful information [6]. This extraction can be formalised as a process in which data from (possibly) heterogenous sources are normalised and combined into a transactional database, in which features or *attributes* are identified, and onto which different techniques are performed to mine the available data.

Association rule mining [6] is a powerful datamining technique which allows to find hidden relationships among attributes in a transactional database. Every transaction consists of a set of items $I = \{i_1, \ldots, i_m\}$ and a transaction identifier. Association rules (AR) are implications of the form $A \Rightarrow B$, where $A \subset I$, $B \subset I$, and $A \cap B = \emptyset$. In addition to the antecedent A (the "if" part) and the consequent B (the "then" part), an AR has several interestingness measures that express the quality of the rule. One relevant measure is called the *support* for the rule, which is simply the number of transactions that include all items in the antecedent and consequent parts of the rule. (i.e., the percentage of transactions in D that contain $A \cup B$). Other important measure is known as the *confidence* of the rule, and corresponds to the ratio of the number of transactions that include all items in the consequent as well as the antecedent (namely, the support) to the number of transactions that include all items in the antecedent. (i.e. the percentage of transactions in D containing A that also contain B). Computing ARs is computationally complex task, and several efficient algorithms (e.g. APRIORI or FP-GROWTH [6]) have been developed. The AR mining process generates usually a huge number of rules, making it necessary to provide powerful query primitives to post-process the generated rulebase, as well as for performing selective, query based generation [14]. Several specialised query languages have been proposed in the literature such as MSQL [14] and DMQL [6], among others.

3   Enhancing Early Prototype Evaluation Through ARs

We have developed an hybrid approach for modelling Qualitative Evaluation in which the elements detailed in Section 1 are integrated with new components for carrying out association rule mining. These new components are depicted in dotted lines in Fig. 1 (left). The traditional use of the results coming from the qualitative usability testing of the prototype (arrow 1 in Fig. 1) is complemented by an AR-based approach (arrow 2). This new hybrid approach intents to generate a more objective and expressive output set of usability problems by minimizing the impact of the interpretation bias of the DT when interpreting ambiguous user statements expressed in natural language that were generated during the Qualitative Evaluation process.

In the proposed framework the input for the process is similar as before (an early prototype design P_i, and its requirement specification R_i). Both quantitative and qualitative usability problems are measured by UCD Evaluation Techniques. Qualitative results are compiled in a set $S_i = \{s_1, \ldots, s_k\}$ of usability problems expressed as natural language sentences. At the same time, all the heterogeneous information coming from the development of the current prototype (e.g. data from the definition of context of use, user profiles or organisational requirements specifications for P_1) are collected in a database DB.[3]

In the new, extended framework the DT can now formulate queries which will provide them with additional information (a list of ranked association rules RAR_i). These ARs express hidden cause-effect relationships among attributes present not only in the set S_i of usability problems but also in the information provided by users during the specification of R_i, stored in DB. This new ranked list RAR_i will help to cope with the impact of the interpretation bias of the DT when analysing ambiguous elements in S_i to redefine R_i into R_{i+1}. In particular, those attributes from DB present in S_i are included in a set A_i and used by the DT members to pose queries expressed in a MSQL language. These queries are processed by a front-end module linked with with the actual DM engine which provides the algorithms required for processing the database DB and obtaining ARs from it. As an output, the front-end module provides a ranked list RAR_i for the prototype P_i. Every item in RAR_i represents a non trivial and hidden cause–effect relationship present in the DB. Adding RAR_i to the original usability problem list S_i provides a new perspective to interpret ambiguous user statements in natural language when contrasting the design of P_i with the conclusions coming from the qualitative usability measure. It must be noted that as the DB collects information coming from users, the UCD perspective of our hybrid approach is reinforced.

4   Experimental Results

In this Section we will summarise the results obtained after using the proposed approach for the development of a web site under a UCD perspective.[4] The web site is intended for educational purposes. The development team DT was formed by two CS students, one usability expert, one CS professional with experience in DM techniques and an interdisciplinary group of six university students (final users). The WEKA [4] platform was available for performing datamining, and its interface was used as a basic MSQL front-end for posing queries.

Experiment (sketch): Following the first part of the methodology shown in Fig. 1, (dotted lines) a first prototype P_1 was developed. An exhaustive poll was carried out on the Web to specify the context of use and the user profiles.

---

[3] Notice that spreadsheets and databases used to compute the quantitative usability can be used when constructing the database DB.

[4] The final version of this web can be found at http://www.mpiua.net. It was developed in the GRIHO Labs at the Universitat de Lleida (Spain).

More than 200 results were compiled in a relational database and used to define the requirement specifications R_1 for P_1. Then the prototype P_1 was designed, including a wide spectrum of resources (such as information, bibliography, etc.), the possibility of registering as a user and having a discussion forum, and restricted access to examples (depending on features provided in the registration, e.g. profession). Next the ES was performed. The design of P_1 was confronted against its requirements R_1 by evaluating the usability of the design P_1. The extended approach proposed in this paper was used to perform the redefinition of requirements in R_1. Quantitative results were summarised into statistical graphics [5]. Qualitative results were compiled as a set $S_1 = \{s_1, \ldots, s_5\}$ generated by means of a Focus-Group [9] and a Stakeholders Meeting [7]. Five elements in S_1 were problematic as different members in the DT had conflicting opinions about their relevance and no clear evidence could be found based on the statistical information. Four of these problems (80%) could be treated with our approach. We will summarise the analysis made by the DT during the contrast between the requirement $r_1 = \{$The web must include a resource called "examples"$\}$ and the usability problem $s_4 = \{$There is no agreement with the necessity of having an hyperlink called "examples": should it be available only for determinate users?$\}$. As the most relevant issue present in the usability problem s_1 was the DB attribute "examples" and this attribute was one of the elements in S_1, the methodology presented in Section 3 could be used this case. The DT defined the following query in MSQL language: GetRulesDB where [Antecedent has {prof=* or sex=*} and Consequent has {e=*} and support > 0.8 and confidence > 0.9] In this query "prof" and "e" stand for "profession" and "examples", resp. The query was adapted for the basic front-end interface provided by the WEKA platform and solved by the WEKA datamining engine using the APRIORI Algorithm [6]. As shown in the above query, the ranking function was a combination of a particular threshold for support and confidence. The final result was the list RAR_1 depicted in Fig. 1 (right). Finally, the DT confronted the usability problem s_4 as well as the elements of the ranked list RAR_1 against the requirement r_1. The evidence provided by RAR_1 was strong enough to disregard the usability problem s_4 and avoid the redefinition of the requirement r_1. The iterative development of the final web continued with the design of next prototype P_2 on the basis of R_2.

5 Related Work. Conclusions

To the best of our knowledge, there is no similar approach to integrate datamining techniques (such as association rules) for performing the Evaluation Stage within other models for software development related to UCD [1,2,9,10,11,12,13] as presented in this paper. Indeed, there are other proposals where association rules are used for assessing usability, but always on fully developed, executable software products (i.e., when the prototype design is no longer an issue), particularly in the context of user interfaces [8]. Datamining techniques have been successfully integrated for interface development in web sites. For example, the

---

[5] To consult quantitative results see http://www.alzado.org/articulo.php?id_art=417).

AWUSA framework [15] presents an automatic tool for evaluating usability in web sites by combining logging techniques and datamining along with the static structure of the web site. Another example is described in [5], where logging techniques are applied based on browsing activities performed by users.

In this paper we have presented a novel approach for integrating association rule mining with the traditional formulation for Prototype Evaluation under UCD. Our experiments have shown that our proposal can be successfully applied to early stages in the life cycle of software developmentcontributing to a better understanding of results from qualitative usability testing for P_i, allowing a more accurate redefinition of its requirements for the next prototype P_{i+1}. Part of our future work is focused on using the proposed approach in professional usability evaluations. In this respect, a prototype of an electronic newspaper related with the ELIN Project[6] and a prototype of a new website for the EPS of the Universitat de Lleida are under evaluation. We are also interested on testing different ranking functions for association rules, evaluating their applicability in early prototyping. In particular, we are interested in rule prioritization by taking into account the cost associated with software development, as suggested in [3]. Research in this direction is currently being pursued.

Acknowledgments. We thank the reviewers for their comments which helped to improve the original version of this paper. This work was partially supported by Cicyt Project ADACO (TIN2004-08000-C03-03), and Project SGR-00881 (Generalitat de Catalunya, Spain).

References

1. Sutcliffe A. *User-Centred Requirements Engineering*. Springer, 2002.
2. Sydner C. *Paper Prototyping: The Fast and Easy Way to Design and Refine User Interfaces*. M. Kaufmann, 2003.
3. Choi D., Ahn B., and Kim S. Prioritization of association rules in DM: Multiple criteria decision approach. *Expert Systems with Applications*, 29:867–878, 2005.
4. Witten I. and Eibe F. *Data Mining: Practical machine learning tools and techniques*. M. Kaufmann, 2005.
5. Alipio J., Poças J., and Azevedo P. Recommendation with Association Rules: a web mining application. *Data Mining and Warehouses Conf. IS-2002*, 2002.
6. Han J. and Kamber M. *Data Mining*. M. Kaufmann, 2001.
7. Dumas J.S. and Redish J. C. *A Practical Guide to Usability Testing*. Intl. Specialized Book Service Inc, 2000.
8. Hornbaek K. Current practice in measuring usability: Challenges to usability studies and research. *Int. Journal of Human-Computer Studies*, page (in press), 2005.
9. Constantine L. and Lockwood L. *Software for Use. A practical Guide to the Models and Methods of Usage-Centered Design*. Addison-Wesley, 1999.
10. Ivory M. Y. and Hearst M. A. The state of the art in automating usability evaluation of user interfaces. *ACM Comput. Surv.*, 33:470–516, 2001.
11. D. J. Mayhew. *The Usability Engineering Lifecicle. A practitioner's handbook for user interface desing*. M. Kaufmann, 1999.

---

[6] See European IST-2000-30188 ELIN Project at http://elin.grupoalamo.com/

12. M. Rosson and J. Carroll. *Usability Engineering: scenario-based developement of HCI*. M. Kaufmann, 2002.
13. Granollers T., Perdrix F., and Lores J. Usability Engineering Process Model. Integration with Software Engineering. *ACM HCI'03*, 2003.
14. Imielinski T. and Virmani A. Msql: A query language for database mining. In Springer Science and Business Media B.V., editors, *Data Mining and Knowledge Discovery*, volume 3, pages 373–408, 1999.
15. Tiedtke T., Märtin C., and Gerth N. Awusa. a tool for automated website usability anlaysis. *9th Int. Workshop DSVIS*, 2002.

Rapid User-Centred Evaluation for Context-Aware Systems

Eleanor O'Neill[1], David Lewis[1], Kris McGlinn[1], and Simon Dobson[2]

[1] Department of Computer Science, Trinity College Dublin IE
[2] Systems Research Group, School of Computer Science and Informatics, UCD Dublin IE
Eleanor.ONeill@cs.tcd.ie

Abstract. This paper describes a platform for the user-centred design and evaluation of adaptive, context-aware services in the wireless, mobile and pervasive computing markets. It focuses on evaluating the user interactions with context-aware adaptive systems while synchronising the control of the environmental context that drives adaptivity and the user's perception of that environment. The platform uses a 3D virtual reality simulation to present the environment to the user and to drive the generation of simulated environmental context. The platform thereby delivers repeatable, instrumented, context-dependent evaluations of adaptive services over a range of contexts. It aims to reduce development costs and facilitate the development of more effective, user-empowering services.

Keywords: User-centred design and evaluation, usability, context-aware services, adaptive services, 3D virtual environment.

1 Introduction

More so than other distributed systems, pervasive computing services and other context-aware mobile services must dynamically adapt to the needs of the user and to the current physical, social and task context in which those needs are formed. For instance a weather forecast service may localize its content based on the user's current location. Alternatively, a news notification service on a user's PDA may adapt the volume of its alerting tone based on the level of ambient noise detected or mute itself if the user's calendar indicates she is in a meeting.

The effectiveness of the exhibited adaptive behaviour is highly dependent on the subjective experience which is influenced by their perception of and interaction with the environmental and social context of the task they are currently attempting. For example, too little adaptivity does not offer any significant benefits; too much means that users cannot predict how the system will behave in a given situation. Developing an effective context-aware adaptive service therefore requires extensive user-centred design and testing as the proposed adaptive functionality for the service evolves.

To produce successful services, developers must be able to exercise services prior to deployment, and to incrementally add (or remove) adaptive behaviours in response

G. Doherty and A. Blandford (Eds.): DSVIS 2006, LNCS 4323, pp. 220–233, 2007.

to feedback from users experiencing that behaviour in a range of context spaces. Developing and testing context-aware services is extremely challenging since there are few effective ways to carry out on-going user evaluation with a controlled, repeatable profile of context-change. It is the large number and type heterogeneity of the independent variables associated with such real-world context, e.g. physical, social and task contexts, that makes testing expensive and thus problematic to integrate into the overall engineering process.

At present mobile service developers address these issues through unit testing and final integration testing. In the case of large systems, integration testing typically occurs immediately prior to deployment without realistic user assessment and ruling out possibility for major change. However progress in rapid prototyping methods and tools has been identified as central to overcoming the barriers to widespread development and deployment of ubiquitous computing applications, according to Davies et al [23].

Here we present a platform for the user-centred evaluation of context-aware services which provides a 3D simulated pervasive computing environment. The simulated environment is sufficiently realistic to accurately convey changing physical and social context to the user through the virtual representation of the environment. In conjunction, the adaptive system under test also receives a simulated electronically sensed view of the environment based on the configuration of embedded simulated sensors in the virtual environment. The service can thus create its own view of the physical and social setting of the user.

The problem of controlling synchronized user and system views of context is addressed through the simulated virtual reality environment An adaptive service model will express the relationship between a service's core behaviour and variation in that behaviour in response to context changes. Ultimately this model will drive the rapid prototyping of the service itself, together with the configuration of the usability evaluation instruments.

In this paper we describe the initial implementation of our platform and report on its usability from the point of view of the experimenter. In section 2 we discuss the state of the art in the evaluation of context-aware adaptive services and in the related use of 3D simulations. We then discuss the current implementation of the platform in section 3. In section 4 we report on our experiences in configuring a complex simulation for evaluating a composite set of adaptive services. In section 5 we describe how we aim to extend the platform to support usability testing for context-aware services, using ontology-based semantics.

2   Relation to State of the Art

Currently, user acceptance testing of mobile services involves expensive field trials where the usage context and the user's experiences may be hard to instrument. Usage tests of pervasive computing services that integrate with situated sensors have been largely lab-based and thus are a poor representation of the variety of real-world context users will encounter in the course of their every day lives. For larger location-aware or pervasive computing applications the cost of user-testing a full service deployment quickly becomes prohibitive [2], especially where the interaction between context variation and the behaviour of the service is still being explored, thereby making effective experimental design problematic.

Groups such as the Future Computing Environments Group at Georgia Institute of Technology working on the "Aware Home" [19] and Tatsuya Yamazaki of National Institute of Information and Communications Technology, Japan working on the "Ubiquitous Home" [18] have completed real-life test home environments for accurate simulation of the home environment. Both groups aim to perfectly emulate a real domestic environment and intend to have test-subjects spend significant periods of time in these simulated home environments carrying out domestic activities. However, such live usage testbeds are expensive and difficult to reconfigure to emulate a wide range of different contexts.

Kerttula and Tokkonen [16] have identified "the total user experience" as an area of concern and aim achieve it through early product and system simulations. This idea moves away from testing in isolation and moves towards a simulation where services are tested in parallel and valued over longer periods of time. This approach uses accurate simulation/prototyping of services focussing on features such as the user interface, audio properties and product behaviour, but not including the user's surrounding physical environment.

Similar to our platform, Huebscher and McCann [17] aim to allow initial testing of context-aware applications without requiring a physical deployment. However Huebscher and McCann are working to simulate sensor data e.g. temperature, humidity or location, from a description of context or a simulation model of contexts. This in turn will be used to test the context-logic of a context-aware application.

In the past, virtual reality simulation of pervasive computing environments has been used in a small number of research efforts, specifically QuakeSim [5] and HP Lab's UbiWise [6]. These have demonstrated that 3D virtual reality computer game engines potentially provide a cost effective platform for simulating pervasive computing environments with sufficient realism to accurately test human interaction with pervasive computing software systems.

More recently Shirehjini and Klar have been developing 3DSim[20], a 3D tool for rapidly prototyping Ambient Intelligence building blocks e.g. situation-recognition, goal-based interaction. 3DSim aids the development of human-ambient-interaction systems such as PDA based control systems, adaptive user interfaces, multimedia output coordination or goal-based interaction systems. During a simulation, sensor data is derived from a 2D GUI and gesture elements which are the result of an avatar can pointing at devices.

The team at GIST U-VR Lab, S. Korea have been working on creating a unified context model and a method for the integration of contexts for unified context-aware applications. To loosen the coupling between services and context, they have developed a unified context that represents user-centric contextual information in terms of 5W1H (Who, What, Where, When, How and Why) [21]. To demonstrate user-centric integration of contexts for a unified context-aware application model (the ubi-UCAM), they created a simple 3D simulated environment [22]. By using the simulator they were able to test the effectiveness of the Context Integrator when there were multiple users working with the service simultaneously. The simulated environment allowed them to assess the capabilities of their Context Integrator before bringing it into a real world situation (ubiHome).

Overall, our platform is distinguished from existing ubiquitous computing simulation approaches in that we focus on providing a flexible and easy to configure platform for the tester/experimenter with the target of integrating seamlessly into a wider rapid prototyping process.

3 An Evaluation Platform for Context-Aware Services

The overall goal of the platform is to provide for the rapid user-centred evaluation of adaptive context-aware services by effectively and efficiently testing and evaluating usability and thus increasing productivity in the development of these services. The platform must support the rapid prototyping of adaptive service behaviour through ease of use in the design, execution and instrumentation of user acceptance tests.

Elements, collectively referred to as contextors, must be provided to sense context both from the physical world (sensors) and gather data from personal and other information (data mining). Individual adaptive behaviours for services, must be provided, the most visible being the user interface [3] but also including adaptive information storage and retrieval and operation of actuators in the pervasive computing environment. A service's behaviour must be verified as remaining within a well-defined behavioural envelope across its exhibited adaptivity [4].

The net effect of the tool is to increase the effectiveness of services by incrementally maximizing user acceptance and thus reducing the risk involved in full scale field trials or deployment.

3.1 Interactive Context Simulator

The interactive context simulator has been implemented to allow a researcher rapidly configure and run an experiment for a prototype of their software, using simulated context generated at runtime. The context generator features a multi-user 3D simulation component, a proxy gateway which interfaces services to the simulated 3D world, the under-lying network infrastructure and a real time execution environment. With many users interacting with the service under conditions set by the tester, this provides the service developer with a sophisticated method for experimenting with collaborative, context-aware systems.

The 3D simulation component of the platform is provided by the Half-Life 2 (HL2) game engine [7] which has been modified to enable extraction of information from the environment in XML encoded messages. The game engine has been further tailored towards a pervasive computing environment through the addition of pervasive computing sensor models. Creating a new simulated pervasive computing environment uses existing HL2 modelling tools to place sensors in the virtual world so that at run-time user activity and movement in the virtual world activates the sensors in accordance with experimental objectives. On activation, a sensor model responds by generating an XML encoded message containing information related to the event e.g. username or location data.

Simulated sensors have been modelled to be visible or invisible. We use visible simulated sensors to represent physical devices e.g. pressure mats or wireless access points. Invisible simulated sensors are used to model the field of view or signal range of these devices where required. Supplementary simulators have also been interfaced to the platform to support this approach by providing realistic simulation of RF signal propagation and location information through triangulation [15].

The sensors are programmed to be event-driven, polling or a combination of the two. For instance, a pressure mat responds to the *event* of a user stepping on it, where as a Bluetooth master *polls* to detect new slaves. Using a game engine allows flexibility in the type and quantity of sensors featured by the test environment. For the most part, this is not yet realisable in the real-world where the expense and logistics are prohibitive.

Fig. 1. Multiplayer Virtual Environment

Interfacing the system-under-test (SUT) to the simulator is done via a Java application or Proxy. The platform can host and manage the connections between multiple services and multiple test environments simultaneously. This allows multiple services to access a single environment, or vice versa, a single service to access multiple environments. Services are not obliged to subscribe to all simulated environments and only receive information about relevant experiments.

Prior to connection, the experiment designer will have created or adapted an already existing 3D map. Hammer 4, a map editor provided as part of the Half-Life 2 SDK (HL2 SDK), is the tool that developers currently use to do this. The flexibility of the HL2 SDK means a wide variety of environments and sensor types can be modelled. These sensors can then be deployed into a map, in the positions, densities and numbers that are required for a particular experiment.

Although developing a large map takes some effort, considerable productivity can be achieved by using a blank version of an existing environment to outline an experiment. The effort to populate blank maps with sensors is minimal by comparison to developing a map of a new environment from scratch. The experimental design and set-up process makes use of reusable resources in keeping with the iterative and incremental approach required by rapid development, testing and experimentation. Among these reusable resources are the map files that define the experimental environment, the sensors and the experiment definition XML profiles for a service.

A new experiment commences when a service contacts the simulator with an experiment configuration file. This configuration file contains an experiment ID, a map name, a game-server address and data subscription information. The service is registered and the simulator creates a new database [8] collection using sensor information parsed from the map file. The simulator invokes a new game-server on the remote host and subsequently establishes a connection with the simulation for experimental data transfer.

At run-time, messages flow between the virtual environment and the adaptive service. Data leaving the simulator becomes the contextual information on which services base their decisions and thus respond to the user's needs. In response, services send asynchronous instructions to alter the state of the environment through device or entity actuation, e.g. opening a door or switching on a light. Only a single connection to game-server hosting the experiment is required since underlying game infrastructure ensures game-clients are also updated in a time that is imperceptible to the player/developer. Ultimately, the sensors will send their information to the services under test *via* a contextual services layer.

4 Experiences in Configuring Experiments on the Platform

Here we report on our experience to date with the Interactive Context Simulator in setting up experiments with a collaborative context-aware service that had been developed as a research prototype by colleagues in our department.

4.1 Modelling the Physical Environment

We have had experience both in successfully importing existing 3D maps and in building maps from scratch. Prior to the experiments described here, a three story office building model was constructed which was an accurate representation of a portion of the Computer Science Department at Trinity College Dublin. The model features 104 rooms comprised of offices, computer labs and lecture rooms. In total these rooms are furnished with 520 desks, 352 chairs and 257 replica desktop computers. An undergraduate intern, untrained in the Hammer map editor, completed this map in 22 working days. The resulting model is a substantial resource, supporting experiments where users can roam on a scale that dwarfs that of indoor lab-based emulations used elsewhere.

We also opted for an accurate population of office furniture over more sparsely furnished rooms, since we wanted to replicate as closely as possible the user's experience of the real spaces so that we could conduct comparative experiment in the real world building at a future date. In the process we gained experience in how to produce such maps more efficiently in future, for instance in the use of overlapping polygons and transparent textures.

4.2 Experimenting with Context-Aware Services

We have uncovered some of the merits and difficulties in using this platform for the evaluation of pervasive computing services under development, by observing colleagues using it to configure usability experiments on context aware systems they have developed. In this context, the system under test is an Instant Messaging (IM) application that can display the location of other users as part of their presence information, but only when permitted through a sophisticated policy-based access control mechanism.

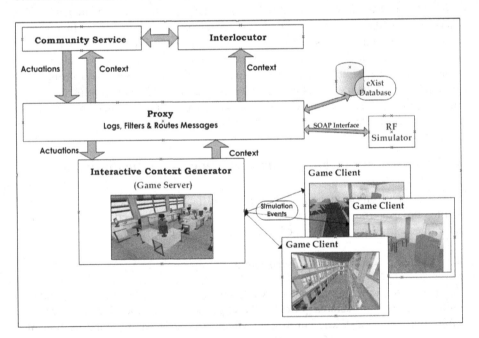

Fig. 2. Experimenting with Context Aware Services

This Location-aware Instant Messaging system extends an existing standard IM server infrastructure, based on JABBER, with a decentralised communications infrastructure employing content-based routing. This adds an additional level of flexibility, allowing applications to subscribe to events of interest based on the event's content rather than overall message type [23]. The IM application allows online users only to view the locations of fellow online members under access control based on policies employing concepts of Community and Trust.

The simulation platform is beneficial as it supplies context in a more dynamic and unanticipated manner since its events are user-invoked and user-controlled. The IM service was tested on an environment where six users were interacting with the environment and service. To enhance location-aware testing, the simulation platform has interfaced to an RF simulator to provide simulated signal propagation values and location information through triangulation of signals [15].

4.3 Experimenting with Policy-Based Access Control

Community Based Policy Management [24] models an organisation's structure as a set of communities. Networks of collaborating users can self-organise because the framework supports dynamic definition of sub-community structure and operational rules. This provides for autonomous sub-communities and allows migration of decision making responsibility to the most appropriate communities in the organisation.

A policy based access control system for the dissemination of location information has been incorporated into the Instant Messaging application above. The policy-based system is characterised by allowing communities of users to agree on policies for the formation of buddy lists, or rosters, in the application. The system also allows policies to be created for determining who is able to monitor the physical location of other users and, in addition, which users can access particular locations (or rooms) in a building. This latter facility was enabled by linking a decision to lock or unlock a door to a request to the access control decision function in this system under test - thus also linking actuation in the simulated environment to the system. The researcher in question wished to determine the ease with which users could collaboratively configure complex access control policies and be satisfied with the operation of those policies as they collectively engaged with the pervasive computing environment.

To evaluate this in situ would only be possible over a long period of use in a location aware environment however the platform provided quick and easy means to designing an experiment to accelerate the usually ponderous interaction of users with policy authoring systems under controlled conditions. This was achieved through experiments where users engage in team games, e.g. catch the flag, in the simulated environment, but using the policy management interface between games/experiments to investigate different rules for the games by changing access control policies for viewing the location of other via the IM application and for enabling room access to the user's avatars. Though the situation is somewhat artificial, the simulator provides a low cost but never-the-less engaging environment for the user in which they can be stimulated into interacting with the adaptive aspects of an application.

4.4 Platform Usability

Based on their experiences, researchers are very receptive to the experimental approach proposed by this tool. The findings from the researchers' use of the platform outline the researchers' opinions on the simulator's usefulness and usability.

Setting up the first version of an experiment, in a new iteration sequence requires the most overhead in terms of time and effort. However, subsequent adjustment to the files is minimal or even non-existent when an experiment is well-defined and fine-tuned. During interviews, researchers reported installation of the simulator, and its accompanying tools, taking on average 30-45 minutes. Further, to initially populate a basic map with sensors and make the XML file associations an additional 60-90 minutes were required. This step partially depends on how powerful the user's computer is. On the grounds that researchers were not at the time familiar with the toolset, i.e. the Hammer map editor, it is expected that these times will improve.

Using the platform, the developer of the location-aware instant messaging service was able to test and debug the system from his desk during the design and development cycle. In particular, it greatly eased the testing of the interaction between the IM application and various configurations of simulated location sensors which the developer confirmed would otherwise have been virtually impossible due primarily to budget constraints. However, even with a substantial equipment budget, the developer would still have faced logistical hurdles regarding deployment of sensors in campus buildings within the college which would be insurmountable at the proof-of-concept stage of development.

A further benefit for the developer meant that it was not necessary to enlist a group of volunteer test users to use a real-deployment of the service. Instead the developer was helped by lab partners to manipulate the location of virtual users in the virtual environment. Since the virtual environment is based on a game engine and very intuitive, the learning curve for new users is minimal. As a result, to run a multi-user experiment required little organisational effort and reduced planning and scheduling of testers and timeslots. These experiments could be run regularly and at short-notice, which was helpful for the debugging process.

5 Extending the Platform

Ultimately, our aim is to combine user-centred design and evaluation. This requires extending the platform as has been implemented to date. Our next steps are to integrate into the platform: support for more sophisticated context processing; more realistic simulation of sensors and adaptive user instrumentation. These extensions are discussed in more detail below.

5.1 Context Services Layer

As is clear from above, one may not treat sensor information as fact but only as evidence of fact, to do otherwise would expose applications directly to all the noise in the environment [9]. This implies that sensor information must be combined with information from other sensors, users models etc, in order to arrive at a stable model of the environment.

A number of approaches to such sensor fusion have been reported in the literature, [10], [11], and [12]. It is not clear that any single approach has yet demonstrated superiority, and within the platform we are experimenting with four complementary approaches; Bayesian networks, fuzzy logic, Dempster-Shaffer evidence theory, and machine learning. Early explorations suggest that each is a plausible candidate for performing high-level context fusion. It is worth noting that, while machine learning may prove extremely useful for adjusting the prior probabilities of sensor events to match observed conditions, these probabilities are functions of context themselves, as mentioned above, and the only criteria for deciding on the accuracy of a sensor observation is the fused result of other sensor observations; a result which itself may not have a strong confidence level.

Our solution to supporting sensor fusion is to run adaptive service tests on top of a contextual services layer based on Construct [13]. Construct provides a highly scalable, distributed platform for collecting and managing contextual information represented using the World Wide Web Consortium Resource Description Framework (RDF). Contextual fusion is supported at the model level, with applications either querying the model or being driven by a truth-maintenance framework. The use of RDF abstracts the details of the sensors underlying a particular installation; sensors write information to the knowledge base under the appropriate ontology, which may be accessed by applications without being aware of the detailed sensor population. This improves the robustness of applications to individual sensor failures and simplifies the addition of new sensor capabilities.

Overall the services under test can be isolated from the fact that their inputs are coming from a virtual environment, they are simply given access to a contextual model to which they can react. The behaviour of the service is less well-abstracted at present, in that some behaviour is targeted directly at devices which must be simulated within the virtual world. Since the models of sensors and their fusion are expressed within the Construct framework, it is straightforward to change the parameters of the simulation to, for example, cause sensors to fail or exhibit more inaccuracy. We conjecture that this will assist in the development of applications that are more robust to sensor noise, sensor failure and uncertain information in general.

The design consists of a closely integrated set of tools and accompanying methodologies, Fig.3. Experimental design involves the tester building a simulation model of the physical environments encountered by the human test subject and populating it with simulated sensors that would provide user driven excitation of the region of context space being investigated. The accurate propagation of realistic context information to the adaptive service under test is mediated by the contextual services layer. The adaptive service model is used to help identify and generate the simulated environment through the identification of experimental goals, test cases and the required control of contextual services. It is also used in generating the user and service evaluation instruments for a test, i.e. which user and service behaviour parameters to monitor and log, along with the structure of user evaluation questioning.

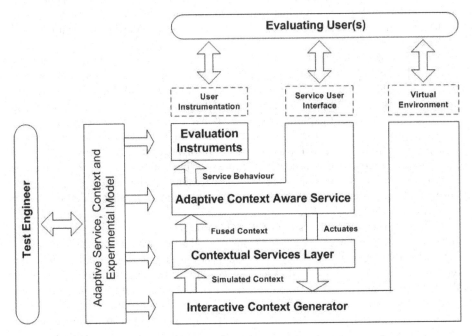

Fig. 3. Overview of Platform Architecture

5.2 Sensor Simulation

Sensors in the platform are implemented as objects in the virtual world, as mentioned above, which expose certain facets of that world to the services under test. The simple approach currently taken in the simulator defines the range and capabilities of a particular sensor, which would then be used by the virtual world to generate sensor events. We recognise, however, that such an approach is naïve for two reasons.

Firstly, all sensors include significant noise components. These manifest themselves as inaccuracies (*i.e.* a location sensor reporting the presence of the wrong person) and imprecision (*i.e.* a location being an area rather than a point). Evaluating a service against such sensors might lead to services that function well in the presence of correct and precise information but which fail when exposed to real-world inaccuracies and imprecision.

Secondly, sensors are themselves sensitive to the context in which they are installed. Two examples illustrate this:

- A wireless communications system will encounter signal reflections and attenuations in buildings with substantial amounts of metal in the walls. These reduce the effective range and bandwidth of the communications channel.

- RFID tag readers frequently fail under heavy load, such as when several people move past a reader in quick succession. This manifests itself as the reader only observing a fraction of the tags that actually come into range.

These two constraints mean that the characteristics of a sensor must take account of both the static and dynamic context into which it is deployed. This is essentially the same problem as encountered in modelling the larger adaptive service, and means that we must provide 'user models' of sensors together with context-aware behaviour, which are then used to generate the information for the services under test.

5.3 User Instrumentation

Integrated user evaluation instruments will be used to conduct tests by allowing the user to roam within and interact with the virtual physical environment. This system will provide task instructions to user test subjects based on context change or adaptive service notification received from the Simulation Infrastructure. It will present the user with evaluation instruments, such as questions or prompts for free style comment.

Responses will be logged aligned to the activities the user has performed in the simulator, the context changes and the adaptive behaviour to which the user has just been exposed. In this way users may interact with the simulation in a non-linear way, exploring the environment and deviated from tasks as the might to in the real world, but the instrumentation of their experience will be recorded in context to assure accurate analysis of the results.

6 Conclusions and Summary of Further Work

To date this Platform has largely been used as a simulator of pervasive computing environments and context generator for experimenting with context aware services. We aim to build on this by exploring the capture of a fuller semantic model for the adaptive behaviour exhibited by a service, beginning with the integration of the contextual service layer with the Interactive Context Simulator. The model will map the context space within which an adaptive service operates to the behaviour space that the service can exhibit. This model will be used both to provide abstractions for rapid, script-based prototyping of new adaptive behaviour, which will thus be integrated, with the ontology-driven experimental design and configuration.

This will lead to improvement in the productivity of the testing and evaluation phase of the rapid development cycle for context-aware adaptive services. This improvement will be achieved through the model-driven configuration of test cases, shorter test development life-cycles, more targeted and relevant user evaluation, a low-cost test infrastructure and the facility for on-line user testing, thereby resulting in a lower overall cost for the test portion of the development cycle.

In line with the range of behaviour exhibited by adaptive services, the aim in evaluation will not be to verify correctness of system behaviour, but to confirm that it operates within a well defined behavioural envelope given for specific regions of the possible context space that corresponds to the overall testing goals. The adaptive service model will be used to identify these experimental goals as well as to identify test cases, and context and control variables. It will also assist in the generation of the simulated environment and user and service evaluation framework through a set of closely integrated tools and methodologies.

Additionally, future development work will fully integrate a set of user evaluation instruments into the simulator to allow online, runtime questioning of users. Usability Engineering offers a number of techniques for evaluating ease of use and user acceptance. Though tool support for the former in mobile services is maturing, in focusing on the latter we address an area where effectiveness remains elusive as evidenced by high-profile failures in mobile data services.

Recent developments allow adaptation of hypermedia documents to be based on the selection of narrative, content and user meta-data [18]. This will be applied to adaptively assemble different evaluation instruments based on questioning style (e.g. factual, opinion, attitude, open/closed ended or Likert style), instrument topic (e.g. adaptive behaviour experienced) and user data (e.g. demography, previous responses).

Extensions to the simulation element of the platform are planned to include integration with a wireless indoor signal propagation simulator. This will allow us to factor in communication performance degradation for both context and service delivery, as well as location sensing inaccuracies for WLAN signal strength based location system. We have performed some initial integration tests with wireless simulators capable of modelling RF reflection and absorption characteristics of different structural materials as well as of the human occupants themselves as they move in the space [15].

Acknowledgements

This work has been partially supported by the Irish Higher Education Authority under the M-Zones programme and by Enterprise Ireland under the PUDECAS [TD 2005 217-A/B] project.

References

1. Czarkowski, M. and Kay, J., (2003). Challenges of Scrutable Adaptivity. In Proceedings of AIED Conference, 11th International Conference on Artificial Intelligence in Education, IOS Press 404 - 407.
2. Yamazaki, T, (2005). Ubiquitous Home: Real-Life Testbed for Home Context-Aware Service. Proceedings of IEEE 1st International Conference on Testbeds and Research Infrastructures for the DEvelopment of NeTworks and COMmunities (Tridentcom 2005).
3. Calvary G., Coutaz, J., Thevenin, D., (2004). A unifying reference framework for the development of plastic user interfaces. In Proceedings of EHCI/DSVIS'04.
4. Dobson, S., Nixon, P. (2004). More principled design of pervasive computing systems. In Proceedings of EHCI/DSVIS'04.
5. Bylund, M., Espinoza, F., (2002). Testing and Demonstrating Context-Aware Services with Quake III Arena. Communications of the ACM, Vol. 45, No 1, pp46-48.
6. Barton, J., Vijayaraghavan. V., (2002). UbiWise, A Ubiquitous Wireless Infrastructure Simulation Environment. HP technical report.
7. Half-Life 2, Valve Corporation (2004). http://www.half-life2.com/

8. eXist, Open Source Native XML Database. http://exist.sourceforge.net/
9. Dobson, S., (2005). Hybridising events and knowledge in an infrastructure for context-adaptive systems. Proceedings of the IJCAI'05 Workshop on Artificial Intelligence and Autonomic Communications.
10. Gonzalez, A. and Ahlers, T., (1999). Context-based representation of intelligent behaviour in training simulations. Transactions of the Society for Computer Simulations International 15(4). March 1999.
11. Henrickson, K. et al, (2002). Modelling context information in pervasive computing systems. Proceedings of Pervasive'02. LNCS 2414. Springer Verlag.
12. Ranganathan, A., Al-Muhtadi, J. and Campbell, R., (2004). Reasoning about uncertain contexts in pervasive computing environments. IEEE Pervasive Computing 3(2). April-June 2004.
13. Stevenson, G., Nixon, P. and Dobson, S., (2005). Towards a reliable wide-are infrastructure for the context-based self-management of communication. Proceedings of the 2nd IFIP Workshop on Autonomic Communications. LNCS. Springer Verlag. 2005. To appear.
14. Dagger, D., Wade, V., Conlan, O., (2004). Developing Active Learning Experiences for Adaptive Personalised eLearning, Third International Conference on Adaptive Hypermedia and Adaptive Web-Based Systems, AH2004, LNCS3137 p55-64
15. O'Neill, E. et al, (2005). A Testbed for Evaluating Human Interaction with Ubiquitous Computing Environments. Proceedings of IEEE 1st International Conference on Testbeds and Research Infrastructures for the DEvelopment of NeTworks and COMmunities (Tridentcom 2005).
16. Kerttula, M. and Tokkonen, T., (2001). The Total User Experience – How to make it Positive in Future Wireless Systems and Services. WWRF Annual Workshop in Paris 2001.
17. Huebscher, M. and McCann, J., (2004). Simulation Model for Self-Adaptive Applications in Pervasive Computing. 2nd International Workshop on Self-Adaptive and Autonomic Computing Systems (SAACS '04).
18. Yamazaki, T., (2005). Ubiquitous home: real-life testbed for home context-aware service. Proceedings of IEEE 1st International Conference on Testbeds and Research Infrastructures for the DEvelopment of NeTworks and COMmunities (Tridentcom 2005).
19. Abowd, G., (2000). Living laboratories: The future computing environments group at the Georgia institute of technology. ACM Conference on Human Factors in Computing Systems, 2000.
20. Nazari Shirehjini, Ali A., Klar, F., (2005). 3DSim: Rapid Prototyping Ambient Intelligence. Joint sOc-EUSAI conference.
21. Seiie Jang, Eun-Jung Ko, and Woontack Woo (2005) Unified User-Centric Context: Who, Where, When, What, How and Why. UbiPCMM: Personalized Context Modelling and Management for Ubicomp Applications.
22. Yoosoo Oh, Woontack Woo (2005). User-centric Integration of Contexts for a Unified Context-aware Application Model. Joint sOc-EUSAI conference.
23. Kenny, A., Lewis, D., O'Sullivan, D., (2006). Interlocutor: Decentralised Infrastructure for Adaptive Interaction. To appear in proceedings of 3rd International Workshop on Managing Ubiquitous Communications and Services (MUCS), 2006.
24. Feeney, K., Lewis, D., Wade V., (2004). Community Based Policy Management for Smart Spaces. Proceedings of 5th IEEE International Workshop on Policies and Distributed Systems and Networks, IEEE, 2004.

Using a Patterns-Based Modelling Language and a Model-Based Adaptation Architecture to Facilitate Adaptive User Interfaces

Erik G. Nilsson, Jacqueline Floch, Svein Hallsteinsen, and Erlend Stav

SINTEF ICT, Norway
{Erik.G.Nilsson, Jacqueline.Floch, Svein.Hallsteinsen,
Erlend.Stav}@sintef.no

Abstract. To design usable mobile applications, exploiting context changes is of vital importance. The rapid context changes in a mobile setting cause the need for flexible and adaptive user interfaces that are multitasking and possibly exploiting multiple modalities. Implementing adaptive user interfaces requires expensive application-specific solutions. Reuse of this type of solutions is difficult or impossible. To make it viable to implement adaptive user interfaces for a broader range of applications, there is both a need for new architecture and middleware, and ways of constructing applications. In this paper, we show how a combination of a patterns-based modelling language using compound user interface components and mapping rules as building blocks, and a generic adaptive architecture based on components with ports and utility functions for finding the optimal configuration in a given situation, facilitates implementation of applications with adaptive user interfaces. First we briefly present our modelling approach, and the adaptive architecture including the generic middleware exploiting architecture models at runtime. With this as a background we show how the presented modelling approach may be combined with the adaptive architecture to facilitate model-based user interface adaptation. Finally, we compare our approach with other approaches for realizing adaptive user interfaces, and we give some conclusions and directions for future research.

Keywords: Model-based design. Interfaces for mobile devices. Adaptive and customizable systems. Patterns-based approaches. Adaptive architecture.

1 Introduction

Limited screen size and interaction mechanisms on mobile equipment make it challenging to design user interfaces on this type of equipment [15, 16]. Compared to a stationary user, the context of a user exploiting a mobile solution changes more often [15, 22]. The context changes are multidimensional, sometimes rapid, and comprise position, light, sound, network connectivity, and possibly biometrics. For example, communication bandwidth changes dynamically in wireless

G. Doherty and A. Blandford (Eds.): DSVIS 2006, LNCS 4323, pp. 234–247, 2007.

communication networks and power is a scarce resource on battery powered devices when outlet power is not available. Furthermore, user interface preferences change when on the move, because light and noise conditions change, or because hands and eyes are occupied elsewhere. Dynamic adaptation is required in order to retain usability, usefulness, and reliability of the application under such circumstances. An important means for enhancing the user experience for mobile users is to exploit information about the changing context in the user interface design [1, 15, 22]. To cater for this, the user interfaces on such solutions need to be adaptive in many cases.

Within model-based user interface research, there has been some interest in mobile user interfaces the last years [e.g., 1, 2, 3, 8, 9, 11, 13, 18, 19, 23, 24]. The focus in most of this work is on using models at design time for specifying either purely mobile UIs or having models that act as specifications across mobile and stationary UIs. If adaptation is present, it is often focusing on adapting the UI to a given platform as part of a code/UI generation process.

Traditionally, adaptive features of a UI have been considered part of the functionality of a UI [1, 17, 20, 21, 22], i.e., it has been the responsibility of the UI itself to find out what kind of changes to perform, and to perform the changes when needed. In our work, we investigate solutions where the adaptation is managed and handled by independent, generic mechanisms, grouped together to an adaptation middleware. By using this model, the adaptation middleware is both responsible for finding out when to perform an adaptation and for doing the actual adaptation. As the middleware is generic, it is made once, and may be used by any application conforming to certain requirements, thus giving clear saving for developers. The price for obtaining this saving, is that the application must be built in a specific way, and that the middleware require some additional specifications for the application.

2 A User Interface Modelling Approach Based on Modelling Patterns and Compound User Interface Components

In this section we give a brief presentation of the modelling approach presented in [13] with focus on the motivation for the modelling approach and its main principles, concepts and features. Below, we will show how this modelling approach together with the adaptive architecture presented in the next section can be used to realize adaptive behaviour at run-time, and how the approach makes development of adaptive user interfaces easier.

Most model-based languages and tools suffer from a combination of two connected characteristics: the languages offer concepts on a too low level of abstraction, and the building blocks are too simple. The building blocks available may be on a certain level of abstraction (like a *choice element* concept that is an abstraction of radio group, drop-down list box, list box, etc.), but are still fairly basic building blocks when a user interface is to be specified. A user interface specification is an instance hierarchy of the given modelling constructs (building blocks). This works well as long as the same instance hierarchy is applicable on all the platforms. If the specification is to work across platforms with a certain level of differences, e.g., with large differences in screen size, having only fairly simple building blocks causes a need to have different instance hierarchies on each platform.

This is often handled by dividing the specification of a given UI in two parts, one describing the commonalities across the platforms and one describing the specialities on each platform. This division must usually be done at a quite early stage in a user interface specification [12]. Furthermore, the amount of specification code for the platform-specific parts tends to be more voluminous than for the common part. In such a situation, it may be just a efficient to develop the user interface on each platform from scratch [14].

Unlike most other model-based languages, the modelling approach presented in [13] uses a combination of compound components and modelling patterns [6, 26]. Compound (or composite) user interface components are used to be able to have equal or similar model instances on platforms with significant differences (including traditional GUI, Web user interfaces and user interfaces on mobile equipment). Modelling patterns are used partly to obtain the necessary level of abstraction to facilitate common models across different platforms, and partly to render it possible to define generic mapping (or transformation) rules from the patterns-based, abstract compound components to concrete user interfaces on different platforms. A mapping rule is a generic and operational description of how a modelling pattern instance should be transformed to a running UI on a given platform, and mapping rules are an important part of the modelling framework. As a modelling pattern usually involves a number of objects, a user interface supporting a modelling pattern must be a *composition* of different user interface components (each being simple or composite). The transformation rules describe how the *modelling patterns* are to be realized on various platforms. This means that the transformation rules must be instantiated with the same concrete classes that the patterns are instantiated with.

To utilize the potential of the modelling approach, it also includes a number of different mapping rules to concrete representations for each abstract compound user interface component on each platform, based on preferences, desired user interface style, modalities, etc. Fig. 1 shows how the different main parts of the modelling approach are connected, expressed using a Unified Modelling Language (UML) class model.

Using this modelling approach, a user interface specification consists of a number of model pattern instances (the abstract representation of the compound UI components), a chosen number of mapping rule instances for each of the pattern instances and additional properties specified for all of these. By mapping rule instance we mean applying a mapping rule to a pattern instance, resulting in a set of UI components (instance hierarchy of concrete UI components) that together constitute the running UI. A specification may also include instances

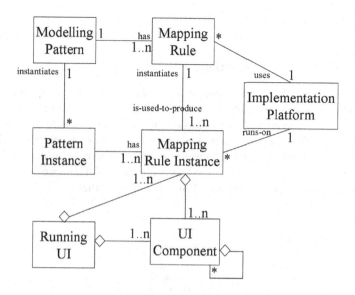

Fig. 1. Main concepts in the modelling approach

of patterns and/or mapping rules that are specified by the systems developer himself/herself. In addition, the modelling framework has features like extensibility (e.g., the possibility to add new building blocks and mapping rules easily) and recursive modelling (e.g., the possibility to construct new building blocks by combining existing ones).

The number of abstract components is limited, to make the modelling language comprehensible and to limit the amount of work needed to define all appropriate mappings. Yet the set is sufficiently comprehensive to render it possible to use the modelling language to specify an arbitrary user interface.

In the section below where we couple the modelling approach and the adaptive architecture we present an example showing how the modelling language may be used to describe two variants of a user interface for mobile users.

3   Adaptive Architecture

To achieve adaptive UIs using the modelling approach just presented, we use the support for handling adaptive applications in the context of mobile computing that we have developed in the FAMOUS[1] project [4, 7]. This work is based on an architecture centric approach where we exploit architecture models to reason about and control adaptation at runtime. To realize the adaptation mechanisms we use generic middleware components [7]. The middleware has three main functions:

---

[1] FAMOUS (Framework for Adaptive Mobile and Ubiquitous Services) is a strategic research programme at SINTEF ICT funded by the Norwegian Research Council.

1. Detect context changes.
2. Reason about these changes and make decisions about what adaptation to perform.
3. Perform the chosen adaptation.

To fulfil these functions, the adaptation middleware requires knowledge of the application structure and constraints, meaning that it should understand the architecture of the software system in question. The architecture models available at runtime describe the information needed by the middleware. Fig. 2 illustrates the middleware architecture (the numbers refer to the three functions just mentioned). The architecture is specified as a component framework [25], allowing middleware services to be composed in a flexible manner.

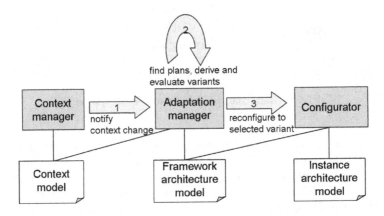

Fig. 2. Middleware architecture and the runtime models

The context and adaptation managers and the configurator are the central components of the adaptation middleware. Below we describe the different parts of the middleware architecture indirectly through the available functionality (the three main functions mentioned above). Before doing this, we explain the runtime models (the boxes in the bottom row in fig. 2) involved.

3.1   Run-Time Models

The *Context model* in fig. 2 represents the current context in terms of relevant context entities and their properties. Context includes execution platform context elements such as network and memory resources, the environment context elements such as light and noise, and user context elements such as location and stress level. The *Framework architecture model* captures the application architecture in terms of component types with alternative implementations annotated with properties and connected together in a possibly hierarchic structure. This model is used do derive application variants best suited for the current context.

Application variants can differ in a number of ways, for example user interface, functional richness, quality properties provided to the user, how the components are deployed on a distributed computing infrastructure, and what resources and quality properties they need from the platform and network environment. The *Instance architecture model* is a run-time representation of the variant that is currently running. This model is used during reconfiguration to perform the transition from the current running variant to a new variant.

The different models are based on a common conceptual model, which is presented in fig. 3. We view a software system and its context as a system of interacting entities. In this case, entities may represent context entities or software components. Entities interact with other entities by providing and making use of services through ports. A port represents a service offered by an entity or a service needed by an entity. Entities may be composed of smaller entities, allowing for a hierarchic structure.

To model variation, both in the application and in its context, we introduce the concept of entity type. An entity type defines a class of entities with equivalent ports which may replace each other in a system. With these concepts we are able to model an adaptive application architecture as a possibly hierarchic composition of entity types, which defines a class of application variants as well as a class of contexts in which they may operate.

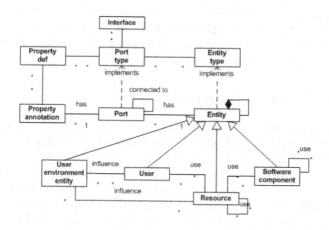

Fig. 3. Adaptation conceptual model

What we need in addition is a way to enable the derivation of the variant that best fits a given context. Our approach is based on property annotations associated with ports. For example, a property annotation might denote the response time of a service provided by an application, the latency of a communication link, the maximum latency tolerated by an application, or the noise level at the current location of the user.

Property annotations allow us to reason about how well an application variant matches its context, by comparing the properties of the services provided by the application with the properties required by the user and the properties expressing the resource needs of the application with the property annotation describing the resources provided by the current computing infrastructure. The match to user needs is expressed in a *utility function*. By default the utility function is a weighted mean of the differences between properties representing user needs and properties describing the service provided by the application, where the weights represent priorities of the user. However, the developer may also provide a tailored utility function for an application.

3.2 Context Change Detection

The *Context manager* represents the active part of the middleware architecture. It is responsible for maintaining an up to date context model and detecting context changes. Context includes execution platform context elements such as network and memory resources, the environment context elements such as light and noise, and user context elements such as location and stress level. This information is collected, represented, and stored using *Context sensors*. There are three main kinds of context sensors: context probes that sense context directly, context reasoners that aim to aggregate, predict and derive new context information, and resource sensors that use resource management services to monitor the resources of the execution platform. Context elements are delivered to the Adaptation Manager component when appropriate. Further details on the context management framework can be found in [10].

3.3 Reasoning About Context Changes

The *Adaptation manager* is responsible for reasoning on the impact of context changes on the application, determining when there is a need to trigger adaptation, and for selecting an application variant that best fits the current context. Based on the framework architecture model it generates all possible variants that can be accommodated with the available resources and selects the one with the highest utility. Then it uses the Configurator to implement the new configuration. The adaptation management is described in more detail in [4].

3.4 Application Reconfiguration

The *Configurator* is responsible for the configuration and reconfiguration of an application. By reasoning on the difference between the instance architecture model of the currently running application variant and the model of the new variant, the Configurator is able to derive the necessary configuration steps to get to the new application variant.

4 Using Modelling Patterns and Compound User Interface Components to Facilitate Adaptive User Interfaces

The adaptive architecture uses models at run time to facilitate any type of adaptive behaviour in an application. In this section we will show how the patterns-based modelling approach may *utilize* the adaptive architecture specifically to ease development of adaptive UIs, facilitating fairly advanced UI adaptation mechanisms at run time.

Normally, a model-based systems development tool does the mapping from the user interface models to concrete user interfaces in the *design phase* (e.g., as a code generation process), i.e., before the system is deployed to the users. The adaptation mechanism may exploit that the modelling approach offers a number of different mapping rules for each modelling pattern. The adaptive functionality is obtained by making the choice of which mapping rule to use at *run time*, i.e., after the system is deployed to the users.

4.1 Using the Adaptive Architecture

As seen above, the adaptive architecture facilitates mechanisms for component based systems to be adapted at run time. To utilize this architecture for the presented modelling approach, a number of mapping rules must be applied at design time, so that the adaptation mechanisms have a number configuration to choose from. This may be done automatically by a code generation facility (at design time). A user interface at run time will thus consist of a number of user interface components arranged in a structure that the adaptation middleware may exploit.

To make both the modelling approach and how it is used for run-time adaptation more concrete, we present an example. In [13] we presented an example focusing on how the modelling approach facilitates cross-platform development. The example in [13] shows how two instantiations of the composite design pattern (file system and system for managing department structure and human resources in an organization) may be mapped to PC and PDA platforms using two different mapping rules on each platform. As we focus on adaptation in this paper, we present a variant of the same example, using only one instantiation of the composite pattern (human resource management) that is mapped to PDA platform using two different mapping rules. Fig. 4 below shows the Composite pattern and the instantiation of it.

The example shows two similar mapping rules for PDA platform, both using a GUI interaction style. The first mapping rule [13] (top part of fig. 5) is optimized for overview, i.e., it will present as many instances as possible on the screen at the same time, and also facilitates flexible navigation. The resulting UI requires that the user utilizes a stylus when operating it. The second mapping (bottom part of fig. 5) is optimized for users focusing on details and not using stylus, i.e., all elements are larger, and the facilities for navigation are on the one side more accessible, but on the other side less flexible. The mapping rule is therefore

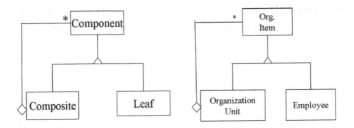

Fig. 4. The Composite Pattern (left) and the Department structure/Human resource mgmt. instantiation of it (right)

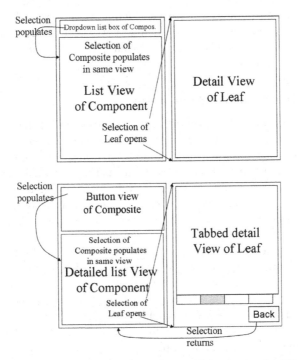

Fig. 5. Stylus (top) and finger (bottom) usage mapping schemes for PDA presentation

designed so that the need for navigation is reduced, e.g., by providing more information in the list view.

The developer chooses that the two mapping rules should be available at run time. This causes the model transformation mechanism that normally would generate one running UI per platform to generate the necessary UI components for both the mapping rules. These UIs would look like figs. 6 and 7.

Each of these UIs consists of an instance hierarchy of concrete UI components. These two instance hierarchies are registered as alternatives in the adaptive architecture. The choice of which variant to use could be determined

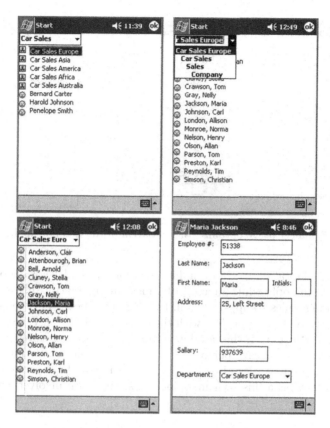

Fig. 6. Stylus usage optimized instantiation of the example application - second view shows navigation to ancestors

by a combination of the users location (obtained from a GPS or RF-ID location sensor), the users task (obtained from the users calendar), and the temperature (obtained from a sensor). For the middleware, this rule is described in the utility function, prescribing when the middleware should choose each alternative. Above, we stated that the utility function is specified by the developer. This is normally the case, but in this special situation where the mapping rules are generic, knowledge about the utility of the individual mapping rules should be available, i.e., describing a mapping rule may include describing (as a utility function) the factors that make the mapping rule best suited. Thus, the developer of the application may be given (i.e., it is generated) a default utility function for each mapping that he may refine for the specific needs of this instantiation. Once the versions are registered in the middleware and the utility function is in place, the application may be started. Which version that will be used at a given time, is depending on the information obtained by the context manager with regards to the utility function, and how the adaptation manager reasons about this information.

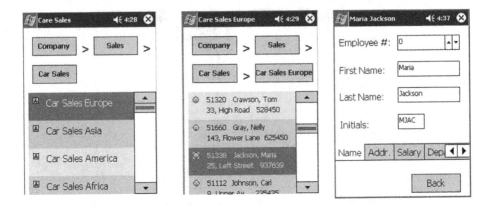

Fig. 7. Finger usage optimized instantiation of the example application

What the adaptation mechanism does at a conceptual level is choosing which mapping rule to apply while an application is running. Of course, the total number of mapping rules to apply (two in the example above) must be decided by the developer. What is appealing with the combination is that it requires almost no additional effort from the developer to offer adaptive features compared to having just one alternative per platform. This is of course only true as long as appropriate mapping rules already exist. If this is not the case, and the developer chooses to make his own mapping rules, the work involved will increase significantly.

4.2   Types of Adaptation

The example above shows a moderate size adaptation, i.e., having two versions of a UI that are similar, but also have significant differences. It is easy to see that adding a third mapping rule changing the UI to a speech driven one, fits easily into the scheme, given that such a mapping rule exists. For the user, this type of adaptation, i.e., one involving a different modality, is more radical.

The most obvious types of adaptations that this approach facilitates are radical changes, i.e., changes regarding the main principles for how the user interface behaves, e.g., changes in the main modality to use or change in the user interface style (e.g., from a forms-based to one using icons and drag-and-drop to a wizard-based one). The reason why these types of changes are most obvious is that this is the most natural aspects to cover in different mapping rules when used for cross-platform development purposes (i.e., to have a set of mapping rules that causes the resulting user interfaces to be different from each other to a certain degree).

As the example above shows, the approach also fits very well for moderate changes. The mapping rules mechanism may also be used to facilitate changes on even a lower level of granularity. Obviously, when the differences between the variants are smaller, the mapping rules become more similar, e.g., different versions of a mapping rule for one modality using a given style. This latter use of the mapping rules mechanism to facilitate smaller differences in the user interface may cause the number of mapping rules to become larger, and if the degree of overlap between the different rules is large, changing one of them may cause the need for doing the same type of change on the parts of the mapping rule that are shared by other mapping rules. A way of handling this is to have a sub typing mechanism that lets different mapping rules inherit from a common ancestor.

In addition to using different mapping rules as a means for adaptation, some low level changes may be done using the pattern instantiation mechanisms (e.g., use a different icon, table headings, sorting of lists, menus, toolbars), this may be viewed as a different way of using the mapping rule, or as an adaptation of the mapping rule, i.e., the changes will not influence the instance hierarchy that the mapping rule was used to generate. This type of adaptation should normally not involve the adaptation middleware, except possibly the context manager that can be used as a trigger mechanism.

5   Related Work

There are three main approaches for adaptive user interfaces, taking a model-based approach more or less into account. The first approach is to handle adaptation at design time [5, 8, 9, 11, 18, 19, 23, 24]. This is the most common way of handling adaptation in model-based UI development environments. The UIs are adapted to different platforms as a part of a UI generation process. This may also be done at run time [2], but still with one UI per platform. This differs from our approach in the way that we also provide adaptation on the individual platforms.

A second approach is to provide some kind of transformation mechanism at run-time [17], i.e., a mechanism that transforms at UI designed for one platform to a fit to a different one. The effect is thus similar to the first approach, only using different means.

A third approach is to provide adaptation mechanisms in the UI itself [1, 20, 21, 22]. As discussed in the introduction, this may cause the same effects as our approach, but requires more efforts for developers, as the adaptation is not handled by generic middleware components. In our work, we investigate solutions where the adaptation is managed and handled by independent, generic mechanisms, grouped together to an adaptation middleware. By using this model, the adaptation middleware is both responsible for finding out when to perform an adaptation and for doing the actual adaptation. Repo et al. [20, 21] also use an independent middleware in their approach, but it is neither based on component frameworks nor a model-based approach for describing the variants of a user interface.

6   Conclusions and Future Work

To design usable mobile applications, exploiting context changes is of vital importance. The rapid context changes in a mobile setting cause the need for flexible and adaptive user interfaces that are multitasking and possibly exploiting multiple modalities. In this paper we have briefly presented a patterns-based modelling approach based on abstract, compound components and mapping rules to various target platforms. As the number of such components (i.e., supported modelling patterns), the number of mappings for each pattern, and the number of target platforms are limited, it is possible to optimise the mappings with regard to usability and exploiting special features on each platform.

We have presented a middleware centric approach to supporting the building of applications capable of adapting to a dynamically varying context as is typical of mobile use. The proposed approach builds on the idea of achieving adaptability by building applications as component frameworks from which variants with different properties can be built dynamically.

In the paper we have shown how the modelling approach may be extended to cover adaptable user interfaces at run time exploiting the adaptation middleware.

At the current stage, the adaptation middleware is more mature than the modelling approach (e.g., we have implemented the adaptation middleware). Still, there are a number of challenges for both. For the adaptation middleware, making the optimization process connected to the utility function more efficient, especially for applications with many components, is both challenging and important. Also the architecture needs further development and experimentation. The modelling approach needs further refinement and details, both regarding the modelling patterns and mapping rules and how they should be used at design time, and how the mapping rules should be used to exploit the adaptation middleware to facilitate adaptive user interfaces at run time.

Acknowledgements. The work on which this paper is based is supported by the projects FAMOUS and UMBRA funded by the Norwegian Research Council.

References

1. G. Calvary et al.: *Plasticity of User Interfaces: A Revised Reference Framework.* Proceedings of TAMODIA 2002
2. T. Clerckx et al.: *Generating Context-Sensitive Multiple Device Interfaces from Design.* Proceedings of CADUI 2004
3. J. Eisenstein et al.: *Applying Model-Based Techniques to the Development of UIs for Mobile Computers.* Proceedings of IUI 2001
4. J. Floch, et al.: *Using architecture models for runtime adaptability.* IEEE Software - special issues on SW architecture., 2006. 23(2): p. 62-70
5. E. Furtado: *KnowiXML: a knowledge-based system generating multiple abstract user interfaces in USIXML.* Proceedings of TAMODIA 2004
6. E. Gamma et al.: *Design Patterns Elements of Reusable Object-Oriented Software.* Addison-Wesley, 1995
7. S. Hallsteinsen et al.: *A Middleware Centric Approach to Building Self-Adapting Systems.* Revised Selected Paper from Software Engineering and Middleware: 4th International Workshop, SEM 2004
8. V. Lpez Jaquero et al.: *Model-Based Design of Adaptive User Interfaces through Connectors.* In Proceedings of DSV-IS 2003

9. K. Luyten et al.: *Migratable User Interface Descriptions in Component-Based Development.* Proceedings DSV-IS 2002

10. M. Mikalsen et al.: *Putting Context in Context: The Role and Design of Context Management in a Mobility and Adaptation Enabling Middleware.* Proceedings of International Workshop on Managing Context Information and Semantics in Mobile Environments (MCISME), Nara, Japan, 2006

11. N. Mitrovic and E. Mena: *Adaptive User Interface for Mobile Devices.* Proceedings of DSV-IS 2002

12. E. G. Nilsson: *Modelling user interfaces challenges, requirements and solutions.* Proceedings of Yggdrasil 2001

13. E. G. Nilsson: *Combining compound conceptual user interface components with modelling patterns a promising direction for model-based cross-platform user interface development.* Proceedings of DSV-IS 2002

14. E. G. Nilsson: *User Interface Modelling and Mobile Applications Are We Solving Real World Problems?* Proceedings of TAMODIA 2002

15. E. G. Nilsson and O.-W. Rahlff: *Mobile and Stationary User Interfaces Differences and Similarities Based on Two Examples.* Proceedings of HCI International 2003

16. E. G. Nilsson: *Design guidelines for mobile applications.* SINTEF Report STF90 A06003, ISBN 82-14-03820-0, 2005

17. S. Nylander et al.: *Ubiquitous service access through adapted user interfaces on multiple devices.* Personal and Ubiquitous Computing 9(3), May 2005, p 123- 33

18. F. Patern and C. Santoro: *One Model, Many Interfaces.* Proceedings of CADUI 2002

19. C. Pribeanu et al.: *Task Modelling for Context-Sensitive User Interfaces.* Proceedings of DSV-IS 2001

20. P. Repo and J. Riekki: *Middleware support for implementing context-aware multimodal user interfaces.* Proceedings of the 3rd international conference on Mobile and ubiquitous multimedia, 2004

21. P. Repo: *Facilitating user interface adaptation to mobile devices.* Proceedings of NordiCHI 2004

22. A. Schmidt et.al.: *Sensor-based Adaptive Mobile User Interfaces.* Proceedings of HCI International 1999

23. A. Seffah and P. Forbrig: *Multiple User Interfaces: Towards a Task-Driven and Patterns-oriented Design Model.* Proceedings of DSV-IS 2002

24. N. Souchon et al.: *Task Modelling in Multiple Contexts of Use.* Proceedings of DSV-IS 2002

25. C. Szyperski: *Component Software: Beyond Object-Oriented Programming.* 2nd ed, Addison-Wesley. 2002

26. H. Trætteberg: *Dialog modelling with interactors and UML Statecharts - A hybrid approach.* Proceedings of DSV-IS 2003

Toward Quality-Driven Development of 3D Computer Games

T.C. Nicholas Graham and Will Roberts

School of Computing, Queen's University, Kingston, Canada, K7L 4L5
graham@cs.queensu.ca, wildwilhelm@gmail.com

Abstract. The development of video games is a complex software engineering activity bringing together large multidisciplinary teams under stringent constraints. While much has been written about how to develop video games, there has been as yet little attempt to view video game development from a quality perspective, attempting to enumerate the quality attributes that must be satisfied by game implementations, and to relate implementation techniques to those quality attributes. In this paper, we discuss desired quality attributes of 3D computer games, and we use the development of our own *Life is a Village* game to illustrate architectural tactics that help achieve these desired qualities.

1 Introduction

Gaming software sales grew to $24.5 billion world wide in 2004 [6], while in the United States alone, 228 million computer games were sold in 2005 [4]. The gaming industry has become a significant part of the software development world.

Games are challenging to develop. They involve complex algorithms in graphics, artificial intelligence, database and distributed systems, have stringent performance, usability and correctness requirements, and at the same time, are developed under aggressive delivery schedules. Game development teams are multidisciplinary, and for top titles include 100 or more people.

As yet, the software engineering literature has had little to say about how to develop games. In this paper, we discuss aspects of why developing games is different from developing other forms of software, and, motivated by a framework suggested by Bass et al. [1], we propose a set of architectural *tactics* that are helpful in game development. These tactics provide guidelines for how to structure games to address their quality requirements. The tactics are motivated and illustrated by our experience with the development of *Life is a Village*, a 3D computer-aided exercise game.

The paper is organized as follows. We first introduce *Life is a Village,* from which our examples will be drawn. We then discuss quality attributes of interest to games. Finally, we introduce our architectural tactics for game development and relate them to those quality attributes.

G. Doherty and A. Blandford (Eds.): DSVIS 2006, LNCS 4323, pp. 248–261, 2007.

Fig. 1. Life is a Village game and player

2 Life Is a Village

Life is a Village is an experimental game testbed intended for exploration of computer-aided exercise [12], in which physical exertion is part of the game play.[1] The goal of the game is to gather resources from a large exterior landscape and use them to build an interesting village. The player traverses the landscape in search of resource nodes (such as wood, stone, etc.) When a node has been found, the player dispatches a villager from his/her village to start harvesting the resource. Once sufficient resources of the correct type have been collected, the player can add a new structure to the village.

The player uses a recumbent exercise bicycle to control the game (figure 1). Players navigate the terrain on their bicycle in the obvious way: pedaling moves forward; pedaling quickly moves forward quickly. Going uphill makes cycling harder; going downhill makes cycling easier. The player uses a handheld, wireless PS2 controller to steer, change gears, and provide button-based commands to the game. Exercise is an integral part of the game; the more players pedal, the faster they find resource nodes, the faster their villagers work, and therefore, the faster they can add to their village.

The core game framework has been implemented, but more work is to be done to make it a "fun" and playable game, such as adding additional village structures and additional resource types. The development of this game motivates the tactics described in the remainder of this paper.

---

[1] More information on Life is a Village can be found at http://dundee.cs.queensu.ca/wiki/index.php/Life_is_a_Village

3   Quality Attributes for 3D Games

In this section, we review a number of quality attributes that are important to game development. This list is far from exhaustive, but serves as a representative set of qualities most important to game developers. Drawing from the presentation of Bass *et al.* [1], we select attributes divided into business time, development time and runtime. In section 4, we will then show how our architectural tactics address these quality attributes.

3.1   Business Qualities: Time to Market

Game developers face significant pressures to bring their products to market quickly. This pressure derives from a number of sources.

Games are often tied to events such as the release of a movie or the start of a sports season. For example, this year's Olympic Winter Games were accompanied by the Torino 2006 game; recent films such as King Kong, Spider-Man 2 and the Lord of the Rings trilogy have all been supported by video game releases. Each year sees the release of a profusion of football, hockey and soccer games featuring that season's players. Games must be released on schedule for the event with which they are associated, or risk losing their appeal.

Games that take a long time to develop risk falling behind the technology curve, leading to a spiral of further delays as artwork and special effects are updated to avoid appearing dated upon release. Additionally, console platforms have an expected lifetime of about five years, meaning that late releases risk catching their chosen platform on the decline.

Finally, the cost to develop a game for the next generation of consoles is estimated at $15-25 million [5]. Given such outlays, publishers face intense pressure to release quickly and begin recouping their investment.

3.2   Development-Time Qualities: Testability, Modifiability, Reusability

Modern computer games are complex and detailed, typically requiring tens of hours to complete. Games are highly graphical, and necessarily have non-deterministic behaviour. Some games have such complex artificial intelligence that their behaviour is "emergent", or unpredictable. All of these factors make games difficult to test. Games have stringent correctness requirements. Console games are distributed and played from a disk, so patches cannot be issued after the game's release. PC games, on the other hand, are routinely supported by patches, costing the publisher significant post-release development resources and distribution costs, as well as damaging its reputation. For example, the game Battlefield 1942, released in 2002, is currently supported by over 270 MB of patches; Rome: Total War, released in 2004, requires over 130 MB of patches for correct play.

Modifiability is an important quality attribute of games. Games may evolve significantly during their development in the search for the elusive "fun" quality.

Games are often extensively modified after their release as game expansions are developed. Massively multiplayer games evolve considerably over their online life, sometimes completely changing their character. Modifiability is a pre-cursor to reusability; the success of projects often relies on reuse of code from earlier projects.

3.3 Runtime Qualities: Usability, Performance

Usability of games differs significantly from that of other kinds of software. The main task of someone playing a game is to be entertained (or simply, to have *fun*.) Fun games routinely violate all normal rules for the design of usable systems. Games often provide players with information in inefficient forms, provide overly complex command interfaces and force players to perform low-level tasks that could quite reasonably be automated. However, a first-person shooter game that provided the player with the location of all enemies, a racing game that prevented players from losing control of their car, or a Tetris game that automatically chose the best location for a falling block would not be *fun*. Game usability must therefore balance the ease of learning and use of the game's interface with the fun that using the interface provides.

The primary performance metric in video games is *frame rate*, measured in frames per second (fps). A minimal value ensuring smooth animation is approximately 30 fps. A maximal value would match the refresh rate of the player's monitor; modern CRT monitors have a refresh rate of 75-85 Hz. Game players claim to be able to perceive the difference of frame rates up to 200 Hz, meaning that high frame rates may be necessary for marketing reasons even in cases where the benefit to game play is not clear.

Both measures of *average frame rate* and *worst frame rate* are important. Average frame rate gives a sense of how well the game is performing in general. Worst frame rate indicates how well the game does when under stress, perhaps the very time that player's require best performance.

4 Tactics for Game Development

Architectural choices can greatly influence a game's quality attributes. The trade literature provides diverse advice on how to architect games (e.g., for sports games [15], for massively multiplayer online games [13] and for real-time strategy games [11]). There is, however, little to help game developers choose broad architectural strategies in a principled manner. We advocate the use of *architectural tactics* [1] to help developers make informed architectural choices. Architectural tactics provide high-level advice for how to structure a software system. Tactics are not code or design patterns, but are higher-level, more generic techniques. Tactics influence quality attributes: a given tactic may improve one attribute while worsening another.

Table 1. Architectural tactics for game development and quality attributes that they influence. '+' indicates a positive influence on the quality attribute, '-' a negative influence, and '⊙' a tuneable influence.

	Time to Market	Testability	Modifiability	Reusability	Usability (Fun)	Performance (FPS)
Create tools allowing non-programmers to engage in development	+			+	+	−
Decompose application into independent components	+	+	+	+		−
Structure application around existing components	+	+	⊙			⊙
Use scripting languages to allow rapid modification of game	+	+	+		⊙	+
Avoid blocking actions in main frame loop						+
Identify opportunities for parallel execution	−	−				+

An architect can therefore analyze which tactics best meet the trade-offs required for his/her project. The approach of linking architectural tactics to software quality attributes has already been applied to human-computer interaction more broadly [2, 7], but not to game development.

Table 1 shows the tactics we propose for game development. This list should be viewed as a starting point; ultimately, our goal is to provide a rich set of tactics that developers can study before committing to a concrete architecture. These tactics were identified as a result of our experience with developing the *Life is a Village* game as well as consulting the game development trade literature. Developing a more complete set of will require the expertise of a wide group of game developers.

In sections 4.1 through 4.6, we review the six tactics presented in table 1, and show how they influence the quality attributes discussed in section 3. The tactics are illustrated with examples from the development of the Life is a Village game.

4.1 Tactic: Create Tools Allowing Non-programmers to Engage in Development

To understand how games are developed, it is useful to consider the structure of game development teams. Table 2 shows the composition of the teams that developed five

Table 2. Breakdown of development teams for five popular computer games

	Battlefield 1942 (2002)	World of Warcraft (2004)	Civilization 4 (2005)	Battle for Middle Earth (2005)	F.E.A.R. (2005)
Producer	2	6	3	8	14
Designer	3	29	2	11	9
Writer			5	2	
Artist	12	41	34	39	18
Programmer	11	29	18	33	24
Audio	3	14		6	9
Video		35		7	3
Quality Assurance	51	114	26	73	56
Actor	18	36	1		16
Total	*100*	*304*	*97*	*179*	*149*

popular video games between 2002 and 2005. (The table was produced by consulting the credits released by the games' publishers. For consistency, all people appearing in development roles in the credits are included in the table; no attempt was made to distinguish between part-time and full-time roles.)

Table 1 reveals three interesting points. First, game development teams for premiere (known as "AAA") games are large, involving upwards of 100 people. Second, these teams are highly interdisciplinary, involving design, story writing, creation of artwork, music, sound effects, voice acting, creation of video cut-scenes, programming and quality assurance. Programmers represent only 10%-20% of the development team. Third, the role of quality assurance is enormous, ranging over 25%-50% of the team's personnel.

The tasks of artists and designers include creating and animating entities that appear in the game world, designing the physical structure and appearance of game "levels" (interior or exterior), and scripting encounters between the players and the environment.

Since all of these tasks involve programming-like activities, one approach is to have the artists/designers specify the behaviour they desire, leaving programmers realize the specification. It is far better to allow non-programmers on the development staff to perform these tasks directly, without the involvement of programmers: artists can get faster turn-around on their ideas, and programmers cease to be a bottleneck in the process. All game development studios purchase at least some commercial tools to help empower artists, for example tools for modeling entities (e.g., Maya and SoftImage XSI) and tools for animation (e.g., Alias MotionBuilder). Larger studios can afford to build custom tools helping with other aspects of development.

This tactic helps with *time to market* by allowing artists/designers to be more productive. It helps *reusability,* since once developed, the tools can be used in future

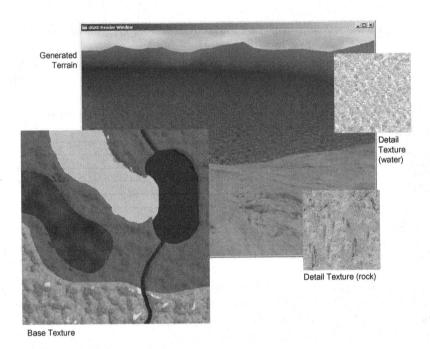

Generated
Terrain

Detail
Texture
(water)

Detail Texture (rock)

Base Texture

Fig. 2. A terrain consists of a polygon mesh with an overlaid base texture and detail texture

projects. *Usability* is enhanced, since designers can more quickly iterate between development and testing. Performance may be hindered as high-level tools may produce less optimized output than hand-crafted code.

4.1.1 Illustration: Landscape Generation in Life Is a Village

We applied this tactic in Life is a Village by developing a tool for procedural generation of landscapes. This allows people without programming skill to quickly develop rich 3D worlds. In 3D games, exterior landscapes are typically represented as a polygon mesh covered in a texture. The polygon mesh is covered in a *base texture*, an image that is stretched over the terrain's area. Often, a *detail texture* is blended with the base texture to give additional detail in the neighborhood close to the camera, reducing blurriness (figure 2).

Terrains can of course be created manually by a programmer by writing the appropriate DirectX or OpenGL commands to create and texture the terrain geometry. More realistically, artists use tools such as Leveller[2] and Terragen[3] to draw the 3D model of the terrain and to paint it with the desired texture. Such tools export a *heightmap* and a texture. The heightmap is a matrix specifying the height y of the terrain at each (x, z) point, and is used to generate the features of the terrain during the game's runtime. Terrain modeling tools such as these can lead to beautiful results, at the cost of significant manual labour.

---

[2] Leveller: http://www.daylongraphics.com/products/leveller
[3] Terragen: http://www.planetside.co.uk/terragen

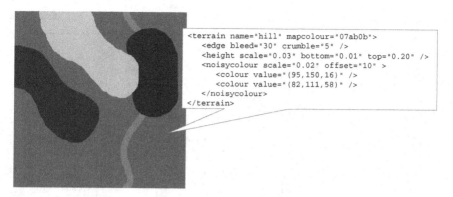

```
<terrain name="hill" mapcolour="07ab0b">
    <edge bleed="30" crumble="5" />
    <height scale="0.03" bottom="0.01" top="0.20" />
    <noisycolour scale="0.02" offset="10" >
        <colour value="(95,150,16)" />
        <colour value="(82,111,58)" />
    </noisycolour>
</terrain>
```

Fig. 3. Landscapes are generated from a terrain map, a simple bitmap image showing where each type of terrain is located

For Life is a Village, we took an alternative approach of generating landscapes procedurally from a high-level description. This approach allows developers to quickly generate landscapes of arbitrary size, reducing time to market. Landscapes consist of numerous terrain types (e.g., hills, mountains, forest), each with differing properties such as height and coloration.

Figure 3 shows the inputs that a developer must provide to the terrain generation tool. The developer uses a paint program to create a bitmap representing where each terrain type appears. In the bitmap, terrain types appear representing mountains, hills, forest, plain, river and lake.

The properties of the terrain types are defined in XML. (Future plans involve building a simple GUI editor for terrain types.) Attributes of terrain types include the range of colours that can appear in the terrain, the height range of the terrain, the "noisiness" of the terrain (e.g., smooth, rolling hills vs jagged peaks), and properties allowing shadows to be pre-computed. The result of running the tool is a heightmap and a base texture. Figure 2 shows the result of running the inputs shown in figure 3, and an example of the rendered terrain.

4.2 Tactic: Decompose Application into Independent Components

This tactic represents one of the fundamental lessons of software engineering, that it is important to decompose software system into components with well-defined interfaces that can be developed by different people. While this tactic is important to all large software products, it is of particular interest to the development of games, where large teams work under intense time pressure. Adopting this tactic, most modern games are based on a well-understood set of core components.

This tactic aids *time to market* by allowing parallel work, *testability* by providing hooks for unit testing, *modifiability* through localization of change, and *reusability* through the provision of components that may be modified for use in other games. *Performance* may be negatively impacted by rigid component interfaces or by components' information hiding, but may also be improved by algorithmic insights afforded by separation of concerns.

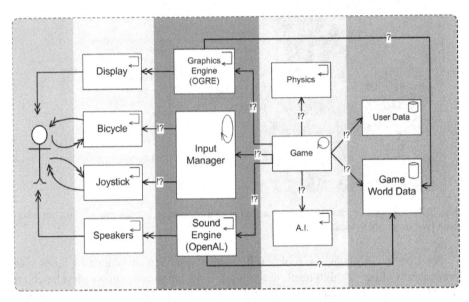

Fig. 4. The architecture of Life is a Village, in Workspace Architecture notation [9]

4.2.1 Illustration: Architecture of Life Is a Village

Figure 4 shows the architecture of the Life is a Village game. This shows how the game is decomposed into high level components that can be given to different development teams. The components present in this architecture are typical of modern 3D games. The architecture is expressed in Workspace Architecture notation [9]. The core of the application is the *Game,* which runs in its own thread. The game takes input from various input devices, such as the bicycle and joystick. The input manager runs asynchronously in its own thread. Output is provided by calls to a *Graphics Engine,* which in turn updates the *Display,* and to a *Sound Engine,* which sends data to the *Speakers.*

The *AI* component is responsible for villager behaviour. The *Physics* component deals with collision detection and realistic behaviour of the player and non-player characters when jumping and falling.

The *User Data* and *Game World Data* components represent data about the player's state and the state of the game world itself.

4.3 Tactic: Structure Application Around Existing Components

A critical strategy for quickly developing complex games is the re-use of components from other projects, or the purchase of third-party components. Examples of highly successful third-party components include the Unreal game engine[4] and the Havok physics engine[5]. Reuse is critical to game development due to the importance of time to market; there simply isn't time to build all components of a game from scratch. A

---

[4] Unreal Engine: http://www.unrealtechnology.com/html/technology/ue30.shtml
[5] Havok Physics Engine: http://www.havok.com

significant part of the value of game development companies is the base of software they have available allowing them to develop new games quickly.

Reuse of components can help *time to market* by reducing code that has to be written, but can also increase time to market if the time to adapt the component to its new use is excessive, or if the component ultimately is a poor match with its requirements. Reuse helps with *testability* if the component has already been extensively tested in other contexts. As above, *modifiability* may be helped through localization of change, and *performance* may be either improved or worsened depending on the details of the components. Reuse may negatively impact usability through locking the developers into a particular style of gaming, or may improve usability by supporting varied and complex interaction styles that would be prohibitive to program from scratch.

4.3.1   Illustration: Use of Open-Source Components
Life is a Village relies heavily on third-party components:

- The Object-Oriented Graphics Rendering Engine (*OGRE*)[6] is an open-source 3D graphics rendering engine that clearly illustrates the trade-offs of component use. While OGRE abstracts the low-level details of DirectX and OpenGL, dramatically reducing the effort of developing 3D graphics code, it has an incomplete feature set, third part add-ons of mixed quality, and difficulty integrating with commercial modeling tools.
- The Open Dynamics Engine (*ODE*)[7] is an open-source physics engine. ODE supports collision detection and correct physical behaviour of objects acting under force.
- *OpenAL*[8] is an open-source 3D sound engine adopted by such well-known titles as Doom 3 and Quake 4.

The gaming world has seen a strong convergence on what predefined components should be used and a perhaps surprisingly strong list of open-source tools. Additionally, an increasing number of companies have created strong niches in the development of third party tools for game development.

4.4   Tactic: Use Scripting Languages to Allow Rapid Modification of Game

Scripting languages have become a common technique for reducing the time to develop games and for reducing the skill level required of game developers. Games almost uniformly use C/C++ for core graphics, low-level AI and networking. Scripting languages such as Python or Lua [8] can then be used to encode the game play itself. Development of custom languages may be appropriate when domain information can be encoded in the language [10], but the cost of developing and maintaining custom languages may exceed their value [14]. Some games open their scripting languages to their player base, leading to a profusion of game enhancements produced and made available by players.

---

[6] OGRE 3D Graphics Engine: http://www.ogre3d.org
[7] Open Dynamics Engine: http://www.ode.org
[8] OpenAL: http://www.openal.org

```
IF at_tree AND NOT chop AND NOT drop_off_wood
   THEN chop AND NOT move

IF at_tree AND chop AND chop_timeout
   THEN NOT chop AND switch_targets
        AND reverse_path AND drop_off_wood AND move

IF drop_off_wood AND at_wood_drop_off
   THEN NOT drop_off_wood AND drop_wood
        AND switch_targets AND reverse_path
        AND go_to_tree AND move

IF NOT chop AND NOT drop_off_wood
   THEN go_to_tree AND move
```

Fig. 5. AI rules for a villager chopping wood and returning it to the village

Scripting languages may improve *time to market*, as it is quicker to write and debug code in high-level languages. Time may be lost, however, to working around an awkward or poorly designed scripting framework, or one that is poorly supported by debugging tools. The *testability* of code may be improved, as scripting languages typically provide more runtime checking than raw C++ code. Scripts are typically high-level and interpreted, therefore more *modifiable* than low-level code. Since they support a fast code-execution cycle, scripts allow quicker refinement of gameplay mechanics, which may increase the *usability* of the final product. Scripting languages are typically slower than compiled code, so excessive use of scripting in time-critical areas may reduce *performance*.

4.4.1 Illustration: AI Scripting

Life is a Village uses a simple scripting language (adapted from Champandard [3]) to define villager behaviour. This allows behaviour to be quickly defined and changed, supporting rapid, experimental development. Figure 5 shows the rules specifying the behaviour of a villager whose job is to walk from the village to a tree, chop wood until his bag is full, then return to the village and drop off the wood.

The language is based on rules specified using propositional logic. A rule is triggered if its antecedent holds. Once triggered, the rule engine ensures that the rule's consequent holds. For example, the rule

```
IF NOT chop AND NOT drop_off_wood
   THEN go_to_tree AND move
```

will be triggered if the villager is not currently chopping wood or dropping off wood in the village. If triggered, the rule ensures that the villager is walking to the tree.

Rules are bound to the application via semantic actions; atoms in the antecedent query the game state, while atoms in the consequent may modify game state in order to make the consequent true.

This language helps collect AI decisions into one place, and allows villager AI to be modified without recompilation of the program. It also, however, illustrates problems with the scripting approach. When developers attempted to add more resources to the game, they discovered difficulties in generalizing the rules, since there is no facility for parameterizing the resource being collected. The possible solutions included making many slightly modified copies of the rules, or burying the problem in the application through more powerful semantic actions. Neither approach was satisfactory, so the scripting language itself must be modified.

4.5 Tactic: Avoid Blocking Actions in Main Frame Loop

Games are driven via a main loop responsible for computing the display for the next frame. The time taken to compute each frame is directly related to the time required to compute each iteration of this loop; e.g., to maintain a frame rate of 20 frames per second, frames must be computed within 50 ms. To optimize worst frame rate, this 50 ms must be treated as a soft real-time bound for each frame rather than an average to be achieved over the execution of the program.

In order to increase the game's frame rate, it is important to architect the main frame loop to contain no excessively lengthy computations, and particularly, no computations of unpredictable length.

4.5.1 Illustration: Input Handling
In traditional graphical user interfaces, input is handled via an event mechanism, where user inputs such as keystrokes and mouse button clicks are transmitted to the application via a callback mechanism (e.g., as provided by Java Swing's listener architecture.) Continuous inputs such as mouse motion are converted into a discrete set of events. In 3D games, inputs are instead handled by polling the input devices within the main frame loop. Thus if a game controller button is depressed or a joystick moved, the game will be able to react to the input within the main frame loop, and modify the game state appropriately. This approach of course requires a sufficiently high frame rate that the devices are polled often enough to provide responsive input.

In Life is a Village, one of our input devices is a Tunturi E6R recumbent bicycle. The bicycle can be polled for inputs representing the speed at which the user is cycling, the current tension of bicycle, what (if any) buttons the user is pushing, and the user's heart rate. Polling is performed via a proprietary protocol via a COM port link between the bicycle and computer.

Polling the bicycle takes a variable amount of time, ranging between 5 ms and 20 ms. Assuming the bicycle is polled once per frame, this time is added to the frame computation cost, unacceptably impacting frame rate. The solution, as shown in figure 4, is to run the input manager in its own thread. The input manager continuously polls the bicycle (and other input devices) in its own thread. When the main frame loop checks the input state, the input manager provides the last value obtained from the input device. Values from the bicycle may therefore be a few milliseconds out of date, but the result can be provided without blocking, and therefore without impacting frame rate.

4.6 Tactic: Identify Opportunities for Parallel Execution

Modern gaming platforms support extensive parallelism. Microsoft's Xbox 360 game console provides three 3.2 GHz dual core PowerPC processors, or six cores in total, in a shared memory environment. Sony's forthcoming PlayStation 3 is built around a 3.2 GHz Cell Processor consisting of seven Synergistic Processing Elements (SPE's), each a 128 bit SIMD RISC processor, all connected by a 10 GBps bus. Desktop PC's are following the trend towards parallel architectures, with both Intel and AMD having scheduled quad-core CPU's for release in 2007. The challenge of programming this next generation of consoles is how to distribute the computation required in the game amongst these many processing elements.

The benefit of parallelism is a potential improvement in *performance*. Parallel programs are harder to write and debug, and therefore may negatively impact *time to market* and *testability*.

4.6.1 Illustration: Pathfinding

Pathfinding involves finding a reasonable path for agents in the game world that have to move from one location to another. For example, if a villager has to move from the village to a tree selected by the player, the game needs to first compute the route that the villager will follow. Path computations can be time-consuming, especially if there are many to do at the same time, and so make a good candidate for parallel execution. Additionally, path computation is not time-sensitive, in that a brief delay in computation will simply cause the villager to wait, playing an idle animation, before moving towards the tree. Pathfinding is mediated via a *CAXVillagerPathManager* component, which maintains a pool of threads that are assigned to a queue of path computation requests.

The six tactics presented in this section have shown how high-level approaches to architecting games can help meet quality requirements. The tactics each address one or more of the quality attributes identified in section 3, sometimes positively, and sometimes negatively. Relating tactics to quality attributes helps developers make reasoned architectural decisions.

5   Conclusion

In this paper, we have discussed quality attributes of interest to 3D video games, and proposed six tactics for addressing these quality attributes. The collection of tactics allows game developers to consider broad approaches to development in the context of how design choices affect game qualities. We illustrated the tactics through examples drawn from the development of the Life is a Village computer-aided exercise game.

Future work includes expanding the list of tactics and the quality attributes addressed. For example, we plan to consider tactics useful in the development of multi-player games.

Acknowledgements

We gratefully acknowledge the support of the National Science and Engineering Research Council in performing this work. The Life is a Village game benefited from the hard work of Irina Skvortsova, Rob Fletcher, Kevin Grad, Kevin Kassil, Joseph Lam, Banani Roy, Paul Schofield, and Sean Richards.

References

1. Len Bass, Paul Clements and Rick Kazman, Software Architecture in Practice, second edition, Addison-Wesley Professional, 2003.
2. Len Bass, Bonnie E. John, Natalia Juristo Juzgado, Maria Isabel Sánchez Segura, Usability-Supporting Architectural Patterns, in *Proceedings of the International Conference on Software Engineering*, pp. 716-717, 2004.
3. Alex J. Champandard, *AI Game Development,* New Riders Publishing, 2003.
4. Entertainment Software Association, *Top 10 Industry Facts,* 2005, Available at http://www.theesa.com/facts/top_10_facts.php
5. John J. Geoghegan, The Console Transition: A Publisher's Perspective, *BusinessWeek Online,* December 14, 2005.
6. Ronald Grover, Cliff Edwards, Ian Rowley and Moon Ihlwan, Game Wars, *BusinessWeek Online,* February 28, 2005.
7. Bonnie E. John, Len Bass, Maria Isabel Sánchez Segura and Rob J. Adams, Bringing Usability Concerns to the Design of Software Architecture. In *Proceedings of EHCI/DSVIS,* pp. 1-19, 2004.
8. Matthew Harmon, Building Lua into Games, in *Game Programming Gems 5,* pp. 115-128, Charles River Media, 2005.
9. W.G. Phillips, T.C.N. Graham and C. Wolfe, A Calculus for the Refinement and Evolution of Multi-User Mobile Applications In *Proceedings of Design, Specification and Verification of Interactive Systems,* Lecture Notes in Computer Science, pp. 137-148, 2005.
10. Falco Poiker, Creating Scripting Languages for Nonprogrammers, *AI Game Programming Wisdom,* Charles River Media, pp. 520-529, 2002.
11. Bob Scott, Architecting an RTS AI, *AI Game Programming Wisdom,* Charles River Media, pp. 397-401, 2002.
12. Brian K. Smith, Physical Fitness in Virtual Worlds, *IEEE Computer,* pp. 101-103, October 2005.
13. Shea Street, Massively Multiplayer Games using a Distributed Services Approach, in *Massively Multiplayer Game Development 2,* Charles River Media, pp. 233-241, 2005.
14. Paul Tozour, The Perils of AI Game Scripting, *AI Game Programming Wisdom,* Charles River Media, pp. 541-554, 2002.
15. Terry Wellmann, Building a Sports AI Architecture, in *AI Game Programming Wisdom 2,* Charles River Media, pp. 505-514, 2004.

Processes: Working Group Report

Stéphane Chatty, José Creissac Campos, María Paula González,
Sophie Lepreux, Erik G. Nilsson, Victor M.R. Penichet, Mónica Santos,
and Jan Van den Bergh

1 Automatic Generation?

It has often been suggested that model-driven development of user interfaces amounted to producing models of user interfaces then using automatic code generation to obtain the final result. However, this may be seen as an extreme interpretation of the model-driven approach. There are examples where that approach is successful, including mobile computing and database management systems. But in many cases automatic generation may be either impossible or may limit the quality of the final interface.

This debate raises the question of where information comes from in the design process:

- at one extreme is straightforward model translation or compilation: all the design information is contained in the model, and the automatic generation just produces the executable code.
- at the other extreme is a fully automated system that incorporates rules able to make the appropriate design choices: adapation to the task, the context and the available hardware.
- in between are more complex situations in which designers must bring additional knowledge and know-how. The process is thus a mix of human design and automated model translation.

Some authors suggest, following the second case above, that one can automatically translate a task model to a concrete user interface. However, task modelling languages currently are not capable of expressing all of the design information that is found in a concrete UI. For instance, some user interfaces rely heavily on the concept of sequence (wizards, for instance) when task modelling languages do not all have such a concept. Consequently, the information must either be encoded in a very rich set of rules, or added by a human designer. Therefore, until such very rich sets of rules are built, processes will most often consist of automatic translations interspersed with additions by human designers.

2 Fitting UI into Larger Scale Processess

The success of big industries relies on their processes, which have to be optimized for return on investment, efficiency and risk management. If one proposes to change existing processes by relying on user-centered methods, one will have

G. Doherty and A. Blandford (Eds.): DSVIS 2006, LNCS 4323, pp. 262–264, 2007.

to provide satisfactory answers to the following questions at least: what is the return on investment? How is the risk added by such methods managed?

– most decision makers are now convinced about the issue of return on investment, thanks to the success of the Web. The Web has been proved to them how better user interfaces yield more traffic, and they are ready to accept that they can improve their business too.
– as for risk, perception depends on the size of companies. Small companies are used to managing larger risks in their projects; therefore they are more open to accepting the potential risk brought by iterative design. Larger companies accept much smaller margins of risk; therefore, one needs to demonstrate that the proposed iterative processes improve the risk margin rather than degrade it.

Among the hurdles identified for integrating UI processes into larger development processes are:

– the fact that in classical software engineering, the architecture of the software is often designed before the analysis of user interface requirements, when there is a strong relationship between software architecture and the type of user interface that can be produced.
– the fact that the business logic is often developed before the user interface is designed, despite the fact that the implementation choices often impose severe constraints on user interaction

3 Communicating with Users

Although an abundant literature is dedicated to the role of users in design processes, there still appears to be a debate as to whether users are able to participate efficiently in the design process. Two opposed schools of thought emerge:

- some group participants consider that users bring a major risk to the design process because they keep changing their minds; these participants advocate processes that are user-centered but not with the actual participation of users;
- other participants contend that users are able to reason about abstract considerations when those have been properly introduced, are able to contribute efficiently to the design solutions when the appropriate prototyping and communication supports are used, and are no more difficult to manage than other actors of a development process.

These two schools of thought lead to very different views of the role of design managers. However, whatever the chosen design process it is important that this process is "self-evident" in that the customer or user knows what is the current phase of the process. In other domains (building architecture for instance), there is no ambiguity between the mock-up phase and the building phase. It should be the same in user interface design, using different levels of fidelity of prototypes.

4   Conclusions

Based on the above discussions, the working group agreed that:

- there is no "silver bullet" process for developing user interfaces, especially not with full automation;
- HCI is about building new objects and not reproducing or evolving existing objects, which means that creativity will always play an important role;
- models should be used only when needed;
- models for communicating within the design and development groups and with users are essential;
- product design is a key activity in software development and its relationship to code development should be clarified.

Usability and Computer Games: Working Group Report

T.C. Nicholas Graham, Paul Curzon, Gavin Doherty, Philippe Palanque,
Richard Potter, Christopher Roast, and Shamus P. Smith

1 Introduction

Computer games are intended to be fun to play. While they are also interactive
systems with sophisticated user interfaces, standard concepts of usability do not
necessarily apply to games. In this workshop, we explored the relationship between
usability and fun. Our central conclusion was that applying standard usability design
guidelines, such as those proposed by Nielson [4], may improve or reduce the fun of a
game, but that for many standard usability guidelines, there exist equivalent
guidelines addressing fun in games.

2 Motivating Examples

Jumpgate [3] and Eve Online [1] are both massively multiplayer online games in
which players pilot through space, mine asteroids for resources, and engage in combat
with other players. While superficially similar, the games provide completely
different user experiences. Jumpgate provides a faithful simulation of Newtonian
physics. Due to conservation of momentum, if a player wishes to slow his ship, he
must rotate it by 180 degrees, and engage his thrusters. Landing a ship in a space
station is a complex and difficult experience. Jumpgate violates many principles of
user-centered design, high among them that the interface does a very poor job of
engineering for errors. Eve Online, on the other hand, provides a very simple
interface: to dock, the player right-clicks that station, and selects the "dock" option
from a menu. The Eve approach does well on the usability scale – there is little
opportunity for error; no memorization is required; and the operation is highly
optimized. The trouble is, it is also thoroughly boring – in Eve, a player can sit for
minutes on end watching the game pilot his ship through space. What makes for good
usability in this case makes for poor gameplay.

Red Alert [2] is a real time strategy game that was released in 1996. Its sequel,
Red Alert 2, was released four years later. In Red Alert, players must attend to a
map in which units fight over territory. At the same time, the player must manage
his production of new units. Some units, such as basic infantry, take only a second
or two to build, making it difficult for the player to multi-task, managing
production and battles at the same time. In Red Alert 2, the concept of a
production queue was introduced, allowing players to issue a lengthy sequence of
production commands to be carried out in sequence. All modern real time strategy
games have adopted this production queue mechanic. In this case, improving the
user interface (by optimizing operations) had a beneficial effect on players'
enjoyment of the game.

G. Doherty and A. Blandford (Eds.): DSVIS 2006, LNCS 4323, pp. 265 – 268, 2007.

**UI Design
Guidelines**   **Game Design Guidelines**

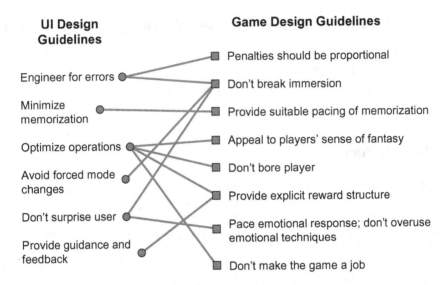

Fig. 1. Pairing usability design guidelines with game design guidelines

From these two examples, we can see that there is no simple relation between usability and enjoyment. Slavishly following usability design guidelines can lead to a tedious gameplay, as ironically, the challenge of games is often the result of poor usability. Alternatively, providing a poor user interface is not a recipe for creating an enjoyable game.

3   Usability Guidelines for Games

User interface design guidelines are commonly used to evaluate the usability of interactive systems. While the above examples motivate that these guidelines are not necessarily applicable to games, we conclude that UI design guidelines can be matched to related game design guidelines. The game design guidelines indicate how UI design guidelines can be reinterpreted in the context of making the game fun. Figure 1 shows examples of this approach of pairing guidelines. We now walk through the guidelines shown in this figure to illustrate the approach.

Engineer for errors: Systems should be engineered to prevent errors where possible, and to allow users to easily recover from the errors they do make. Errors are a fundamental part of games, however – the game should not prevent the player from driving into a wall, attacking an enemy that's a little too tough, or passing the football to the wrong player. When the player does make such an error, the *penalties should be proportional to the error made.* Games have many ways of softening the penalties for errors: crashing a car might lead to a time penalty as opposed to fiery death; death from fighting a too-powerful enemy might to a modest experience point reduction as opposed to having to start the game again. Making the penalty for an error too harsh increases frustration, and encourages players to be overly cautious.

Similarly, when errors occur, they should *not break immersion.* A typical approach to player death is to require re-loading the game from a saved checkpoint. The player then replays the failed scenario over and over until finally he solves it. This breaks immersion, as the player interacts with an out-of-game mechanic to resolve the in-game event. The approach of experience point penalty is more immersive, as the player never leaves the game world.

Minimize memorization: This guideline encourages the provision of information where it is required, so that users do not have to memorize information from earlier interactions. Memorization is often key to the fun of a game. Card games often rely on memorization of what cards have already been played; role-playing games often require players to remember earlier situations. Instead, games should *suitably pace memorization* to be fun rather than overwhelming.

Optimize operations: User interfaces should allow frequent tasks to be performed efficiently. Applying this guideline in games can lead to the effect of travel in Eve Online, where the interface is so optimized that the game almost plays itself. Conversely, failing to optimize operations can lead to annoying repetitiveness. Games should optimize sufficiently to *avoid boredom,* and should counter tedium by *providing an explicit reward structure* that encourages the player to continue. Over all, the game should *appeal to players' sense of fantasy* – players should feel that they are piloting a space ship (or race car or horse), not operating a user interface. Finally, failure to optimize operations can lead to so much repetition that *the game feels like a job.* Effective game design will require balancing these conflicting guidelines.

Avoid forced mode changes: Mode changes cause confusion and interrupt users' flow. This guideline applies equally well to games: a player running towards a local town should not receive a pop-up informing him that the terrain is too rocky to pass through. Such information should be conveyed directly within the game (e.g., through not permitting the player to move in the rocky direction) in order to *not break immersion.*

Don't surprise the user: While an excellent guideline for traditional systems, games often rely on surprise: a trap door may suddenly open, a monster may jump out from hiding, or cresting a hill may reveal a beautiful landscape. Surprises should be plausible and consistent with the game world to *avoid breaking immersion.* Use of surprise should be *paced*; overuse of the same technique will lessen its impact.

Provide guidance and feedback: A well-designed user interface will give the user information about how to proceed, and provide feedback to indicate that operations have been performed correctly. Many games make good use of this principle, providing tutorial modes, or in-game help options. Providing too much guidance can remove the challenge or sense of exploration from a game. One way of giving feedback to players is through an *explicit reward structure* that indicates when progress is being made.

4 Conclusions

The fundamental conclusion of the workshop is that while many usability guidelines are not directly applicable to games, the underlying problems that the guidelines address do exist in some form in games. New game design guidelines help us understand the tradeoffs of applying usability guidelines, providing game-specific interpretations.

The game design guidelines presented here should be considered a first step. Future research would include refining these guidelines, and exploring their tradeoffs in more depth using concrete examples from games.

References

1. CCP. Eve Online. http://www.eve-online.com
2. Electronic Arts. Red Alert 2. http://www.ea.com/official/cc/redalert2/english/features.jsp
3. NetDevil. Jumpgate. http://www.jossh.com
4. J. Nielsen. Usability Engineering. Morgan Kaufmann, 1994.

Author Index

Back, Jonathan   123
Barboni, Eric   25
Blandford, Ann   123

Campos, José Creissac   137, 262
Chatty, Stéphane   262
Coninx, Karin   81, 95
Conversy, Stéphane   25
Cuppens, Erwin   95
Curzon, Paul   123, 265

De Boeck, Joan   95
Dobson, Simon   220
Doherty, Gavin   265

Faconti, G.   185
Falcão e Cunha, João   39
Floch, Jacqueline   234

Gallud, J.A.   67
González, María Paula   213, 262
Graham, T.C. Nicholas   248, 265
Granollers, Toni   213
Gulliksen, Jan   1

Hallsteinsen, Svein   234
Huypens, Steven   81

Khazaei, Babak   109

Lepreux, Sophie   157, 262
Lewis, David   220
Lorés, Jesús   213
Lozano, Maria D.   67

Massink, Mieke   185
McGlinn, Kris   220
Michotte, Benjamin   157

Navarre, David   25
Nilsson, Erik G.   234, 262

O'Neill, Eleanor   220

Palanque, Philippe   25, 265
Paternò, Fabio   67
Penichet, Victor M.R.   67, 262
Pereira, Altamiro da Costa   39
Petrie, Jennifer N.   199
Potter, Richard   151, 265

Raymaekers, Chris   95
Roast, Christopher   109, 265
Roberts, Will   248
Rukšėnas, Rimvydas   123

Santos, Mónica Sara   39, 262
Saraiva, João   137
Schneider, Kevin A.   199
Silva, J.C.   137
Smith, Shamus P.   171, 265
Stav, Erlend   234

Thimbleby, Harold   11, 52

Van den Bergh, Jan   81, 262
Vanderdonckt, Jean   157

Wright, Helen   151

Lecture Notes in Computer Science

For information about Vols. 1–4277

please contact your bookseller or Springer

Vol. 4377: M. Abe (Ed.), Topics in Cryptology – CT-RSA 2007. XI, 403 pages. 2006.

Vol. 4371: K. Inoue, K. Satoh, F. Toni (Eds.), Computational Logic in Multi-Agent Systems. X, 315 pages. 2007. (Sublibrary LNAI).

Vol. 4369: M. Umeda, A. Wolf, O. Bartenstein, U. Geske, D. Seipel, O. Takata (Eds.), Declarative Programming for Knowledge Management. X, 229 pages. 2006. (Sublibrary LNAI).

Vol. 4368: T. Erlebach, C. Kaklamanis (Eds.), Approximation and Online Algorithms. X, 345 pages. 2006.

Vol. 4367: K. De Bosschere, D. Kaeli, P. Stenström, D. Whalley, T. Ungerer (Eds.), High Performance Embedded Architectures and Compilers. XI, 307 pages. 2007.

Vol. 4364: T. Kühne (Ed.), Workshops and Symposia at MoDELS 2006. XI, 332 pages. 2007.

Vol. 4362: J. van Leeuwen, G.F. Italiano, W. van der Hoek, C. Meinel, H. Sack, F. Plášil (Eds.), SOFSEM 2007: Theory and Practice of Computer Science. XXI, 937 pages. 2006.

Vol. 4361: H.J. Hoogeboom, G. Păun, G. Rozenberg, A. Salomaa (Eds.), Membrane Computing. IX, 555 pages. 2006.

Vol. 4360: W. Dubitzky, A. Schuster, P.M.A. Sloot, M. Schroeder, M. Romberg (Eds.), Distributed, High-Performance, and Grid Computing in Computational Biology. X, 192 pages. 2007. (Sublibrary LNBI).

Vol. 4357: L. Buttyán, V. Gligor, D. Westhoff (Eds.), Security and Privacy in Ad-Hoc and Sensor Networks. X, 193 pages. 2006.

Vol. 4355: J. Julliand, O. Kouchnarenko (Eds.), B 2007: Formal Specification and Development in B. XIII, 293 pages. 2006.

Vol. 4354: M. Hanus (Ed.), Practical Aspects of Declarative Languages. X, 335 pages. 2006.

Vol. 4353: T. Schwentick, D. Suciu (Eds.), Database Theory – ICDT 2007. XI, 419 pages. 2006.

Vol. 4352: T.-J. Cham, J. Cai, C. Dorai, D. Rajan, T.-S. Chua, L.-T. Chia (Eds.), Advances in Multimedia Modeling, Part II. XVIII, 743 pages. 2006.

Vol. 4351: T.-J. Cham, J. Cai, C. Dorai, D. Rajan, T.-S. Chua, L.-T. Chia (Eds.), Advances in Multimedia Modeling, Part I. XIX, 797 pages. 2006.

Vol. 4349: B. Cook, A. Podelski (Eds.), Verification, Model Checking, and Abstract Interpretation. XI, 395 pages. 2006.

Vol. 4348: S.T. Taft, R.A. Duff, R.L. Brukardt, E. Ploedereder, P. Leroy (Eds.), Ada 2005 Reference Manual. XXII, 765 pages. 2006.

Vol. 4347: J. Lopez (Ed.), Critical Information Infrastructures Security. X, 286 pages. 2006.

Vol. 4345: N. Maglaveras, I. Chouvarda, V. Koutkias, R. Brause (Eds.), Biological and Medical Data Analysis. XIII, 496 pages. 2006. (Sublibrary LNBI).

Vol. 4344: V. Gruhn, F. Oquendo (Eds.), Software Architecture. X, 245 pages. 2006.

Vol. 4342: H. de Swart, E. Orłowska, G. Schmidt, M. Roubens (Eds.), Theory and Applications of Relational Structures as Knowledge Instruments II. X, 373 pages. 2006. (Sublibrary LNAI).

Vol. 4341: P.Q. Nguyen (Ed.), Progress in Cryptology - VIETCRYPT 2006. XI, 385 pages. 2006.

Vol. 4340: R. Prodan, T. Fahringer, Grid Computing. XXIII, 317 pages. 2006.

Vol. 4339: E. Ayguadé, G. Baumgartner, J. Ramanujam, P. Sadayappan (Eds.), Languages and Compilers for Parallel Computing. XI, 476 pages. 2006.

Vol. 4338: P. Kalra, S. Peleg (Eds.), Computer Vision, Graphics and Image Processing. XV, 965 pages. 2006.

Vol. 4337: S. Arun-Kumar, N. Garg (Eds.), FSTTCS 2006: Foundations of Software Technology and Theoretical Computer Science. XIII, 430 pages. 2006.

Vol. 4334: B. Beckert, R. Hähnle, P.H. Schmitt (Eds.), Verification of Object-Oriented Software. XXIX, 658 pages. 2007. (Sublibrary LNAI).

Vol. 4333: U. Reimer, D. Karagiannis (Eds.), Practical Aspects of Knowledge Management. XII, 338 pages. 2006. (Sublibrary LNAI).

Vol. 4332: A. Bagchi, V. Atluri (Eds.), Information Systems Security. XV, 382 pages. 2006.

Vol. 4331: G. Min, B. Di Martino, L.T. Yang, M. Guo, G. Ruenger (Eds.), Frontiers of High Performance Computing and Networking – ISPA 2006 Workshops. XXXVII, 1141 pages. 2006.

Vol. 4330: M. Guo, L.T. Yang, B. Di Martino, H.P. Zima, J. Dongarra, F. Tang (Eds.), Parallel and Distributed Processing and Applications. XVIII, 953 pages. 2006.

Vol. 4329: R. Barua, T. Lange (Eds.), Progress in Cryptology - INDOCRYPT 2006. X, 454 pages. 2006.

Vol. 4328: D. Penkler, M. Reitenspiess, F. Tam (Eds.), Service Availability. X, 289 pages. 2006.

Vol. 4327: M. Baldoni, U. Endriss (Eds.), Declarative Agent Languages and Technologies IV. VIII, 257 pages. 2006. (Sublibrary LNAI).

Vol. 4326: S. Göbel, R. Malkewitz, I. Iurgel (Eds.), Technologies for Interactive Digital Storytelling and Entertainment. X, 384 pages. 2006.

Vol. 4325: J. Cao, I. Stojmenovic, X. Jia, S.K. Das (Eds.), Mobile Ad-hoc and Sensor Networks. XIX, 887 pages. 2006.

Vol. 4323: G. Doherty, A. Blandford (Eds.), Interactive Systems. XI, 269 pages. 2007.

Vol. 4320: R. Gotzhein, R. Reed (Eds.), System Analysis and Modeling: Language Profiles. X, 229 pages. 2006.

Vol. 4319: L.-W. Chang, W.-N. Lie (Eds.), Advances in Image and Video Technology. XXVI, 1347 pages. 2006.

Vol. 4318: H. Lipmaa, M. Yung, D. Lin (Eds.), Information Security and Cryptology. XI, 305 pages. 2006.

Vol. 4317: S.K. Madria, K.T. Claypool, R. Kannan, P. Uppuluri, M.M. Gore (Eds.), Distributed Computing and Internet Technology. XIX, 466 pages. 2006.

Vol. 4316: M.M. Dalkilic, S. Kim, J. Yang (Eds.), Data Mining and Bioinformatics. VIII, 197 pages. 2006. (Sublibrary LNBI).

Vol. 4313: T. Margaria, B. Steffen (Eds.), Leveraging Applications of Formal Methods. IX, 197 pages. 2006.

Vol. 4312: S. Sugimoto, J. Hunter, A. Rauber, A. Morishima (Eds.), Digital Libraries: Achievements, Challenges and Opportunities. XVIII, 571 pages. 2006.

Vol. 4311: K. Cho, P. Jacquet (Eds.), Technologies for Advanced Heterogeneous Networks II. XI, 253 pages. 2006.

Vol. 4309: P. Inverardi, M. Jazayeri (Eds.), Software Engineering Education in the Modern Age. VIII, 207 pages. 2006.

Vol. 4308: S. Chaudhuri, S.R. Das, H.S. Paul, S. Tirthapura (Eds.), Distributed Computing and Networking. XIX, 608 pages. 2006.

Vol. 4307: P. Ning, S. Qing, N. Li (Eds.), Information and Communications Security. XIV, 558 pages. 2006.

Vol. 4306: Y. Avrithis, Y. Kompatsiaris, S. Staab, N.E. O'Connor (Eds.), Semantic Multimedia. XII, 241 pages. 2006.

Vol. 4305: A.A. Shvartsman (Ed.), Principles of Distributed Systems. XIII, 441 pages. 2006.

Vol. 4304: A. Sattar, B.-H. Kang (Eds.), AI 2006: Advances in Artificial Intelligence. XXVII, 1303 pages. 2006. (Sublibrary LNAI).

Vol. 4303: A. Hoffmann, B.-H. Kang, D. Richards, S. Tsumoto (Eds.), Advances in Knowledge Acquisition and Management. XI, 259 pages. 2006. (Sublibrary LNAI).

Vol. 4302: J. Domingo-Ferrer, L. Franconi (Eds.), Privacy in Statistical Databases. XI, 383 pages. 2006.

Vol. 4301: D. Pointcheval, Y. Mu, K. Chen (Eds.), Cryptology and Network Security. XIII, 381 pages. 2006.

Vol. 4300: Y.Q. Shi (Ed.), Transactions on Data Hiding and Multimedia Security I. IX, 139 pages. 2006.

Vol. 4299: S. Renals, S. Bengio, J.G. Fiscus (Eds.), Machine Learning for Multimodal Interaction. XII, 470 pages. 2006.

Vol. 4297: Y. Robert, M. Parashar, R. Badrinath, V.K. Prasanna (Eds.), High Performance Computing - HiPC 2006. XXIV, 642 pages. 2006.

Vol. 4296: M.S. Rhee, B. Lee (Eds.), Information Security and Cryptology – ICISC 2006. XIII, 358 pages. 2006.

Vol. 4295: J.D. Carswell, T. Tezuka (Eds.), Web and Wireless Geographical Information Systems. XI, 269 pages. 2006.

Vol. 4294: A. Dan, W. Lamersdorf (Eds.), Service-Oriented Computing – ICSOC 2006. XIX, 653 pages. 2006.

Vol. 4293: A. Gelbukh, C.A. Reyes-Garcia (Eds.), MICAI 2006: Advances in Artificial Intelligence. XXVIII, 1232 pages. 2006. (Sublibrary LNAI).

Vol. 4292: G. Bebis, R. Boyle, B. Parvin, D. Koracin, P. Remagnino, A. Nefian, G. Meenakshisundaram, V. Pascucci, J. Zara, J. Molineros, H. Theisel, T. Malzbender (Eds.), Advances in Visual Computing, Part II. XXXII, 906 pages. 2006.

Vol. 4291: G. Bebis, R. Boyle, B. Parvin, D. Koracin, P. Remagnino, A. Nefian, G. Meenakshisundaram, V. Pascucci, J. Zara, J. Molineros, H. Theisel, T. Malzbender (Eds.), Advances in Visual Computing, Part I. XXXI, 916 pages. 2006.

Vol. 4290: M. van Steen, M. Henning (Eds.), Middleware 2006. XIII, 425 pages. 2006.

Vol. 4289: M. Ackermann, B. Berendt, M. Grobelnik, A. Hotho, D. Mladenič, G. Semeraro, M. Spiliopoulou, G. Stumme, V. Svátek, M. van Someren (Eds.), Semantics, Web and Mining. X, 197 pages. 2006. (Sublibrary LNAI).

Vol. 4288: T. Asano (Ed.), Algorithms and Computation. XX, 766 pages. 2006.

Vol. 4287: C. Mao, T. Yokomori (Eds.), DNA Computing. XII, 440 pages. 2006.

Vol. 4286: P.G. Spirakis, M. Mavronicolas, S.C. Kontogiannis (Eds.), Internet and Network Economics. XI, 401 pages. 2006.

Vol. 4285: Y. Matsumoto, R.W. Sproat, K.-F. Wong, M. Zhang (Eds.), Computer Processing of Oriental Languages. XVII, 544 pages. 2006. (Sublibrary LNAI).

Vol. 4284: X. Lai, K. Chen (Eds.), Advances in Cryptology – ASIACRYPT 2006. XIV, 468 pages. 2006.

Vol. 4283: Y.Q. Shi, B. Jeon (Eds.), Digital Watermarking. XII, 474 pages. 2006.

Vol. 4282: Z. Pan, A. Cheok, M. Haller, R.W.H. Lau, H. Saito, R. Liang (Eds.), Advances in Artificial Reality and Tele-Existence. XXIII, 1347 pages. 2006.

Vol. 4281: K. Barkaoui, A. Cavalcanti, A. Cerone (Eds.), Theoretical Aspects of Computing - ICTAC 2006. XV, 371 pages. 2006.

Vol. 4280: A.K. Datta, M. Gradinariu (Eds.), Stabilization, Safety, and Security of Distributed Systems. XVII, 590 pages. 2006.

Vol. 4279: N. Kobayashi (Ed.), Programming Languages and Systems. XI, 423 pages. 2006.

Vol. 4278: R. Meersman, Z. Tari, P. Herrero (Eds.), On the Move to Meaningful Internet Systems 2006: OTM 2006 Workshops, Part II. XLV, 1004 pages. 2006.